Japanese American
World War II Evacuation
Oral History Project

Part II: Administrators

Japanese American
World War II Evacuation
Oral History Project

Edited by Arthur A. Hansen

Part 1:   Internees
ISBN 0-88736-539-6   1991   CIP

Part 2:   Administrators
ISBN 0-88736-540-X   1991   CIP

Part 3:   Analysts
ISBN 0-88736-696-1   1991   CIP

Part 4:   Resisters
ISBN 0-88736-697-X   1991   CIP

Part 5:   Guards and Townspeople
ISBN 0-88736-698-8   1992   CIP

Japanese American World War II Evacuation Oral History Project

Part II: Administrators

Edited by
Arthur A. Hansen
California State University, Fullerton

Meckler
Westport · London

Library of Congress Cataloging-in-Publication Data

Japanese American World War II evacuation oral history project /
    edited by Arthur A. Hansen.
        p. cm.
    Includes index.
    Contents: -- pt. 2. Administrators.
    ISBN 0-88736-540-X (v. 2: alk. paper) : $
    1. Japanese Americans--Evacuation and relocation--1942-1945.
  2. World War, 1939-1945--Concentration camps--United States.
  3. Prisons--United States--Officials and employees--Interviews.
  4. Oral history.   I. Hansen, Arthur A.   II. Title: Japanese
American World War 2 evacuation oral history project.
  D769.8.A6J363   1991
  940.53'1503956073--dc20   90-6180
                                                         CIP

British Library Cataloguing in Publication Data

Japanese American World War II evacuation oral history
    project.
    Pt. II, Administrators
    1. United States. Japanese Americans. Internment, 1939-1945
    I. Hansen, Arthur A.
    940.53170973

    ISBN 0-88736-540-X

Meckler Publishing, the publishing division of Meckler Corporation,
    11 Ferry Lane West, Westport, CT 06880.
Meckler Ltd., 247-249 Vauxhall Bridge Road,
    London SW1V 1HQ, U.K.

Printed on acid free paper.
Printed and bound in the United States of America.

11866256

Contents

Preface

Consistent with the student-based philosophy and practice of the Oral History Program (OHP) at California State University, Fullerton (CSUF), its extensive Japanese American Project was launched in 1972 at the urging of a then CSUF undergraduate history major, Betty E. Mitson. Mitson was enrolled concurrently in an introductory oral history class taught by Professor Gary L. Shumway, the founding director of the CSUF program and a pioneer in the national oral history movement, and in a historical methodology class under my tutelage. Coincidentally, she had chosen, with Shumway's guidance, to sharpen her technical processing skills in oral history by transcribing, editing, and indexing a series of tape-recorded interviews in the OHP collection pertinent to the World War II Japanese American Evacuation, the very topic I had selected for investigation by the students in my Historical Methods class.

At this point, I knew virtually nothing about either the method of oral history or the subject of the Evacuation. My motivation for assigning each student in my class to write a research paper on some aspect of the wartime removal and incarceration of West Coast Japanese Americans was that the thirty-year anniversary of this event afforded a convenient way of imparting historical perspective to the contemporary concern with civil liberties, human rights, and ethnic consciousness. Mitson, a senior reentry student, soon convinced me that, because only the previous semester she had completed a research paper centered upon the Evacuation in another of her classes, she could spend her time for my class more profitably by doubling her processing efforts relative to the Evacuation tapes and by collecting and collating research materials for exploitation by her classmates.

One immediate result of this arrangement was that, in reviewing Mitson's processing work, I was drawn--or rather, I was plunged--into every facet of the oral history process via the topic of the Japanese American Evacuation. Before long I found myself becoming less Mitson's teacher than her student, as she instructed me both in the art of oral history interviewing and transcript editing. Moreover, the dynamic, dialogical character of the oral history data that I was working with had the effect of deepening my understanding of and stimulating my curiosity about the entire subject of the Evacuation. Mitson then encouraged me to suggest to Professor Shumway that the OHP formally constitute a project pivoting upon the history and culture of Japanese Americans, with particular attention being paid to the events surrounding World War II. Upon receiving Shumway's enthusiastic endorsement for this idea, the Japanese American Project, with Mitson as associate director and myself as director, became a reality.

During its seventeen-year history, the project has evolved through three discernible stages of development. The first stage extended through 1975, at which time Mitson accepted an appointment as the oral historian for the Forest History Society in Santa Cruz, California, and I succeeded Shumway as the CSUF-OHP's second director. The high tide of this stage was reached late in 1974 with the publication of Voices Long Silent: Oral History and the Japanese American Evacuation (coedited by Mitson and myself), an anthology of project interviews, interpretive essays grounded in these interviews, and taped lectures delivered by selected interviewees in a University of California, Irvine, Extended Education series which I coordinated. The annotated bibliography of project holdings that we prepared for that volume is instructive. It shows that the project had inherited thirteen interviews conducted for the OHP between 1966 and 1972, all with individuals residing in Orange County, California, who, for the most part, were of Japanese ancestry and had been interned during the war in the Poston War Relocation Center in southwestern Arizona. More importantly, it indicates that within the next two years project members generated seventy-three new interviews, and that these taped recollections encompassed the Evacuation experiences of Japanese Americans and non-Japanese Americans from all over California, though particularly from the Los Angeles area--the prewar residential, commercial, and cultural center of the mainland Japanese American community. In addition to addressing the situations prevalent for evacuees at the nine other War Relocation Authority (WRA) centers apart from Poston, especially the Manzanar center in eastern California that housed primarily evacuees from Los Angeles County, these interviews embraced the reminiscences of: (1) Japanese Americans who had been detained temporarily in many of the fifteen assembly centers managed by the Wartime Civil Control Administration (WCCA); (2) resident Japanese aliens deemed "potentially dangerous" who were interned in one or more of the several centers administered by the United States Department of Justice; (3) children and grandchildren of the evacuees capitalizing upon the symbolic meaning of the Evacuation as activists in contemporary movements of ethnic consciousness-cum-cultural politics; (4) Caucasians who had been employed by the WRA as camp administrators; and (5) non-Japanese residents of the small communities in the regions close to the sites of the former California camps of Manzanar and Tule Lake. The latter was located near the Oregon border and was converted during the war from a regular relocation center to a segregation center for Japanese Americans deemed "disloyal."

What is less clear from perusing the annotated bibliography in Voices Long Silent is how this profusion of new interviews came into existence. Although Mitson and I were directly responsible for the production of a substantial number of them, the bulk of the interviews derived from students enrolled in successive seminars on the Evacuation taught by the two of us (after Mitson's matriculation into the CSUF Department of History graduate studies program and her appointment as my teaching assistant). During this interval, individual and group forays into the field by project members netted an array of oral memoirs falling into the categories noted above. The two most prominent student interviewers during this phase of the project, David Bertagnoli and Sherry Turner, undertook prolonged fieldwork with the aforementioned townspeople living adjacent, respectively, to the Manzanar and Tule Lake campsites. Then, too, other undergraduate student interviewers, notably David Hacker and Ronald Larson, substantially enlarged and enhanced the project's holdings by conducting key interviews with controversial personalities involved in intracamp politics at the Manzanar center. Finally, two other undergraduate interviewers, Janis Gennawey and Pat Tashima, played important roles during this period through the multiple interviews each added to the project's mushrooming archival collection.

The next stage of the project's development extended through 1980. This stage saw the addition of some thirty-five interviews, falling largely within one of four topical foci: (1) internees and administrators of alien internment centers; (2) celebrated dissidents at WRA centers; (3) Japanese American community leaders in Orange County, California; and (4) residents of the southwestern Arizona communities proximate to the former Poston War Relocation Center. The interviews comprising the last two categories were collected, respectively, under the aegis of seminars which I taught in conjunction with Ronald Larson and Jessie Suzuki Garrett in 1976, and with David Hacker in 1978. Along with Susan McNamara, Eleanor Amigo, Paul Clark, and Betty Mitson, each of these individuals, at one or another time during this phase of the project, saw service as the project's director.

More central and, perhaps, more consequential than interviewing in this period, however, was the technical processing and interpretation of the amassed oral data. Owing to a contractual arrangement between the OHP and Microfilming Corporation of America (MCA), a New York Times subsidiary, project personnel were obliged to transcribe, edit, and index our holdings so that they could be disseminated internationally by MCA in a microfilm edition. In addition to the project directors indicated above, three other project members, Paula Hacker, Elizabeth Stein, and Mary Reando, were instrumental in converting raw tapings into polished archival documents.

With respect to the interpretive work accomplished in this stage, project members produced not only two more published anthologies of its interviews, but also two unpublished CSUF Department of History master's theses and one lengthy scholarly monograph based upon project material. The first of the anthologies, Japanese Americans in Orange County: Oral Perspectives, was edited with an introduction by Eleanor Amigo in 1976. More ambitious in scope, as well as more controversial in nature, was the 1977 anthology, coedited and introduced by Jessie Garrett and Ronald Larson and showcasing the interviews transacted by David Bertagnoli and myself, entitled Camp and Community: Manzanar and the Owens Valley. The two theses, authored by Paul Clark and David Hacker, were completed in 1980 under my supervision. Clark's study, "Those Other Camps: An Oral History Analysis of Japanese Alien Enemy Internment during World War II," revolved around interviews he recorded (some with the translation assistance of Mariko Yamashita, a Japanese exchange student at CSUF affiliated with the project) with former internees and administrators of Department of Justice camps for enemy aliens. The thesis by Hacker, "A Culture Resisted, A Culture Revived: The Loyalty Crisis of 1943 at the Manzanar War Relocation Center," was informed by the many interviews in the project impinging upon developments at Manzanar, particularly an intensive three-day interview conducted jointly by Hacker and myself in the spring of 1978 in Norman, Oklahoma, with Dr. Morris Opler. A professor emeritus of anthropology at both Cornell University and the University of Oklahoma, Opler, during World War II, had headed Manzanar's Community Analysis Section. As for the unpublished monograph, "Doho: The Japanese American 'Communist' Press, 1937-1942," it was authored by Ronald Larson and anchored by interviews done by himself and other project members.

The project's third stage, persisting into the present and encompassing some thirty-five new interviews, has been characterized by cooperative ventures undertaken with outside agencies and individuals. The first of these had its origins in a 1976 project interview with the central figure in the so-called Manzanar Riot of December 1942, Harry Y. Ueno. This endeavor was capped by a widely circulated and critically acclaimed 1986 project publication, Manzanar Martyr: An Interview with Harry Y. Ueno, coedited and introduced by Embrey, the wartime editor of the camp newspaper at Manzanar and the founding chair of the Manzanar Committee (a Los Angeles-based activist group known principally for leading an annual pilgrimage to the Manzanar campsite in the Owens Valley), Betty Mitson, and myself.

The second shared venture, done in conjunction with the Japanese American Council (JAC) of the Historical and Cultural Foundation of Orange County, consisted of fifteen interviews with pioneer family residents of the Japanese American community of Orange County, California. Of these interviews, which were done by enrollees in a CSUF Department of History community oral history class composed about equally of CSUF students and JAC members, seven were with predominantly Japanese-speaking Issei (immigrant-generation Japanese Americans), whose transaction and processing necessitated the services of competent bilingualists. Fortunately, these were provided on a volunteer basis by college-educated wives in Orange County's large overseas Japanese business community who were affiliated with the JAC. Published as fully bilingual volumes including introductions, photo captions, and indexes, these interviews, along with eight other ones done exclusively in English with Nisei (citizen-generation Japanese Americans) comprised the first phase of the ongoing Honorable Stephen K. Tamura Orange County Japanese American Oral History Project, named after the founding cochair of the JAC in recognition of his rise from his roots in the local Japanese American community to appointment in 1966 as the first Japanese American appellate judge in the continental United States.

A third set of cooperative undertakings during the project's last phase has been the publication of two novels penned by project interviewees dramatizing the Japanese American World War II experience from contrasting perspectives. The first of these novels, The Harvest of Hate, was written by Georgia Day Robertson, an Orange Countian who supervised the high school mathematics teachers at the three camps in the Poston War Relocation Center during the war. Although submitted originally by Robertson for publication consideration in 1946, its ultimate publication did not occur until forty years thereafter in 1986. Issued jointly with the JAC as a hardcover volume (in June 1989, it was released by Lynx Books of New York as a mass-market paperback), this novel depicts the crisis of the Evacuation through the eyes of the several members of the fictional Sato family, who farmed in the San Diego area prior to being interned at Poston. The second novel, Seki-nin (Duty Bound), saw print in 1989 under the dual copyright aegis of the project and its Nisei novelist, George Nakagawa. Also published in hardcover form, this novel focuses upon the plight of a Seattle-area Nisei who, out of deference to parental fears for his future, forsakes his native country in 1940 to accompany his parents back to Japan, only to be drafted three years later into the Japanese army and sent to fight, and be killed, in China. Both of these novels, appended with portions of project interviews with their authors, have been widely reviewed in the mainstream and vernacular press.

In addition to these cooperative publication activities, the project has continued to extend and diversify its archival holdings. Consistent with its established pattern of collection, the project added more interviews with Japanese American wartime evacuees, especially those who took part in resistance movements; WRA appointed personnel; and social scientists who studied the Evacuation. But while these older categories were augmented, they were also broadened and variegated. For example, a 1982 interview with a Nisei teacher turned social activist, Hannah Tomiko Holmes, took up her wartime evacuation from the School for the Deaf in Berkeley, California, her incarceration at the Manzanar and Tule Lake centers, and her resettlement in Chicago as a student at the Illinois School for the Deaf. Then, too, a 1987 interview with a WRA administrator, Paul S. Robertson, highlights his seven-month directorship of the isolation center for alleged Nisei "troublemakers" established by the WRA in the spring of 1943 at Leupp, Arizona, on the Navajo reservation. Instead of recording further interviews with those "applied" social scientists employed by the WRA through its Community Analysis Section, the project branched out to interview three social-scientific observers connected with the theoretically-attuned University of California sponsored Evacuation and Resettlement Study (ERS): Robert F. Spencer, an emeritus professor of anthropology at the University of Minnesota, who served as a field anthropologist at the Gila Relocation Center in Arizona; Charles Kikuchi, a retired Veterans Administration social worker who was an ERS participant-observer at Tanforan (California) Assembly Center and Gila Relocation Center and also collected life histories in Chicago among resettled evacuees; and James M. Sakoda, an emeritus professor of social psychology and statistics at Brown University, who carried on participant-observation for JERS at Tulare Assembly Center and the relocation centers at Tule Lake and Minidoka, Idaho.

Finally, this phase in the project's development has witnessed the production, in 1989, of two more CSUF History Department M.A. theses by project members. The first, "Medicine in a Crisis Situation: The Effect of Culture on Health Care in the World War II Japanese American Detention Center," by Michelle Gutierrez, makes resourceful use of existing project interviews with an Issei, Dr. Yoriyuki Kikuchi, Chief of the Dental Clinic at Manzanar, and Frank Chuman, the Nisei director of the Manzanar hospital. The second, "Interned Without: The Military Police at the Tule Lake Relocation/Segregation Center, 1942-46," by Reagan Bell, is heavily reliant upon interviews he transacted for the project with soldiers who were stationed at the Tule Lake Center as well as with a man who served there as one of its assistant directors. Both Gutierrez and Bell illustrate a practice increasingly being followed in the project: that of employing mature students rich in beneficial life experiences as interviewers, editors, and interpreters. In the case of the former, she graduated from a university with a degree in microbiology and worked for a decade as a laboratory technician at the University of Southern California/Los Angeles County Hospital prior to matriculating in the graduate history program at CSUF; as for the latter, a World War II veteran who witnessed his southern California classmates at Tustin Union High School being evacuated to Poston and other centers in 1942, he finished a twenty-year U.S. Army career, including considerable guard duty, prior to completing his B.A. in history and commencing graduate history studies at CSUF.

During the course of its seventeen-year tenure, the Japanese American Project has been fortunate to have the dedicated service and support of countless individuals. Apart from those already named, a number of other people associated in one or another significant way with the project deserve specific recognition for their contributions. Dr. Kinji K. Yada, a colleague in the CSUF Department of History and a wartime internee at the Manzanar center, has assisted the project as a resource person from its inception through the present; not only has he provided timely translations and trenchant advice, but also taught classes taken by project personnel in Japanese and Japanese American history and shaped and sharpened the M.A. theses of a selected few of them. Elizabeth Stein, now a faculty member in the CSUF Department of English, gave unstintingly of her time and editorial talents as an undergraduate while discharging her duties as the project's associate director during its second stage of development. Others who were important to the project for their promotional work in this same period were Duff Griffith and Reed Holderman. Since 1980, the project has benefited greatly, particularly in connection with its work on the Honorable Stephen K. Tamura Orange County Japanese American Project, by the efforts of volunteers drawn from Orange County's Japanese American population and the county's overseas Japanese business community. Noteworthy in the former category were the following individuals: Myrtle Asahino, Yasko Gamo, Susan Hori, Charles Ishii, Gale Itagaki, Hiroshi Kamei, James Kanno, Carol Kawanami, Grace Muruyama, Dr. Ernest Nagamatsu, Clarence Nishizu, Shi and Mary Nomura, Iku Watanabe, Dorothy Wing, and Rae Yasumura. The latter category was headed up by Masako Hanada and Yukiko Sato, who coordinated the team of translators, transcribers, and editors associated with the production of the bilingual volumes in the Tamura collection. Members of this team included: Keiko Akashi, Kokonoe Baba, Kazuko Horie, Hisako Maruoka, Etsu Matsuo, Setsuko Naiki, Kyoko Okamoto, Yoko Tateuchi, Yumiko Wakabayashi, and Chiharu Yawata. CSUF students instrumental during this third phase of the project have been Phillip Brigandi, Jeanie Corral, Richard Imon, and Ann Uyeda. Although the CSUF Oral History Program staff, spearheaded by its able and indefatigable associate director/archivist Shirley E. Stephenson, has facilitated the work of the project in a panoply of ways from its beginning, in recent years the role of staff members, Kathleen Frazee, Shirley de Graaf, Debra Gold Hansen, Gaye Kouyoumjian, and Garnette Long, especially in the area of technical processing, has been both spirited and substantial. During the 1980s, the project has enjoyed the support of two new OHP directors, Professors Lawrence de Graaf and Michael Onorato, both faculty members in the CSUF Department of History, the OHP's administrative parent. Finally, the four History Department chairs during the life of the project--Professors George Giacumakis, Thomas Flickema, Robert Feldman, and James Woodward--have demonstrated leadership beneficial to its growth and development.

Throughout its existence, the project has been largely self-supporting as a result of the sale of its assorted publications. In its formative years, a small amount of subsidization was provided by the CSUF School of Social Sciences and Humanities and a series of research grants awarded to student project members through the university's Departmental Association Council. The largest infusion of funds into the project came about, however, during its second developmental stage via Comprehensive Employment Training Act (CETA) salary payments for trainees attached to the project. In recent years, financial assistance has flowed from several sources: (1) the Japanese American Council of the Historical and Cultural Foundation of Orange County; (2) the MAC NEEL PIERCE FOUNDATION, with student scholarships; (3) CSUF faculty research and travel grants; and (4) donations from project interviewees and their families.

Almost from its outset, project holdings and personnel have been consulted by a variety of researchers, from affiliates of local historical societies and agencies, both within and outside of the Japanese American community, through writers of doctoral dissertations and scholarly studies. The media have also turned to the project for assistance on a regular basis, extending from area newspapers through network television stations in Japan and the United Kingdom, and from low-budget documentary film makers through producers of mass-circulation feature films. Although the contemporary movement for redress/reparations to Japanese American survivors of the Evacuation has dramatized the value of project documents, it is likely that they will continue to be deemed valuable by researchers for many years to come, even after the project as an institutional entity has come to its inevitable end.

California State University, Fullerton   ARTHUR A. HANSEN

Introduction

As stated in my prefatory note, the World War II Japanese American Evacuation experience is central to the collection of interviews comprising the Japanese American Project of the Oral History Program at California State University, Fullerton. While most of the interviews focused upon this event are with interned Japanese Americans, a sizeable number recount the Evacuation from the perspective of those who served as administrators in the several varieties of centers established by the U.S. government for the wartime detention of people of Japanese ancestry. Thus, this volume of the Japanese American World War II Evacuation Oral History Project consists of interviews transacted with seven of these administrators. Collectively, these interviews, which possess an intertextual compatibility, evoke a broad range of administrative responses to the challenges posed by the U.S. government's decision to incarcerate resident aliens and citizens of Japanese ancestry.

Opening the volume are interviews with Richard S. Dockum, Abner Schreiber, and Amy N. Stannard, all of whom were high-ranking officials at alien internment camps. Each of these individuals were interviewed in connection with former Japanese American Project member Paul Clark's 1980 CSUF History Department thesis, "Those Other Camps: An Oral History Analysis of Japanese Alien Enemy Internment During World War II." These interviews have been reproduced here along with slightly abridged and amended versions of the introductions and endnotes Clark prepared for them in his thesis.

The interview with Richard Dockum, the adjutant (i.e., second in command) of the U.S. Army managed internment camp at Lordsburg, New Mexico, was done in 1977 at the interviewee's home in Lordsburg, with the assistance of local historian Mollie M. Pressler. Because Dockum was at the camp during the first year of its operation, his commentary contains vital information about the settling in of the camp community, encompassing internee relationships with camp officials--including a number of violent encounters with the military police--and residents of the nearby town of Lordsburg. Dockum also relates revealing facts about the two commandants under whom he served at Lordsburg, the "culture" of the camp administration, and the customs and ceremonies of the imprisoned Japanese aliens.

Like Dockum, the telephonic interview conducted by Clark in 1979 with Abner Schreiber is with a second-ranking official in a World War II alien internment camp in New Mexico who, after the war, returned to make his home in that state. But unlike Dockum, Schreiber's administrative role was discharged at the Santa Fe Internment Center, which was operated, not by the Army, but by the federal Immigration and Naturalization Service. Whereas Dockum had a military background, Schreiber was a product of a legal education and prewar employment in the U.S. Department of Justice's Border Patrol. Moreover, it was when Dockum was departing Lordsburg, in the spring of 1943, that Schreiber was dispatched to the Santa Fe camp, just then beginning its operations. As with Dockum's interview, Schreiber's contains valuable insights into the personality and leadership style of his superiors, the activities of the internees, and administrative-internee relations. Perhaps the most important information contained in Schreiber's interview, however, is his depiction of the riot that occurred in the Santa Fe camp on March 12, 1945, following the transfer to the camp of dissident citizen renunciants from the tumultuous Tule Lake Segregation Center.

The interview with Dr. Amy N. Stannard, the sole woman to head an alien internment facility during World War II, was conducted by Paul Clark at her retirement community residence in northern California in 1978. Stannard's training was neither in the military or the law, but rather in psychiatry. In her interview, she describes her 1940 appointment to the Bureau of Prisons at the new Federal Reformatory for Women at Seagoville, Texas, explains how in the spring of 1942 that facility was converted into an alien enemy detention center under the joint supervision of the Bureau of Prisons and the Immigration and Naturalization Service, and relates her successive experiences as Seagoville's superintendent and officer-in-charge. Although in declining health at the time of the interview, Stannard was able nonetheless to convey the precise dimensions and physical layout of the camp, delineate the different national, ethnic, chronological, and gender components of the interned population, and explore the special problems attendant upon being a woman administrator within a system dominated by men.

The remaining four interviews in this volume are with appointed personnel of the War Relocation Authority (WRA), the agency charged with administering the ten semipermanent centers housing the evacuated West Coast population of Japanese American citizens and resident aliens. The first two, with Robert L. Brown and Ned Campbell, are with men who served as assistant project directors at the Manzanar Relocation Center in eastern California's Owens Valley. In his interview, done with me in 1973-1974, Brown clarifies the circumstances that led to the selection of the Inyo County site for Manzanar and his role, as the secretary of the Inyo-Mono Association, in this process. He explains, further, how his prewar experience as a publicist for the area prompted his appointment as the public relations officer for the Owens Valley Reception Center, the official designation for the Manzanar camp during the period of March 21 to May 31, 1942, when managed by the Wartime Civil Control Administration (WCCA), a quasi-civilian U.S. Army agency headed by Colonel Karl Bendetsen and charged with supervising seventeen assembly and reception centers for the temporary detention of evacuated people of Japanese ancestry. Brown, who was appointed the camp's reports officer by the WRA once this agency assumed command from the WCCA on June 1, 1942, and renamed the site the Manzanar War Relocation Center, discusses in depth the demands of his job, including supervising the production of the Manzanar Free Press, the camp newspaper, accommodating the administrative agenda and styles of five directors or acting directors during the camp's first eight months of operation, and acting as a liaison relative to the camp's relations with surrounding Owens Valley communities. Finally, Brown's interview is notable for his depiction of prominent administrative and internee personalities and factions and how these were implicated in the tragic Manzanar Riot of December 6, 1942, an event that led to the death of two internees, the wounding of nine others, and the elevation of Robert Brown to the position of Manzanar's assistant director.

Brown's predecessor as assistant director, Ned Campbell, covers much the same ground as Brown in his interview, though with a decidedly different twist. With Texas roots, a legal education, and disaster relief experience with the Red Cross, Campbell was employed on the Navajo reservation when, in the wake of Pearl Harbor, the superintendent of the reservation, E. Reesman "Si" Fryer, was appointed the director of the regional WRA office in San Francisco and, at a sizeable increase in salary, made Campbell the agency's organizational man. Charged first with assisting in the preparation of the three camps comprising the Poston center in Arizona, Campbell, with the WRA takeover of Manzanar, was made assistant to the director, Roy Nash. As his interview indicates, Campbell continued in his post through Nash's short directorship and the still shorter tenures of acting directors Harvey Coverley and Solon Kimball, a situation which, in effect, rendered him as the camp's dominant authority figure. A close associate and confidante of Robert Brown's, Campbell became increasingly larded in controversy with conflicting internee factions, culminating in the accusation by Harry Ueno, head of the Mess Hall Workers Union, that he and Joseph Winchester, the camp's chief steward, were stealing rationed supplies designated for internees and selling them on the black market. The upshot of this accusation was the arrest of Ueno and his removal from the camp to a local town jail, allegedly because of his involvement in the beating of an unpopular internee spokesman, and a series of mass demonstrations that led to Ueno being returned to the Manzanar jail and, shortly thereafter, to a confrontation between military police and internees that ended in the tragic Manzanar Riot. Of interest is Campbell's contention that Manzanar's new director, Ralph Merritt, "a cold-blooded egoist," used the pretext of the riot to replace him with "his boy" Robert Brown, who had persuaded Campbell to join forces with him to promote Merritt's application for the vacant directorship. Quite apart from its contribution to an understanding of events at Manzanar, this account suggests that political in-fighting in the WRA camps was by no means limited to the interned population.

On the other hand, the interviews with Ed. H. Runcorn and Paul S. Robertson tend to belie any blanket condemnation of WRA appointed personnel as callous bureaucrats interested more in self-advancement than in the well-being of their interned charges. Both highly religious men concerned with putting their principles into practice, Runcorn and Robertson became associates and close friends during their days together at the Tule Lake Segregation Center in northern California after the former was appointed to supervise its cooperative stores and the latter to be one of its assistant directors. Runcorn, who was interviewed in 1973 by Janis Gennawey, grounds the discussion of his activities pertinent to the co-ops at Tule Lake and at the Granada center in Colorado in the larger context of the co-op movement, the comparative perspective afforded him as the WRA's associate superintendent of cooperative enterprises, and the overarching socioreligious mission incumbent upon him as a Quaker. That the camp co-ops were implicated in controversy in the camps is underscored by Runcorn's allusion to the brutal murder of the internee head of the Tule Lake co-op, Yaozo Hitomi.

Paul Robertson's interview, transacted by Reagan Bell and myself in 1987 at his home in Carmichael, California, embraces virtually the entire wartime existence of the WRA. Raised as a Methodist and schooled in architecture at Yale University, it was as a state of California agricultural official with wide and varied contacts among the Japanese American farm population that Robertson captured the attention of the WRA regional office in San Francisco, which in 1942 appointed him to a staff position. With the WRA's increasing commitment to relocation as against detention, Robertson was assigned to the national WRA office in Washington, D.C., to facilitate this objective. After the WRA deemed it necessary in 1943, following a protracted strike at Poston and the riot at Manzanar, to isolate citizen internees like Harry Ueno, whom project directors at the ten WRA centers designated as "troublemakers," Robertson was made director of the Tule Lake Segregation Center by Dillon Myer. Robertson's interview discusses how he was alerted to the essentially groundless and unsubstantiated charges against the men sent to Leupp, and how this knowledge conditioned the WRA's decision to close that center and transfer the majority of the internees to Tule Lake, along with Robertson himself. Robertson's recounting of his life and work at the WRA's isolation and segregation centers and his relationships with the reputed recalcitrant and/or disloyal internees at both places is singularly placid in content and tone. Somewhat more stormy is his depiction of his post-Tule Lake WRA employment as the supervising officer of the agency's efforts to assist the resettlement of Japanese Americans in southern California, an area still rife with the same racist feelings that had fueled and sustained the Evacuation.

California State University, Fullerton   ARTHUR A. HANSEN

An Interview with
RICHARD S. DOCKUM
Conducted by Paul F. Clark and Mollie M. Pressler
on March 18, 1977
for the
California State University, Fullerton
Oral History Program
Japanese American Project

(United States Army Internment Camps Administration Experiences
and Army Career, O. H. 1612)

1

This is a slightly edited transcription of an interview conducted for the Oral History Program, sponsored by the California State University, Fullerton. The reader should realize that an oral history document is spontaneous in nature, and portrays information and impressions as recalled by the interviewee.

Interview Introduction

For two years after Pearl Harbor, the United States Army maintained official custody of interned alien enemy males. This interview with Richard S. Dockum explores the administration of the army internment camp located at Lordsburg, New Mexico. Dockum's assignment there spans much of the period of the Japanese occupancy of that facility. As the camp's adjutant, or second in command, he is able to impart firsthand information and impressions of this early period of army internment responsibility.

Dockum's army career is closely associated with the military's reserve program. A civil engineer by college education, he drilled with the Texas A&M University Reserve Officers' Training Corps in the late 1920s. Called to active duty with the coming of the Second World War, he transferred among a number of duties during these hostilities, including an interesting postwar term in Portugal as an aide in negotiations with that nation. In August 1946, he finally left active military service to rejoin his family in New Mexico.

In the later postwar years, Dockum resettled in Lordsburg and established a business there. Through the courtesy of Mollie M. Pressler, a local schoolteacher, Paul Clark met and arranged this interview with Dockum while visiting Lordsburg in 1977. Previously, Pressler had written an unpublished paper on the Lordsburg encampment covering its entire wartime history. Pressler not only contacted Dockum, but also served as cointerviewer during the interview, which involved one evening session lasting a little over one hour. The interviewee's wife was also present at the interview. Subsequent to the taping session, Dockum reviewed the corresponding transcript of the interview; while limiting himself largely to small changes, he did add some significant material that had not been brought out when the interview was recorded.

CALIFORNIA STATE UNIVERSITY, FULLERTON

ORAL HISTORY PROGRAM

Japanese American Project

INTERVIEWEE: RICHARD S. DOCKUM

INTERVIEWER: Paul F. Clark and Mollie M. Pressler

SUBJECT: United States Army Internment Camps
                  Administration Experiences and Army Career

DATE: March 18, 1977

PC: This is an interview with Richard S. Dockum for the California State University, Fullerton, Oral History Program's Japanese American Project. The interview is being conducted in Mr. Dockum's home in Lordsburg, New Mexico, on March 18, 1977, and the interviewers are Paul F. Clark and Mollie M. Pressler.

Good evening, Mr. Dockum. We are pleased to be in your home tonight to interview you about your memories of the Lordsburg Internment Camp. Perhaps, before we talk about the camp, we should discuss your early career as an [United States] Army officer before coming to Lordsburg.

RD: Well, I was commissioned into the cavalry in 1930 upon graduation from Texas A&M University. I held a second lieutenant's commission for a number of years. Then, several years prior to the outbreak of war in 1941, I was commissioned first lieutenant. I held that rank when I came to Lordsburg in June 1942. My degree from Texas A&M was in civil engineering which I practiced privately and with the state highway department in Corsicana, Texas, for several years prior to the war.

Of course, the war interrupted all that type of thing. I was called into the service while working in Dallas, Texas. I went to Camp Walters Reception Center at Mineral Wells, Texas. From there, I went to Clovis, New Mexico, where we opened a railroad battalion training base. I stayed there until June [1942] when I was sent to Lordsburg.

My wife and I drove into Lordsburg on a hot, June Sunday, and when we took one look at it, we decided we didn't want to stay here. (laughter) So we got busy and wrote letters, trying to get transferred out, but the [United States] War Department didn't pay any attention to us. We were assigned to the internment camp here at Lordsburg. The camp was still under construction at the time I came. Shortly after that, when it was completed, I was made adjutant under Colonel Clyde Lundy, who was the camp commander. It wasn't long before we began receiving Japanese internees.

PC: You mentioned that you were in Clovis in the early part of the war. About what period do you recall that you were in Clovis?

RD: Well, I believe that was from about March until June of 1942.

PC: Do you recall if formerly there were any Japanese in Clovis that had been removed?

RD: No, not that I know of.[1] At Camp walters in Mineral Wells, we had the Nisei Japs. The armed forces had centralized them into labor battalions, and they worked on housekeeping chores there at Camp Walters. One interesting person there was a Negro mess sergeant. He had these Japanese out there mashing cans for salvage. They accidentally broke the ax handles and hadn't anything to mash the cans with, so he had them jumping on them. He said, "Mash 'em flat, you sonsabitches. If it wasn't for you, I wouldn't be here!" (laughter)

PC: I understand that Colonel Lundy, the first commander of Lordsburg, was a pretty colorful individual. What was he like? Can you recall anything in particular about him?

RD: Well, he was rather typical "Army." Of course, he was a regular Army officer, having come up from the ranks. He started out as an enlisted man, but he rose rather rapidly. I'm not positive about this, but I think he was commissioned not long before the war broke out. He came to the camp as a lieutenant colonel and was later promoted to full colonel while I was here.

He [Colonel Lundy] was a very colorful character. He liked to be the typical Army officer, wearing his boots and carrying a riding crop. And to round out the picture, he got himself a dog. He'd take this dog with him and let the dog sleep under his desk. He liked to walk around with his riding crop, his boots, and so forth, putting on a show. He liked very much the old, formal entertaining that the Army had always had in peacetime. He wanted a party every Saturday night at the officers' club. His wife stayed in El Paso because they had a daughter who had rheumatic fever. Because his wife stayed there most of the time, it fell to my wife to be the official hostess at these parties. Every Saturday night we'd have a big party in the officers' club and always had receiving lines--same people, same officers, same everything. Well, we had some colorful parties and entertainment: masquerade-type things, as well as rather formal dances. He was always a great one for show and doing things the way he wanted to do them.

I remember when he first received and unloaded his equipment and brought his personal effects into his office. He unpacked his Army regulations, put them on the shelf, and said, "See all those books? Regulations are made to be broken in my book." (laughter) That was the way he looked at it. So we had quite a time there with Colonel Lundy.

Under his administration, half of the officers were required to stay on the base for two or three nights. Then they would switch, and the other half would be required to stay. He had me make up the roster of those that he wanted to stay on a particular night, because that was when he liked to play poker. We had the ones who were congenial in the poker games stay in one group, and all the others would be in the other group.

When I first arrived at the camp, as I mentioned, it was under construction and, of course, there was not very much for the military personnel to do. Lieutenant [James E.] Hughes was the adjutant at the time and was the only one who had the combination to the office safe. Almost every afternoon when it was time to lower the flag, Colonel Lundy would come into the headquarters and say, "Lieutenant, the flag is down and it is time for a drink." Lieutenant Hughes would open the safe, and I saw that it contained nothing but liquor. Colonel Lundy was very positive about no one drinking before the flag went down, but after that, the sky was the limit.[2]

PC: I understand, though, that he was relieved of command because of irregularities.

RD: Well, yes, he was. At that time, the Army still had this system of rationed savings--like in the old days. To feed the companies, they were allowed so much cash per day per man. If they saved any money on that, it went into a fund for the entertainment of the men, or for recreational purposes.

The companies in those days also had their own PX [post exchange] that they would operate as a company function. Any money they made from that went into their recreational fund, too. When we started the camp here, they were still under the system where they had rationed savings. This meant that you had so much for the men in the Army and, also, the same amount for the Japanese [internees]. Well, when the rations were issued, they were counted out and divided on that basis. The colonel was a little bit liberal with the Army personnel and short-changed the Japanese some. The rationed savings that accumulated wasn't always used to their best advantage. In other words, he was a little bit more inclined to bring things up to the officers' club than to put them down for the enlisted men, or to put them into the compound where the Japanese were.

Eventually, some of that was investigated and brought out against him. One thing in particular, when the International Red Cross[3] sent some band instruments in for the Japanese, the colonel had those taken up to the officers' club. Of course, when the Red Cross came and checked up, they very quickly had us move them in the compound. However, I don't think anything in Colonel Lundy's administration was too awful but, of course, these violations were charged against him. When the inspector general's department came in and made an investigation, he was relieved of duty. In fact, he was allowed to retire rather than having any formal charges brought against him. He was, however, relieved of his command here at Lordsburg prior to his retirement.

PC: I understand that his successor was one of those who helped expose the irregularities.

RD: Yes, Colonel [Louis A.] Ledbetter came in to relieve him. He was formerly adjutant general for the state of Oklahoma and as such was in command of the Oklahoma National Guard. He had been called into active duty as a brigadier general and then was later relieved and put on inactive status. At this time, he was called back to duty as a full colonel, or given the choice to come back, which he accepted. He was sent in to relieve Colonel Lundy. Apparently, he was told to look for certain things when he came here, which he did. He went through the records pretty thoroughly and came up with some of these violations that I've mentioned. Then he requested the inspector general's department to come in and make a thorough investigation. This was done, of course, after Colonel Lundy was gone. I never did see Colonel Lundy again after he was relieved of command.

PC: Do you mean that Colonel Ledbetter did this checking after Colonel Lundy was relieved?

RD: Yes. Apparently the Eighth [Army] Corps Headquarters had some information. That was the reason they had sent Colonel Ledbetter in. They had some specific things for him to look for. But we--the other officers and personnel--weren't informed of that. You could see Colonel Ledbetter going through the records. He would ask me various questions about this, that, and the other. It wasn't long before he found out what he was after.

PC: Were Colonel Lundy and Colonel Ledbetter the two main commandants here at Lordsburg while the Japanese were here?

RD: Yes. Colonel Ledbetter was still here when I was transferred out. I think he stayed the full time the Japanese were here, but I could be wrong.

PC: What was their relationship to the Japanese? You mentioned Colonel Lundy's irregularities. However, besides that, what kind of program did he try to provide for the Japanese?

RD: Well, I would say that the Japanese were treated very well. They were not abused in any way. When I mentioned the fact that some of the rations were diverted from the compound to the enlisted mess or to the officers' mess, that sounds worse than it really was. The Japanese preferred their own type of cooking. They would prefer fish for certain meals, or they would prefer the bony parts of chicken and that sort of thing, in making up their dishes, rather than the best meat parts. So the Colonel considered their likes and dislikes by taking the best and giving them the other. (laughter) That's not really the case. Actually, they didn't suffer from that. From outward appearances, it did seem that they were being taken advantage of and not given things they should have had. But the Japanese were treated well and not abused in any way.

They were given baseball equipment, too. I can't think of any other recreational equipment. They had their recreational programs that they could follow if they wanted to. They did that pretty much on their own. The Japanese were very industrious people, and a lot of them put in gardens and raised various produce there. They were also very good at making things out of wood. They would take old mesquite roots and things like that, polish them up and carve them into various objects. They made these sandal affairs--what do you call them? You slipped your feet in, like this.

MP: Like a clog?

RD: Clogs, yes, that type of thing. They also did a lot of stone polishing, making various things out of stone and cement. They were pretty busy and kept occupied. I'd like to say, except for being confined, they led a pretty good life. It wasn't bad at all.

PC: Did they organize themselves?

RD: Well, I don't remember much detail of the organization in the compounds. They had barrack leaders, and they had a mayor--if you could call him a mayor--for the compound. They would go through the chain of command for any complaints they had or for anything that they needed. Of course, we had officers who were assigned for this purpose, who took care of and looked after the Japanese. They were in consultation all the time as things came up.[4]

PC: As adjutant of the camp, what were your particular duties?

RD: Well, mostly being a flunky for the colonel. (laughter) In the first place, I was commanding officer of the headquarters company, which took in all the headquarters personnel: the message center, the clerks, the headquarters company mess, the VIPs, and all that. I'd make out the daily roster and so forth of all the headquarters company. Also, we had the hospital orderlies and the medical personnel in the headquarters company. Aside from that, I supervised all the work in the headquarters myself, and I was on call for the colonel for any particular sandwich or anything special. All the mail came through my hands. I sorted that out and passed on to the colonel anything I thought needed his particular attention. I also took care of all the switchboards and telephones, and the installation of the telephones.

I know that several years ago there was an article in the Lordsburg paper [Lordsburg Liberal], that they couldn't understand why so many phones had been installed in a particular year. We [Dockum and wife] looked at that and traced it back. Well, that was the time when we were installing telephones in the camp and they told me they wanted so many phones in the barracks and so many up at the hospital. I went through and marked "Xs" on the walls. Everywhere I put an "X", that's where a phone was put in. They installed about eight hundred new phones that particular year. Not all of them were out there at the camp, but the majority were. We had one of the old-fashioned switchboards with about four men on duty all the time taking calls.

PC: What kind of relationship existed between the camp and the people of Lordsburg?

RD: Well, as far as my personal feelings go, it was a very good relationship between the camp and the people of Lordsburg. Of course, any time you have an Army installation, or a group like that, you're going to have some unfortunate experiences. Of course, we'd have some of the boys come down there [to town], and they'd get drunk and get in fights, or one thing or another. But I'd say there was very little of that. We had the military police pretty well-organized and they'd keep track of the boys pretty well. They would stop anything that would come up pretty quick. We had our curfews and they'd see that they were all rounded up and on the bus back to camp.

We had one provost marshal who was an Englishman. He talked like a Britisher, you know. You might say he was a soldier of fortune. How he wound up in this particular assignment, I don't know. One night he was down at the Blue Moon Bar when a fight started. It wasn't between the soldiers, but among the civilians. One of them knocked another one out--knocked him on the floor--and he was kicking him and one thing and another. This Englishman said, "Don't do that!" So this old boy just turned around and cold-cocked him right there. (laughter) Next thing he [the Englishman] said, "That taught me to keep my nose out of somebody else's business." (laughter) On the whole, the relationship with the people in Lordsburg was very good.

PC: I understand Colonel Lundy often did invite the townsfolk to the parties.

RD: Oh, yes. Quite a few of the local people were invited out to these Saturday night parties and dances, the ranchers more so than the townspeople.

PC: Were the Japanese ever used as servants or waiters at these parties?

RD: No. They were in their compounds. I'm not quite sure of this, but I think some of them helped out in the hospital. They were not required to do any outside labor. They were offered a chance to work outside if they wanted to, and a few did work outside a little bit. But they didn't go for that very much.

PC: You mentioned that the Red Cross made a number of visits to the camp. Do you recall visits by other organizations, like the Quakers?

RD: I think the Red Cross was the only one I remember coming in.

PC: Mollie, is there anything you would like to ask?

MP: Well, about these parties. Do you remember anyone in particular that you would like to describe?

RD: (laughter) I don't know what you're getting at?

MP: How about the barn dance?

RD: Do you want me to describe myself?

MP: Why not?

RD: Well, there was this barn dance there. We fixed up the officers' club with bales of hay and so forth. We had the old artillery horses and wagons which were used by the quartermaster as the only means of transportation around the camp. We'd use those to haul supplies. On this particular night, we had these wagons meet the guests at the gate. They came to the building in hay-filled wagons. Then they had to crawl through a tunnel of hay going into the officers' club. Some local musicians--cowboys who played the fiddle and all--furnished the music. We had some cages with chickens and pigs all around to give it an authentic look. I was dressed as the old black mountaineer, barefooted, with a beard, hat shotgun, and a jug. My date for the night was Mrs. [Marie] Smart, a lieutenant's wife. She weighed about two hundred pounds. She had on a regular apron affair with sunbonnet, a corncob pipe, and GI [government issue] shoes. We were together most of the evening. We had square dancing and so forth. Colonel Baker was the doctor who ran the hospital. He dressed as one of the Japanese internees, and he would say, "So solly, please." (laughter)

Sergeant Moore was the cook for the officers' club. He had been General [John J.] Pershing's private chef, while Pershing was in retirement and recuperating over in Arizona. He was quite a good cook. He prepared the food and had the table very lavishly supplied for the evening with two or three different kinds of meat and all sorts of accoutrements. They fixed a "well" over in one corner with buckets, you know, that you draw up. One bucket had Manhattans and another had martinis. (laughter)

We invited the boys from the Deming Air Base[5] over for the occasion, and quite a few of them came. Lieutenant [E. W.] Mitchell's wife--Singee, we called her--dressed up as Daisy Mae. She had a little skit she put on imitating playing the old bass fiddle. She'd make the sounds and play the fiddle. Mrs. Causey, who was a civilian in town, came out and sang "Just a Bird in a Gilded Cage." I was so taken by all that; _e way she sang it brought tears to my eyes. While I was squatted down there wiping the tears from my eyes, one of these boys from the Deming Air Base slipped up behind me and tried to give me a hotfoot. (laughter) But it didn't take; for some reason I never did feel it. Finally, the fiddler became drunk enough to fall off a bale of hay and that put an end to the dancing. (laughter)

PC: Did the Japanese there have access to liquor?

RD: No. They had their PX where they could buy toilet articles, shaving supplies, some cigarettes and candy, and things of that kind. But they had no liquor.

PC: No beer even?

RD: No.[6]

PC: When the Japanese originally came on the trains, how were they brought out to camp?

RD: Well, the trains came on this railroad [Southern Pacific] right out here on the El Morris Siding. The trains stopped there usually at two or three o'clock in the morning. When it stopped, of course, the guards came to meet them there, and they would unload them and march them over to the camp--about two miles. They'd march them up there, and they'd be fed and bedded down in the compounds by daylight.

PC: What were the procedures of admitting new internees? What would you have them go through?

RD: Well, they were processed. They'd come in late at night, and they were fed and bedded down first. The next day they were processed through the custodial officer, Lieutenant Hughes. He took all their valuables from them--of course, giving them receipts for it. All the money was deposited in the bank. They were processed as far as where they were from and all sorts of similar historical data on them before they were actually turned loose to go their way in the compound.

PC: Do you remember any particular problems with the Japanese that may have occurred while they were being brought to the camp?

RD: Well, of course, there were two or three incidents. The main incident was when two were shot trying to escape. The guards were marching a group up from the train one night, and two of them tried to escape. The guard called to them to halt. They didn't, so he shot them. There has been a lot of controversy over that, particularly recently. I've had occasion to talk to some local people about it, and they thought it was a pretty bad thing in that, if they had escaped, there wouldn't have been anyplace for them to go. They'd have been very easily apprehended. They thought it was pretty bad that they were shot. Still, the guard was under orders not to let them escape. He called to them to halt three times, as was specified, and they didn't halt. Well, he shot them.

We had our Colonel Bell, who was from the Eighth Army Corps Headquarters in camp at the time, making an inspection. He went down the next morning to look around and picked up the shells as souvenirs. He told Colonel Lundy that they ought to strike a medal for this boy who did the shooting. The people in town just really went wild over it. They took up a collection around town and gave him free meals, free drinks, and all that.

Well, as soon as the information was passed on to Eighth Army Corps Headquarters, we were ordered to put the man under arrest, confine him to his barracks, and court-martial him. Of course, that's just actually a routine that is followed in order to clear the man. Unfortunately, he didn't get a chance to take advantage of all the free stuff in town because he was kept confined to the post. He did, however, get the money that was taken up for him, eventually. I don't remember how much it was; it was a pretty good sum. He was court-martialed and, of course, cleared. He was shooting in the line of duty.[7]

Another little incident that I was telling Mollie about was, one day some of the Japs were coming out of their PX, and one of the GI boys, for no apparent reason at all, jumped on one of the Japanese with a penknife and started stabbing him. Of course, he was pulled off very quickly, and he was punished for it. But we still don't know why or what provoked him to do anything like that. It was just one of those things. The old boy just cracked, I guess. These are the only incidents that I recall of any violence with the Japanese.[8]

We had, at one time, when a mistake was made, about fifty Japanese naval prisoners of war [POWs]. The Lordsburg Camp was strictly an internment camp for enemy aliens and not for POWs, and, as such, we did not have the required security to take care of POWs. These naval POWs were shipped to us by mistake when they were supposed to go to Sugarland, Texas, I believe. They were a pretty sullen bunch, and of course, being put in with the civilians was a bad thing. Our camp commander notified the headquarters, and when the error was discovered, they were transferred out almost immediately. They were here, though, for a couple of days. The Japanese internees really took on over these prisoners and made heroes out of them. They ran a Japanese flag out over the barracks and things like that. Of course, the colonel sent a man in and took the flag down and, more or less, put the guards under strict security orders for awhile until we could get those POWs out of there.

It was a rather tense time when all of this was taking place, you know. We didn't know whether there was going to be any kind of an uprising or not, so everyone was on guard to see if anything might happen.

PC: I've heard that the Japanese POWs performed some sort of ceremony and shouted, "Banzai." Do you recall that?

RD: I don't recall that, particularly. Like I said, they ran the flag up, and there was quite a bit of commotion. I don't particularly remember that, but I do recall that it was a pretty tense time for all of us.[9]

PC: Back to the shooting incident. Do you recall how many Japanese were in the group that was being taken up there?

RD: Oh, not specifically, but I imagine there were around one hundred.

PC: Do you believe that the guard force was sufficient for that number of Japanese?

RD: Oh, yes.

PC: About how many guards did you usually have?

RD: Well, let's see. We had three guard companies with about a hundred and fifty men in each company. They were assigned various duties, and they'd rotate on guarding the Japanese around the compounds and meeting the trains. I don't remember, specifically, how many guards they had, but they had an officer in charge of a platoon, maybe twenty-five men to meet the train and bring them to camp.

PC: What happened to the two individuals who were shot?

RD: I believe that those particular ones were cremated. Their next of kin were notified and they [the next of kin] supplied the money to ship their ashes to them.

PC: I understand that three individuals are still buried there at Lordsburg?

RD: We'll take Mollie's word for that; I don't know.[10]   Most of them wanted to be cremated when they died.   Several died, and they wanted to be cremated and their ashes sent to their families.   In some cases they weren't able to raise the money to have it done, so we couldn't ship them [the deceased] to Albuquerque to be cremated. If the money couldn't be raised, they were buried here.   Later, I understand, some were dug up and cremated.   But I never did know how many were left.

MP: There's Judge [H. Vearle] Payne who cited two examples.   He stated that two had been shot, and he went out with Mr. [Jack] Heather to bury the two.

RD: Jack Heather was the mortician.   Dr. [James H.] Baxter was here then, and he always helped to get things together and taken care of.   That's how I first got to know Dr. Baxter.   (laughter)

PC: Did some of the Japanese try to tell these other individuals who'd run away to come back?

RD: I really don't know.   I wasn't there, personally, at the time.   Of course, since I don't speak Japanese, I couldn't have understood them anyhow.

PC: Do you know what kind of reaction the Japanese had to the shooting incident?

RD: Well, they didn't like it, of course.   They resented it and they felt that they'd been taken advantage of.   As far as any strong showing in their conduct, well, I don't recall anything out of the way.

PC: Did the Spanish Embassy make any investigation?

RD: No, not to my knowledge.   I think the International Red Cross checked it out.   A Swiss came here with the International Red Cross several times.   I could be wrong on that, but it seems to me that they did make an investigation through the Red Cross.   But I don't remember any embassy personnel coming in.

The [United States] State Department came in and had some hearings at different times.   They called in some of the Japanese for interrogation and the FBI [Federal Bureau of Investigation] was there.[11]

PC: Do you know anything about these FBI hearings?

RD: No, except that they were, of course, investigating all personnel who were potential enemies of the country.   They were checking out the records on quite a few of the internees.   At that time, I remember being very much impressed with the thoroughness of the investigation, and of the files that they had on these men.   I was really proud of the work our FBI had done in assembling the data on these different people.

Of course, in later years, particularly just the last couple of years, there has been a lot of criticism of Americans for mistreating the Japanese and breaking up their families and putting them into these camps.   It's a funny thing, but at the time I never even thought of these people as having families.   They were enemy aliens and they were picked up because they were potentially subversive people.   They were isolated and put into this camp.   As far as we were concerned, they were enemies to the American people.   They were treated as enemies, although they were not abused in any way, shape, or form. They had on occasion shown where their sympathies were. They were very sympathetic to Japan's cause. They were elated over any news that they could get that Japan was winning. I'm sure there were some mistakes made in rounding these people up. But I'd have to say that the FBI did a darn good job in having the information on the people and in isolating them so that they were not able to do any damage as far as the war cause was concerned.

MP: Do you remember if you had any Nisei here? Were Issei the only ones here?

RD: Well, no. I'm confused on Issei, Nisei, and that sort of thing. The Nisei, as I understand it, are the ones who were born in this country. We didn't have any of the younger ones. In Camp Walters, we did. There were Nisei Japs, the younger ones, there in the Army. At Lordsburg, they were all older people and they were not naturalized citizens. They were over here doing business on the West Coast, Hawaii, and Alaska and in a position to do damage to the country, if the opportunity presented itself. Their sympathies were all with the Japanese nation and their war.

I can't go along with the present thinking that the Americans were treating the Japanese so badly. This was all-out war; we had to protect ourselves and I think the FBI and the Army and all did a darn good job in rounding these people up and placing them in a situation where they couldn't do damage to the country.

PC: Did the Japanese internees display their loyalty to Japan in ceremonies or any other particular way?

RD: Like I say, when they would get any news of a Japanese victory or anything of that kind, they would show their elation over it. They would show that they were very pleased. They'd talk to us and let us know that we were losing the war and that sort of thing.

Of course, when the naval prisoners of war came in, well, they were all heroes. They [the internees] just really took on over them, showing their loyalty to their country.[12]

PC: Do you know of any cultural activities that they may have put on?

RD: Yes, they put on some skits there in the compounds. I remember one time in particular. Captain [Phillip] Bond was a doctor in the Army hospital who had quite a good baritone voice. So they invited him to come to the compound and hear their musical renditions. He asked me to go with him, and we went into the compound where they put on their play. I can't say that I enjoyed it too much, except that it was a curiosity. They had their five-string instruments, and they played this off-key "noise," so to speak, and their vocalizing was more of a chanting than anything like singing. It was very interesting just from that standpoint. When they finished, they asked Captain Bond to sing for them, so he sang "Home on the Range" and one or two other songs. That was the only time that I personally attended anything like that in the compound, but they did that every so often.

At Christmastime, they had their own ceremonies that weren't anything like ours. They dressed up in fantastic costumes and masks. They had their bells and gongs, and they paraded around and made these noises. They went through the hospital, particularly, making noise and parading.

MP: What about their burial ceremonies?

RD: They had their own burial ceremonies. I can't describe them to you vividly, except that they were unusual from our standpoint. One time, they wanted to cremate this fellow, and they couldn't raise the money. So they started a procession. They had their noisemakers and their Shinto priests, and the procession was starting toward the cemetery. In the meantime, his friends in the compound were taking up a collection of coupons that they were given to spend in the PX, trying to raise enough money to have him cremated. So they'd stop the procession and count the coupons. Well, there wouldn't be enough, and the colonel would say, "Bury him!" Off they would go again starting the procession about three times, and they never did collect enough money to cremate the fellow. They went on and buried him. He may be one that was exhumed later or he still may be out there.

That afternoon we were supposed to come over to Fay Clayton's house--where we were living--for a party. I had trouble getting away from headquarters because this procession was delayed so many times. Well, finally, when I did, a train had been coming on the tracks down here. Somebody said that it had derailed and that a coffin had fallen off, and I said, "My God! There's that Jap again!" (laughter)

PC: Do you remember a newspaper that the Japanese put out? I believe it was called the Lordsburg Times.

RD: No, I don't recall a newspaper.[13]

PC: Did the soldiers there put out any type of publication?

RD: Not that I recall.

PC: What was your impression of the type of guards at the camp? What kind of fellows were they, in general?

RD: Well, for the most part they were good people. They were older men who were not qualified for war duty. They were older and some of them disabled more or less. They had things that were keeping them from serving in the troops and going overseas. On the whole, they were a very good bunch of men, easily controlled, and that sort of thing.

MP: What about the monotony of that camp? I recall that you told me of one attempt at breaking the monotony.

RD: Yes, you're referring to guard duty, which is very boring. It's very boring business being in guard towers all around the compound. The soldiers had to watch the fences and all to see that the Japs didn't try to get out. They'd get so bored they didn't know what to do while sitting up in those guard towers. So one night when I was officer of the day I heard shooting going on out there and then the calling, "Corporal of the guard! Corporal of the guard!" I grabbed my pistol and ran out to see what was going on. A guard up in the tower had been shooting at the rabbits. (laughter) So in the report, of course, they had to make a report of it, he said that he just became so damn tired of seeing those rabbits running around that guard tower that he couldn't keep from shooting at them. (laughter)

MP: Were there any attempts to escape?

RD: Not that I recall, no. We didn't have any attempted escapes from the compounds; at least it didn't amount to anything, if they did. We had another case that was kind of funny: the Japanese would be out in the recreational area, and just out of boredom they would get too close to the fence. They'd been told to stay at least ten feet back from the fence. One Jap went out there and walked up to the fence post, and the guard called to him, "Move back." The internee just leaned against the post and looked up at him with a smile on his face like, "What the hell are you going to do about it?" So the guard just raised his rifle and put a hole through the fence post. The last time I saw the Jap, he'd gone around the corner of the barrack. He didn't slow down![14]

PC: How long were you stationed at Lordsburg?

RD: From June 1942 until Easter Sunday of 1943.

PC: And after that, where were you transferred?

RD: I was transferred to Fort Riley, Kansas. I was put on a horse and trained on a horse for awhile. (laughter)

MP: You were there on a horse at twenty below?

RD: It wasn't comfortable, but it wasn't, of course, twenty below. We trained on horses there for awhile, in the reception center. Later, I went through the cavalry school. Of course, at that time, they were changing everything over to a mechanized cavalry. In the school, we used the mechanized equipment, the personnel carriers and tanks. Until they decided to send us through school, we went down and played nursemaid to the horses and drilled on the horses.

PC: Were you ever sent overseas?

RD: Yes, from Fort Riley, Kansas I was put into the Eighth Army Corps Area Headquarters, and went through about three months of training with the inspector general's department. I was then sent to Fort Hood, Texas, where I stayed about a year. From Fort Hood, I was sent overseas to the Azores until 1946.

The war in Europe was over soon after I arrived there. We were occupying Terceira Island jointly with the British. On Santa Maria Island, we built our own base. Of course, it caused quite a bit of rancor among the Germans and all because we were allowed to come into the Azores there--Portugal being a neutral country. But after the war in Europe was over, the United States wanted to continue the use of these bases for some time. So we were negotiating with Portugal on the continued use of the bases. I was very fortunate in being able to enter into those negotiations.

During the lapses in negotiations, I spent quite a bit of time in Lisbon with our commanding general [A. W. Kissner] there and in various different places. We toured Europe to see what damage had been done. Our commanding general had been with the Eighth Air Force stationed in England which had done the bombing of Germany. He was anxious to see it. So we went from Portugal to Paris, then to Wiesbaden, Germany, and to Berlin, then back around to Hamburg. We flew over the Normandy Beach where they had the big invasion on D-Day, and all the ships and everything were still there. Then we went into London, back to where his headquarters was, on one of the big estates called Elvendon Hall.

The headquarters had taken over the main building on the estate, and the people who owned it had moved into one of their smaller houses. The general wanted to see them, so we went down to call on them. Quonset huts that the troops had been stationed in were still scattered around the estate there and back into the trees. In order to protect the main building, the manor house, they had put Sheetrock over the walls. I know there was a big map of America on the wall and they had a great big map of Texas on it, and then the rest was called "unexplored territory." (laughter) We went down to the little church, there on this estate, that the general and the men in the Eighth Air Force had put a stained glass window into. The general wanted to see if it had been done properly.

PC: Would you like to talk about the negotiations with Portugal a bit?

RD: Well, I was, of course, very, very silent. I was, more or less, an aide to the general and, as the negotiations proceeded, to different members of the State Department who were sent in to help. One little incident occurred because I became kind of fed up with the way that we would write our agreements up and send them to [Antonio de Oliveira] Salazar who was the prime minister of Portugal.[15] The Portuguese people just don't operate like we do. They don't work eight to five, six days a week. On Thursday or Friday the weekend starts, and they go off to the mountains for Friday, Saturday, Sunday, and Monday, and come back on Tuesday. Then perhaps they don't feel like doing anything on Tuesday, so maybe they'll work on Wednesday and Thursday. We'd send these things in and he [Salazar] would be tending to other business, so he wouldn't even read it. Well, we'd sit around cooling our heels and get no response, so we'd rewrite it. The first thing you know, we were giving in all the time. One time we were flying from Paris back to Lisbon on General Lawrence Kuter's plane, and he could tell that I didn't approve of what was going on. He just handed me a tablet and a pencil and said, "Well, you write it." (laughter) So I wrote it straight from the shoulder the way I thought it should be. I handed it back to him; he just kind of smiled and tucked it in his bag, and that was the last of that. (laughter) I wasn't very diplomatic.

Another thing that I didn't know until several years after I was back in the States was that General Kuter was with Roosevelt and Churchill at the Yalta Conference.[16] He was the military adviser with them and I didn't know that. He was our commanding general with the North Atlantic Wing of the Air Transport Command. He came in on those negotiations and I didn't know that he was in on the Yalta Conference. I saw the photograph later, and there he was, big as life, right up with the rest of them.

Also, while I was there, we had an opportunity one weekend to take General Kuter's plane and fly over to Casablanca. We stayed in the same hotel that they, Roosevelt and all of them, did when they had their big Casablanca meeting.[17]

Mrs. D: Where was it that they thought you were a general?

RD: Well, they didn't think I was a general, but we had to wear civilian clothes in Portugal. So we'd get out there and you wouldn't know if I was a private or what. One or two mistakes were made. When we were coming back to the Azores, there was a lieutenant who was going back to the United States, and he rode with us to the Azores. I was in civilian clothes. A major met us there, and I said something to him about taking care of the lieutenant. The major said, "Yes, sir; yes, sir!" I was just a captain. (laughter) One other time, I went from Kansas down to New Orleans to see my brother. I went on a general's plane there, and it was raining. While the general was waiting for a car to come out to get him, I got off in the rain and they were all standing at attention when I got off.

PC: Would you like to recount anything else about your Army life? You're retired now, I assume.

RD: Well, I'm still in the inactive reserve. Of course, I was commissioned in 1930 when they had these pay raises every three years, and they were called "fogies." You could have only five fogies in one grade; that would be the tops. Then you had to get a promotion and you could start in again. I had fifteen years of service completed when I was over there in Portugal, and these guys who fixed my paycheck all thought I was in the regular Army. (laughter)

PC: Oh, at that time you were in the negotiation in Portugal, you were a reserve?

RD: Well, I was a reserve on active duty, you see. Originally, they didn't count reserve time on your pay. You had to have so much active duty time to get these fogies. In the reserve ranks, each fogie was five years. Active duty was three years. I had three fogies, or fifteen years, showing on my record. Well, later, they made it so that all reserve time counted on your pay, so that helped us quite a bit. When I was drawing my pay over there, I had fifteen years as a commissioned officer. Not many reserves had that; most of them were just starting.

PC: You seem to have come full circle, in a way. You spent time in Lordsburg during the war. How did you happen to come back to Lordsburg again?

RD: Well, I was over in the Azores with General Kissner and I was due to get out of the service. Still, I was taking these trips, and it was all very interesting work, and the general didn't want to let me go. He wanted me to stay in there. In fact, he wanted me to go into the regular Army, you see. But Mary was at home with our little girl, and she got tired of staying at home and just going to church. So she decided to get in the car and go to Santa Fe, [New Mexico]. She wrote me a letter and said, "Either you're having such a good time that you don't want to come home, or else the general is taking advantage of you. Either way, I'm going to Santa Fe, and you can come home when you're damn good and ready!" (laughter) So I showed it to the general and he said, "Maybe you'd better go home." I came back on August 26, 1946 and went to Santa Fe. We stayed up there awhile.

Then I joined this Lieutenant Mitchell who was the intelligence officer here at the camp. His family had a feed business in Roswell, [New Mexico]. So I got in touch with him. He wanted me to come and work for him, so we went to Roswell. I worked for him for several months. In the meantime, this Fay Clayton kept thinking there was a good opening here to get into a kind of ranch supply store. So we came back here to investigate that, and we ended up staying here. During the war, we had made a lot of good friends among the ranchers and people here and liked it. So we didn't mind coming back.

MP: Well, this is a good climate.

PC: So you came back here.

RD: Yes, we came back and then ended up buying this propane business. I was in that from 1948 until November 1974. Since then I have been retired and playing golf when I can. (laughter)

PC: Is there anything else about your experiences at the Lordsburg camp that you'd like to say, anything that might come to mind?

RD: Yes. One Sunday a group of people came out to visit the camp. Among them was Mrs. Sage, the wife of General Sage who, as adjutant general, took the New Mexico

National Guard into war in the Hawaiian Islands. He was later captured, and was on the infamous death march in the Philippines. She, particularly, was furious at the good treatment the Japs were receiving and particularly because they were getting cokes and things like that which were not available to the average citizen.

I think that about covers it.

PC: One thing comes to my mind. What kind of relationships, if any, did you have with, say, the Immigration and Naturalization Service or with other departments within the government that handled these internees?

RD: Well, I don't remember any immigration people, as such. We did have some border guards, and that was Army. You may have heard or know of these old Army posts that were stationed all up and down the Mexican border: Fort Brown at Brownsville, Fort Clark at Brackettville, Fort Bliss at El Paso, and Fort Huachuca over in Arizona. Those forts were the old cavalry posts all up and down the Mexican border.

While I was taking the ROTC [Reserve Officers' Training Corps] training in school, we always trained at Fort Clark in Brackettville. During the First World War, those posts were very active and patrolled the border. They started out with horse patrols in the Second World War, and then they were changed to mechanized. They patrolled the border from one end to the other with jeeps and whatnot. We used to see those boys when they'd come into camp every so often and stay a day or two and then go back to the border. But the Immigration Service people, as such, I don't remember.

PC: Where were you born, sir?

RD: In Corsicana, Navarro County, Texas.

PC: May I ask the date?

RD: On November 15, 1907.

PC: What school did you attend?

RD: Corsicana schools and then to Texas A&M University.

PC: While there, is that when you went into the ROTC?

RD: I was in ROTC during college, yes.

PC: Is there anything that you'd like to add, Mollie, before we close?

MP: No.

PC: Okay. I'd like to thank you very much, Mr. Dockum, on behalf of the Japanese American Oral History Project at California State University, Fullerton, for taking time this evening to tell us about you Army experiences.

RD: You're welcome.

END OF INTERVIEW

NOTES

1. At the time that the United States and Japan became embroiled in World War II, there was in Clovis a small group of resident Japanese aliens, all employees of the Santa Fe Railroad, and their families (ten men, five women, and seventeen children) who lived together in a compound owned by the railroad. In January 1942, the U.S. government removed them to the Old Raton Ranch, an abandoned Civilian Conservation Corps camp located twelve miles from Fort Stanton in the northeast corner of New Mexico. In December 1942, they were transferred to War Relocation Authority camps in Utah (Topaz) and Arizona (Poston and Gila River) for internment. For an interesting overview of this situation and the forces shaping it, see John J. Culley, "World War II and a Western Town: The Internment of Japanese Railroad Workers of Clovis, New Mexico," Western Historical Quarterly 13 (January 1982): 43-61.

2. For a differing perspective of the drinking at Lordsburg, see the interview with Herbert Nicholson by Betty E. Mitson in Voices Long Silent: An Oral Inquiry into the Japanese American Evacuation, ed., Arthur A. Hansen and Betty E. Mitson (Fullerton, Calif.: Japanese American Project of the Oral History Program at California State University, Fullerton, 1974), 128-29, 130.

3. The International Red Cross originated from the Geneva Convention of 1864. Later treaties amended and strengthened this protocol; for example, the Geneva Convention of 1929 gave the International Red Cross special status in dealing with war prisoners. The International Committee of the Red Cross serves as the organizations coordinating body.

4. The internee self-government structure was laid out in military fashion. The camp was divided into three "battalions" headed by an elected governor; in turn, these battalions were subdivided into four "companies" supervised by an internee mayor. See Michi Weglyn and Betty E. Mitson, eds., Valiant Odyssey: Herbert Nicholson in and out of America's Concentration Camps (Upland, Calif.: Brunk's Printing, 1978), 69.

5. The town of Deming, New Mexico, is located approximately fifty-five miles east of Lordsburg.

6. The availability of beer in the internee canteen is mentioned in a letter from Masaru Akahori to his family, dated May 1943, after Dockum had been transferred from the Lordsburg camp. See folder 7, box 9, Akahori Family Papers, Japanese American Research Project (JARP), Department of Special Collections, University of California, Los Angeles (UCLA).

7. A number of sources detail this incident, including Weglyn and Mitson, 69-70. Both the Japanese protest and the American reply are contained in an official contemporary source. Reads the first: "A party of Japanese subjects numbering 147 were transferred from Bismarck Internment Camp in North Dakota to Lordsburg Internment Camp in New Mexico. Under escort of American soldiers they arrived 27th July, 1942 at 1:45 AM at a station on Plateau near Lordsburg. Two men of party, Shiro Kobata and Hirota Insomura, who were invalids aged nearly sixty years, former suffering from tuberculosis and latter from spinal disease caused by injury while at work in fishing boat, were unable to walk any further, and had to follow party in automobile escorted by soldiers. Party felt uneasy about these two persons, as they failed to join them at Lordsburg Camp. Moreover reports of gun heard in direction of station gave them evil forebodings. So they made inquiries at camp office and office of army surgeon, but no definite information was given. It was announced by camp office next morning two invalids had been shot at dawn 27th on charge of attempt to escape. It is inconceivable that aged invalids hardly able to walk should while under

military escort have attempted to escape. The person who escorted two men, it is learnt, was committed for trial by court-martial, but was acquitted." Ran the American reply: "The proceedings of the board appointed to investigate the matter revealed that in the early hours of July 27, 1942, one hundred and forty-seven internees arrived at the Lordsburg Railroad Station from Bismarck and were escorted by military police to the camp. The two internees, Toshiro Kobata and Hirota Isomura, who were reported to be unable to keep up with the column on the march to the compound were permitted to walk behind at their own pace, accompanied by a guard. They were ordered to keep on the main highway in the center of the road, but were permitted from time to time to rest. At times they walked slowly, at other times they proceeded rapidly. Before coming to the main gate of the military reservation where the internment camp is located the men appeared to be arguing between themselves. After they entered the reservation but before they were within the camp enclosure, they suddenly made a break and started running toward the boundary of the reservation. The guard shouted to them twice to halt and when his order was not obeyed he fired in accordance with his standing instructions. Hirota Isomura died instantly and Toshiro Kobata a few hours later. An inquiry into the circumstances was conducted at once. The court-martial of the guard was vigorously prosecuted and all the facts were developed. An acquittal of the guard resulted." See U.S. Department of State, Bureau of Public Affairs, Foreign Relations of the United States: Diplomatic Papers 1944, V (Washington, D.C.: Government Printing Office, 1965): 1104; 1131. For a firsthand, albeit vague, account, see also the 1966 interview with Masao Itano by Joe Grant Masaoka, tape 95, box 384, JARP, UCLA. For a recent account of this and related incidents, see Tetsuden Kashima, "American Mistreatment of Internees During World War II: Enemy Alien Japanese," in Japanese Americans: From Relocation to Redress, ed. Roger Daniels, Sandra C. Taylor, and Harry H. L. Kitano (Salt Lake City: University of Utah Press, 1986), 52-56.

8. This incident is treated in an official Japanese protest and an American reply registered during the war. According to the first: "During 1942 some 20 American convict soldiers were interned at Lordsburg Camp. Japanese internees requested Commandant to remove these convicts to another place, but request was not complied with. On Thanksgiving Day one of the convicts, under influence of liquor, intruded into Japanese internees quarters, used abusive language, sat astride Doctor Uyehara, and wounded him in back with a knife." Stated the American response: "Several American military personnel who were prisoners were confined at Lordsburg Internment Camp. On November 26, 1942, one of these American prisoners became disorderly, and in the fracas Dr. Uyehara was knocked down, but was not injured to an extent requiring medical attention. After this incident, the prisoner who created the disturbance, together with all other American garrison prisoners, was removed and confined elsewhere. The prisoner was tried for this offense by special court-martial on December 31, 1942, and the commanding officer of the Lordsburg Internment Camp was subsequently removed from command." See Foreign Relations, 1944, 1105; 1132.

9. Herbert Nicholson writes of a conversation he had with a Lordsburg officer about this occurrence while visiting the camp. According to him, the Japanese prisoners wished to celebrate the emperor's birthday and painted a Japanese flag and shouted "Tenno heika, Banzai." See Herbert Nicholson, Treasure in Earthen Vessels (Whittier, Calif.: Penn Lithographics, 1974), 68.

10. Toshiro Kobata's ashes were sent to friends interned at the Poston War Relocation Center in Arizona. In 1946, after the closure of the Lordsburg camp, the remains of Hirota Isomura and three others were exhumed and reburied at the Fort Bliss, Texas, National Cemetery, Post Section. See letter of James McFarland to Isamu Kantaniguchi, copy in possession of Paul F. Clark.

11. The United States Department of State was not connected with the internee's "loyalty" hearings, but rather, assisted when representatives of the protecting powers appointed under the Geneva Convention visited the internment camps.

12. Before the formal establishment of an internee newsletter at Lordsburg in the summer of 1942, English speaking internees would translate news items orally into Japanese. According to one authoritative source, "some internees became excited when they heard good news for Japan." See Japanese Chamber of Commerce in Southern California, Japanese in Southern California: A History of 70 Years (Los Angeles: Japanese Chamber of Commerce of Southern California, 1960), 869.

13. The internee newspaper, the Lordsburg Times, began publication on August 26, 1942 and functioned until November 6, 1943 when the last Japanese internees were removed to Immigration and Naturalization Service camps.

14. A reference in an American reply, published in Foreign Relations, 1944, 1131-32, reads similar to Dockum's description of this incident: "The allegation contained in the memorandum from the Spanish Embassy that an internee was fired at when requesting a sentry to fetch a golf ball, was reported not to be based upon facts. The only occasion when a sentry at Lordsburg Internment Camp fired in the direction of a Japanese internee was at a time when the guard had been alerted to expect an attempted escape by the internees. On that occasion, when an internee approached one of the gates during the evening, a sentry fired a warning shot at a nearby telephone post. The camp authorities on learning of the incident investigated the circumstances and as a result the sentry was relieved from further duty of this nature."

15. Salazar became Portugal's finance minister in 1928, and prime minister in 1932. He fell from power in 1968 and died two years later.

16. Among the items on the agenda of the Yalta Conference, which lasted from 4 to 11 February 1942, was the settlement of the division of postwar Germany and Japan.

17. At the Casablanca Conference, which took place in January 1943, the Allied leaders declared that the war would end only with unconditional surrender of the Axis nations, and plans were laid for the invasion of Sicily and Italy.

Index

An Interview with
ABNER SCHREIBER
Conducted by Paul F. Clark
on March 19, 1979
for the
California State University, Fullerton
Oral History Program
Japanese American Project

(Department of Justice Internment Camps
Administration Experience, O. H. 1613)

This is a slightly edited transcription of an interview conducted for the Oral History Program, sponsored by the California State University, Fullerton. The reader should realize that an oral history document is spontaneous in nature, and portrays information and impressions as recalled by the interviewee.

Scholars are welcome to utilize short excerpts from any of the transcriptions without obtaining permission as long as proper credit is given to the interviewee, the interviewer, and the University. Scholars must, however, obtain permission from California State University, Fullerton, before making more extensive use of the transcriptions and related materials. None of these materials may be duplicated or reproduced by any party without permission from the Oral History Program, California State University, Fullerton, California, 92634.

Interview Introduction

In this interview, Abner Schreiber focuses on his experiences as the second in command of the Immigration and Naturalization Service internment camp at Santa Fe, New Mexico. This facility contained the largest number of interned Japanese outside of the camp designated for family internment at Crystal City, Texas. In March 1945, the only incident of mass violence among the internment camps occurred at Santa Fe, and herein Schreiber recounts this event from his perspective as an administrator. Also of interest is Schreiber's recollection of other aspects of the U.S. Justice Department's internment program, such as providing security forces for the U.S. State Department's detention compounds that held enemy diplomats.

Schreiber's career has centered on the justice system. He holds several law degrees from New York institutions, all obtained prior to World War II. After the war, he settled in New Mexico and was employed for a time with the Atomic Energy Commission at Los Alamos. Today, in 1989, he maintains a private law practice in that community.

Schreiber's strategic position with respect to the administration of the Santa Fe internment camp as well as his direct involvement in the March 1945 riot there immediately recommended him as a prime interview subject to Paul Clark at the time that he was doing research for his study on Japanese enemy alien internment during World War II. However, due to time and financial limitations, an in-person interview was not possible. Instead, Clark utilized the telephone recording equipment available at the California State University, Fullerton campus to conduct this interview. Previous experience with telephone interviewing in relation to a study of recreational history in the California Desert for the Bureau of Land Management had trained him in this inexpensive although admittedly somewhat impersonal mode of oral history. Notwithstanding this constraint, the interview presents information and reflections that otherwise might not be available to researchers. Owing to restrictions imposed by the interviewee, scholars wishing to quote and likewise use material from this interview must obtain written permission in advance from the archivist of the Oral History Program at California State University, Fullerton.

CALIFORNIA STATE UNIVERSITY, FULLERTON

ORAL HISTORY PROGRAM

Japanese American Project

INTERVIEWEE: ABNER SCHREIBER

INTERVIEWER: Paul F. Clark

SUBJECT: Department of Justice Internment Camps
Administration Experience

DATE: March 19, 1979

PC: This is a telephone interview with Abner Schreiber for the Japanese American Project of the California State University, Fullerton, Oral History Program. The date is March 19, 1979, and the time is approximately 5:30 p.m. The interviewer is Paul F. Clark.

Good afternoon, Mr. Schreiber.

AS: Good afternoon.

PC: Before we go into your experience at Santa Fe, I'd be interested in knowing something about your personal background before the war. Could you tell me a little bit about that?

AS: I was with the [United States] Border Patrol prior to the war.[1] I was assigned to the northern part of New York. I spent some time at El Paso prior to that time, mostly going to the border patrol school down there. In the summer of 1940, I was appointed a border patrol inspector, as I believe they called them in those days. Prior to all this, I was involved in some practice of law, and I did some investigative work in New York City. I was a graduate of Fordham Law School with an LL.D. [Doctor of Laws] from that school in 1935, and I received a Master of Law degree from Brooklyn Law School at Saint Lawrence University in 1936. I was admitted to the bar in New York in 1936 or thereabouts.

PC: I understand that you were involved with the Vichy French ambassador.

AS: Yes. For background, we might just as well get into it. I can remember pretty well the day the war broke out. The day after, I was ordered by radio to stand by and wait for the chief inspector to come on by. He came on by, and told me I was on my way down to Baltimore in charge of a detail of some eight men, as I recall. We were going to assist the Bureau [Federal Bureau of Investigation] there in picking up alien enemies.

You've got to recall one thing, that was forty years ago, and this is all from memory. You understand this.

PC: Yes.

AS: We went around down there, and we filled the local jails when it was determined that we had several hundred detainees. They were called detainees before they were given hearings. After the hearings, the ones who were held in custody were termed internees and dangerous enemy aliens.

The next situation was that they started to make a detention center, a camp out at Fort Howard, about twenty or thirty miles from Baltimore. I was detailed out there with several border patrolmen to assist in setting us up. We were given a copy of the Geneva Convention, and we then took most of our people out of the local jails and into the detention center. We had Germans, Japanese, and Italians there. They were given hearings. Some of our German prisoners were taken out of the penitentiaries. I recall we had quite a number of people who were employed around Baltimore as chefs and one thing and another in the hotels. There weren't too many Japanese in that area. We had a few Italians, but most of the detainees there were German. Let's see, we did have, as time went on, the detainees from, I think it was the German ship <u>Columbus</u>.[2] The ship, I guess, was in some South American port at the outbreak of the war with us and they shipped them up to the United States. We had them there for awhile. Later, they went down around the Fort Stanton camp [in New Mexico].

Again, this is starting to come back to me.

PC: That's pretty interesting.

AS: Is that the type of thing you want to know about?

PC: Yes, this is very interesting.

AS: I was second in command at that camp. They had an immigration inspector that was a fellow in charge who was a veteran of the First [World] War. We had civilian guards and border patrolmen.

PC: Do you recall approximately how many detainees you had at Fort Howard?

AS: I believe the number somewhat fluctuated. We also had the Baltimore office use us, to some degree, for some of their illegally entered aliens there. We kept them separate. Our total prison population, as I recall, was somewhere in the area of about five hundred then.

PC: Did your facility there at Fort Howard last very long, or did it close down?

AS: No, it lasted long after I left there, I know that. A lot of those people were interned. They, as I recall, finally had their hearings before these boards set up by the United States Attorney General [Francis Biddle]. Again, this is almost thirty or forty some odd years past, and this is my recollection of what transpired at that time.

PC: Sure, I understand that.

AS: This all leads into that Vichy French situation you were talking about, but is there anything else you want to discuss relative to the Fort Howard operation?

PC: I think that pretty well covers it.

AS: Yes, that's background. The next thing that transpired was at our headquarters. Willard Kelly was in charge of the internment. He asked me to get down to headquarters, and he then asked me to run out to Hershey, Pennsylvania, where they proposed to take over the Hershey Hotel--a very nice, luxurious hotel, I might add. The reason being that the United States had picked up or was in the process of picking up the Vichy French ambassador and their various counsels throughout the country. This included families as well. They wanted this hotel prepared as a detention center for these people pending their repatriation, just as I understand our [diplomatic] people in France had been picked up.[3] I was assigned to get out there and set up the situation for these people to come in. In the meantime, they were going to send up fifty or a hundred or more border patrolmen, but they wouldn't be in for a time. This was close to Harrisburg, [Pennsylvania]. I saw the chief of police, chief of the state patrol, and the [Home Guard] colonel. They were very cooperative. I told them what our problem was. They put on loan to us fifty or seventy-five of their state patrolmen pending our people coming in. They were transferring these French consulate people and the ambassador from around the country. We set the place up and got it ready to go, then I made my report to the chief, who was deputy commissioner Willard Kelly, in charge of the border patrol. He said, "This is very good. If you want it back, you're the commanding officer." So (chuckle) I went on back there and these people started to come in and we set up posts around. It wasn't the same type of thing as Fort Howard or some of the other internment camps. These were [United States] State Department people. In fact, I was the commanding officer, or officer-in-charge, I guess is what they called them of this operation to get everything going there. They also sent out a man from the State Department who presumably was the diplomat of the two of us--presumably; I'm kidding. We joked a lot about that, but he was representing the State Department and I was, of course, representing the Immigration [and Naturalization Service] and the [United States] Border Patrol.

The people came on and came on. Gaston Henry-Haye was the ambassador, I remember well. He had a fire dog, a Dalmatian. They were well taken care of. The ambassador had a luxurious suite. His other people had luxurious quarters, too. They ate in the dining room of the hotel. The hotel was, of course, closed and you couldn't get out or in without going through our people. It was very good, very luxurious living, just as I assume our people had in France. Prior to that time--you may know from your research--we had some people down at the Greenbrier Hotel, [White Sulphur Springs, West Virginia]; Ambassador [Kichisaburo] Nomura was in the same type of quarters.[4] This occurred at the end of 1942.

PC: Is there anything you care to comment upon in the way of either problems or interesting highlights of your service there with the Vichy French?

AS: The Vichy French, no. There were many titled people, generals, counts, dukes, and so on and so forth. Of course, every time you saw them there was a handshake. There wasn't any difficulty involved in that situation at all. After getting the administrative situation all set, such as the guard personnel chosen, I was ready to sit back and start enjoying the place, when I was called back to headquarters; they had another detai. for me. (laughter) I was there about six weeks, and then they ordered me to turn it over to one of the chief inspectors and get onto another deal. In fact, I went back and had a little excitement, I guess, over at Fort Howard. I went there to give them an assist.

After that, I was sent down to Fort Stanton to organize a similar type of setup for the receipt of the Nazi generals who were picked up in that African campaign. They wanted to treat them pretty nice, I guess, so we went down and took over the country club down there. I wrote up a report, but I did not participate in setting that up or in the receipt of the officers out of that African campaign. I understand that my recommendations were taken and they set up a camp there. I think it was the Stanton Country Club.

Then the next thing I was assigned to was at Santa Fe, [New Mexico]. I was called into headquarters and they told me that they were reopening the Santa Fe camp. It initially was a detention camp, of course, similar to what we had at Fort Howard. I think that the Army had these people beforehand. You were talking about this guy out of Lordsburg [Richard Dockum].[5] When did they turn that bunch over? Do you recall from your conversation with the adjutant officer at Lordsburg?

PC: I understand that they started transferring the civilians back around the summer of 1943.

AS: Well, then, that was after I got there because they had some in there then. I know at that time the Army wanted the border patrol to take that over because I guess they were beginning to become involved with other POWs. That I don't know, but I do remember I got out there as the chief liaison officer sometime in March or April of 1943. [Lloyd] Jensen was then the officer-in-charge.[6] As I recall there were just a few hundred people there when I got there. My job was to take care of the inside of the camp, to be in charge of the censors and to keep the lid on from the inside standpoint. A few months later I was promoted to executive officer or assistant officer-in-charge. Jensen then took off for another job and Ivan Williams came in. I guess that was about a year or so after and then Ivan was assigned to some other camps out on the coast where they were having some difficulties. He's quite a guy. He was on the assignment for a year or a year and a half, and I was, of course, the acting officer-in-charge during that time. He came back for awhile, and then was sent on to another detail. Anyway, I guess we had about a little over two thousand prisoners, or internees, at any one time.

We didn't have too much difficulty with our internees. In fact, we had very little. We adhered to the Geneva Convention. The Geneva Convention was the bible. Philosophically, I think, those of us who were in charge of the camp felt that if we gave the internees more than what they usually were entitled to as to food, space, and other things under the Geneva Convention we would have something to take back as a punitive measure if they got out of line. In other words, we could say, "If you don't straighten out, why, here's what we're going to do."

PC: I see.

AS: Psychologically, it worked well. We didn't really have to do any of that except one time after that riot; then we did. Now we had there a fair-sized hospital which, I notice, is mentioned in Katsuma Mukaeda's interview.[7] These were real nice people [most of the internees]. They were people that came from middle-class life and so on. Well, I'm not going to apologize for them. They were declared to be dangerous enemy aliens and they were potentially dangerous, and that was why they were there.

PC: I was wondering, in some of these camps when it came to the interpretation of the Geneva Convention, I've heard a complaint about some of the internees, who were sometimes called barrack lawyers, who occasionally presented a problem to the administration.

AS: Well, that may be so. We always had people who were fomenting, and who sought to foment difficulties. These were people who I would assume felt that they were furthering the war effort of their respective countries, Germany and Japan. Yes, you had this type of persons. (chuckle) We had our visits from the Spanish diplomatic corps quite routinely. The Swiss came out, too. Of course, we'd make available rooms for them, barracks, and they [the internees] had their opportunity to discuss their grievances. Usually these people would take up with us what they thought was something that possibly should be corrected, and we'd explain it to them or correct it if it was something we had no knowledge of. We didn't have too much difficulty in regard to the so-called barrack lawyers,[8] or whatever you designated them. There were always people who wrote letters and made complaints. We thought we were giving them, and obviously we were giving them, everything that the Geneva Convention required. We treated them as persons, as people. They, unfortunately, found themselves in that situation, but they were human beings. Some camps may not have. There was trouble in some POW locations. I think I read that in [Jerre] Mangione's book which I have had occasion to look at not too long ago.[9] Of course, we had meetings from time to time, and one camp would know what was going on in the other. Some of them had a rough time. In fact, we had a camp at Fort Stanton in New Mexico, which was, I guess they called it, the "sinker camp." They had some of the troublemakers down there.[10]

PC: Well, I understand that Fort Stanton was what they called a segregation camp.

AS: It wasn't so much a segregation camp. They had that Columbus crew I told you about. I was down there once or twice to help them on some matters, but I just stayed for a day or two. They did have some people who were involved in causing fomentation. Again, as I remember it.

PC: Since we're somewhat touching on the subject, maybe we could go into the riot that occurred in Santa Fe on March 12, 1945. I understand that was primarily the work of the Tule Lake [Segregation Center] people.

AS: Yes. We had had what I thought was a fairly smooth operation. So did everyone else. Under the circumstances, we had very little difficulty with any situation there [at Santa Fe]. We had several hundred people who had been apparently, backgroundwise, sent over to Japan when they were five or six years old for an education so they would not lose their background. I guess that's what their parents felt. They had caused a lot of trouble probably at the Tule Lake War Relocation/[Segregation] Camp. You know the difference between the war relocation centers?[11]

PC: Yes.

AS: It was during the relocation where they took these citizens, and they emptied out the West Coast and other places and put them in these war relocation camps. Well, I won't comment more on that. You can tell from my name that, after all, Schreiber, my background is German and Austrian. (chuckle) So you wondered, you know.

Anyway, they got these people out of the war relocation centers. Of course, the immigration service previously could do nothing with them because we only dealt with aliens. Apparently they[12] were inured to a great extent, having been in Japan from a tender age up until they were early in their twenties. So, they were instilled, I would assume, with patriotism for Japan. Anyway, that was part of the situation. They shaved their heads. I think a good cross section felt strongly that it was unfortunate they were not in the Japanese army. I don't know this for a fact. The next thing, they wanted to show their patriotism and they renounced their American citizenship. Well, as soon as they did that, they became aliens. I guess they knew what they were doing and why they were doing it. Of course, the immigration service was then able to bring them into the internee war program. They sent them up to North Dakota, too. They apparently had caused a lot of difficulty and trouble at Tule Lake.

I think I may have touched on this thing in my recent conversation, but when they came in some of them were rather, oh, surly. I remember I did address them and suggested to them that we'd had an operation that had gone along smoothly as far as we were concerned, and we hoped they would fit in and be gentlemen. We knew their background, but if they wanted to get tough, we could get tough, you know, and so forth. Well, that was that. A few weeks went by, and, the next thing that happened, we were informed that there was quite a bit of fomentation.

We had little if any difficulty with the older people like Mukaeda. We never had. In fact, we kind of enjoyed conversations with them. We tried to give them make-work. They had details going out. We had about eleven to fifteen acres under cultivation, and they sure could grow the stuff. (chuckle) It seemed like every other week or so we had to dig another root cellar in order to store the vegetables and one thing and another they were able to grow. We had some details out to the Santa Fe Golf Course to help them straighten that out, maybe a dozen or two dozen people.[13] That was part of the program. They did this with the German war prisoners, too; I mean fellows who were actually from the battleground. I think they received eighty cents a day or something of that kind.

PC: The internees you sent out to the golf course didn't go out there to play golf, they went out there to work?

AS: Oh, no. They were sent out under guard. (laughter) They were paid eighty cents a day for their assisting in getting that cultivated and so on. No, they weren't sent out to play golf, no.

PC: They were gardening?

AS: Yes, they were. During the war years, there weren't the usual number of people available. We tried to make work for these people. There's nothing more boring than people sitting around with nothing to do.

PC: Did most of the older internees, before the Tule Lake people, of course, go for this type of make-work or did most of them just sort of stay in the compounds?

AS: Oh, I think they felt it was a privilege really to get into this type of thing. They built themselves a little miniature golf course there within the fences. It was just a sand thing where they had a few holes. Yes, I would say anybody who was interned there for two or three years--my god!--wanted to do something. They made pets out of birds. They had classes. They had a stage and they put on shows and Japanese plays for themselves there. We showed them a lot of movies and so on. Of course, when we talk about the older people, you had people who were anywhere from their twenties on up to middle age and beyond.

These new people came in, and we kind of felt that something was going on. We asked for some border patrolmen to be sent up from El Paso to back up our guard force, which, of course, was recruited from the civilian population, you might say. They did, and I don't recall if that was the first time or the second time. I think Williams was there then, too. He'd come back from one of his details. In fact, I know he was. Anyway, they were waving flags, Japanese flags, blowing bugles and so on. Now under the rules of the Geneva Convention, in any other POW situation, nobody could assemble without permission of the authorities, not more than three people. We were called out and we had them break it up. They did, and we confiscated the flag.

PC: I understood that they wore some sort of sweatshirt with something on it.

AS: They may have painted that stuff on their sweatshirts. I remember I saw the rising sun flag flying around. (chuckle) Of course, that was easy enough to manufacture. They had sewing machines.

PC: So they were engaging in marching?

AS: They were engaging in what was obviously a drill. They were doing exercises more than anything else. Anyway, I don't want to suggest that they were going to attack the authorities or the United States, but they were involved in at least a quasi-military operation there including exercises and so on.

We felt this bode no good, so we ordered them to cease and desist. There were a bunch of them who were of a surly nature. Anyway, they did that again, I guess, a few days later. Where the dickens did they get all those bugles! (chuckle) I think they did that again a few days later, and we pulled out several of their ringleaders.

It's also my recollection that we never had any reason to use a camp outside the regular compound, but we got one together and had them sit there pending being taken down to Fort Stanton. Of course, these people all gathered and they were surly, to use the word again. It was self-evident--if you've been in this kind of business as I have been--that something was ready to pop. They gathered up at the wire at the northern part, as I recall, of our enclosure and we asked them, "Break it up." I was in charge of that operation, and I made darn sure that the record was replete for a lot of reasons at that time. You're familiar from your history that the Japanese were doing a hell of a lot to our people over there without any reason. I had notes taken on warnings to them, and I think I repeated the thing about four or five times. We'll say we repeated the thing four or five times. I like to be incognito.

PC: I understand that tear gas was thrown and a platoon was sent in.

AS: Oh, yes. We'd been asking them to disperse. There were several hundred up at the wire. They didn't. I remember I was testing the air there because if you threw tear gas and the wind was blowing in the wrong direction, you'd get it back in your face. (laughter) We had some billies and we had tear gas canisters, and we doubled the guard on our towers. Finally, about the fourth or fifth time, we made mention, "If you don't, we're forced to take whatever action is indicated." We made sure the stenos were getting this, and we then let some of the stuff go, and the wind was right. They backed off, and the next thing that happened was out came the stones and rocks and other things at us, and some of us got hit in the head. We had a lot of women around, you know, in the headquarters building. Then we sent some people down to the south gate, and I got some border patrol guys to follow me. In those days, I was young and didn't have enough sense to say, "Go in and do the job." This you can erase. (laughter) Well, we went in there in the worse shape. They had a heck of a lot of iron pipe and one thing and another. There were about fifteen or twenty of us, I guess, who went in there, and they started to come after us. Now, I might say--backgroundwise--we never had any reason to have night sticks, so we went and borrowed them from the MPs over at Bruns Hospital--that was a military hospital.

They did have some Italian POWs over there who were assistant medical personnel. We borrowed some night sticks to reinforce our position because it doesn't pay to go into a prison compound with firearms! They'll usually take them away from you and you've had it. The only thing we went in with was billies and gas grenades. We also had these night sticks. In fact, I had one of them, and they were kind of balsa wood affairs. I can remember when they came after us with rocks and these crowbars that it was peculiar to see the night sticks used. Instead of the guy falling down, the night sticks broke. (laughter) So they weren't very effective, not the sticks. In fact, we later ordered some night sticks. We were fortunate we never had to use them.

PC: Apparently you were able to break it up and get them into their barracks.

AS: Oh, yes, we broke it up. There were a few guys lying around there after it was over. We were able to break it up without too much difficulty. But after that, we got these so-called shaved heads, the Tule Lake bunch, and put them into a portion of the camp that we segregated off. They were in there for quite awhile, oh, a week or so. We limited our operation to just what the Geneva Convention called for, maybe a little less. After awhile, they sent some delegations up to the headquarters and asked to go back to the way things were. Ultimately they did.

PC: I understand there was a bit of a strike or a work slowdown. Do you know anything about that?

AS: By whom?

PC: By the internees in the camp after the riot.

AS: Well, there may have been. There was sympathy, I'm sure. There may have been a work slowdown, but there wasn't much work for them to do. We had about two thousand people there, and I guess a hundred people could have done the cooking for themselves and one thing and another. Here again, I think I did read that in Mukaeda's interview. As I recall, he [Mukaeda] seemed to be a very sensible guy. These [older] people were not involved in the isolation, you know, or the segregation. I can just envision one or two who were fomenting a lot among the older people, and who we knew had their allegiance to Japan very definitely and thought they should be doing something for the mother or father country, whatever they called it. But by and large, I have no real recollection of any slowdown as such. I think that the older hands weren't too sympathetic. I may be wrong about that. What I'm trying to say is that my recollection is that the older people, aside from all the excitement, just continued along the same line. They always continued with the exception of these few hundred who had been involved in, or were associated in some way with, that [Tule Lake] operation or were extremely sympathetic. They came from the same group. There may have been a slowdown, but it wasn't noticeable to me. But I don't want to debate that issue, not by any means. (chuckle)

PC: Okay. (chuckle) That pretty well covers what I had to ask you on the strike and the riot. To maybe go back a little bit, I might ask if it seemed to you that the Tule Lake people were quite separate from the other, older, internees?

AS: Yes, I got that impression. They [the Tule Lake people] were the more militant. There was no question about it. They were younger, they were instilled with patriotism from the mother country, for Japan. After that, we had little difficulty with that operation. We didn't have any difficulty after that at all with these people, as I recall. In fact, Ivan Williams talked with them. He did a hell of a good job. Well, he was an outstanding man--is an outstanding man. He then left, and I remember they repatriated quite a bunch of them. He [Williams] left for another detail. I have no recollection of having any more difficulty, except with just the usual misconduct or orneriness of individuals. Well, they were incarcerated there. I wouldn't want to be exposed to that for a number of years. These guys were. There was sympathy, but some of them were real nice people, really; real nice people. I enjoyed knowing them. They were intelligent people. I guess most of them spoke some English. I would talk with them at some length. I'm sure the other officers would. They had their problems. They were real nice people, a lot of them. A heck of a lot of them were.

PC: I'm interested in your relationship with the central office and the regional offices of the Immigration [and Naturalization] Service. How much autonomy did they give you to run the camp?

AS: Oh, they gave us a pretty large degree of autonomy. Everything had to be reported to the central office and we had a fine staff. As I mentioned, Willard Kelly was in charge of it and he made his visits regularly. We had autonomy. You know, it's like any other operation, they have officers who know what they are doing, but if they got out of line, or if they didn't know what they were doing, they'd replace them. (laughter)   The central office would get its reports regularly as to population, expenditures, et cetera, from all of the camps, presumably. We went to meetings from time to time--not too often--that the central office held. Now, some camps had more problems, some had less; we didn't.

PC: Did you feel that your general record keeping was excessively burdensome?

AS: No, I don't think we had too much of a problem there, at least I didn't feel it was. We had to keep records. We had to justify amounts and expenditures. I was directly involved in the thing for over a year and a half. When I say directly involved, I'm talking about in charge of it, and I saw nothing excessive about it that I can recall. I thought everything was reasonable. I was very proud of our "big honcho," the boss, Willard Kelly, and the rest of the gang. They were reasonable people.

PC: You never felt that they were meddling in the camp's affairs or anything?

AS: No. It was their job to meddle if that was indicated; they had to make damn sure what was going on. They'd be doing less than their job if they didn't get their periodic reports, but we had an open line both ways. I can't speak anything but very highly for the so-called central office operation as far as the camps were concerned. Kelly was an outstanding man. He had an outstanding staff.

PC: I understand that there was a press blackout.

AS: Oh, yes. I laid a little foundation earlier in this thing about that; you can go on and on with these things and just scratch the surface, you might say. Yes, we were ordered not to disclose this. We got a central office, coded message by radio. We did talk to all our personnel telling them about this. The reason being, as I stated earlier in this conversation, since our people were getting killed and beheaded and one thing and another in the death marches and so on without any rhyme or reason, that could have been a propaganda stroke for the enemy. That was my understanding of the reason. In this day and age, we'd have had all the media and the Supreme Court in there, wouldn't we? (laughter)

PC: So you primarily kept the press blackout to keep down the feelings of the local people, so that they wouldn't misunderstand what was going on?

AS: Oh, no, no. That's not what I said. You're talking about the press situation as the same pertained to that riot?

PC: No.

AS: Oh, you're generalizing?

PC: Yes.

AS: Oh, no. I thought you were tying it in with the riot and the gas. No, that was where we were instructed to put the lid on. We had no specific instruction that I recall, about a lid on everything. I don't recall any of that. In fact, from time to time we'd get an editorial about these people eating better than most people around and something like that. We'd usually call the newspaper guys in and try to establish a rapport and tell them about the Geneva Convention. They were usually reasonable.

I thought you were talking about the news blackout in regard to that riot. We did get instructions not to let that one out. We were very proud that nothing leaked on that--to my knowledge--until after the war was over, when we gave full accounts to the press about it. Yes, they came in and they wanted to know about anything they should know about. In fact, during the war years we would trade off some of the meat and stuff that these people were allowed for fish from Bruns Hospital. The Japanese, they're not big meat eaters, as you probably know. They prefer vegetables, fish, rice and so on. No, while there wasn't ready access into the campsite, there wasn't any blackout that I recall.[14]

PC: I see.

AS: There wasn't anything to black out. (laughter)

There were a lot of strong feelings around, especially earlier in the war, among the people in New Mexico because a hell of a lot of people who were on the death march out of Bataan were from New Mexico. The Japanese, you know, were not kind. I don't know whether you are familiar with that from your research. They were not kind. I'm talking about the armed forces of Japan. They were not kind to our people at all. In fact, they were merciless. The press, of course, was replete with those events; the Ernie Pyles and the foreign correspondents let it be known that our people were on the death march. They lost hundreds, I mean thousands of people during this thing. The food they were given was negligible. The Japanese militaristic operation, from what I gather and what I was able to determine thereafter, was not a kindly operation, nor did they adhere to the Geneva Convention. Now, that was none of our business. Well, when I say none of our business, I mean in connection with the operation of these internment camps. We operated under the Geneva Convention. I think we were kind to these people. They were nice people, a hell of a lot of them, and they were treated as nice people. If they wanted to get tough, I guess we could get tough, too. After all, it was wartime. We had, other than what we talked bout there, very little difficulty, no difficulty.

Does that answer your question?

PC: Yes.

AS: You wanted me to editorialize there. Why the pointed question about blackout? I'm not sure that I understand that.

PC: Well, I understand from a newspaper clipping from the <u>Santa Fe New Mexican</u> that when the camp was closed in 1946, they mentioned a news blackout. Perhaps they're referring to the riot.

AS: I believe that was what they were doing. Was that a Will Harrison column?

PC: I don't recall. I know it was in the <u>Santa Fe New Mexican</u>.[15]

AS: I think that was what they meant. Of course, the papers did state time and time again that there was a blackout, which was so. When I say, "which was so," I don't mean there was a news blackout per se, but we could not just throw the gates open or anything like that for any reporters or newspapers. There was definitely a news blackout and I thought that's what you were talking about in connection with that riot, for the reasons stated.

PC: Well, to sort of sum up here, maybe I could cover just some of the personalities of the camp. I understand that there was a fellow by the name of Clarence Uyematsu who was the translator and censor. Do you recall that person?

AS: Yes, I remember Clarence very well. Do you know anything about him?

PC: No, I don't. I'd like to know something about him.

AS: There was Yoto, too. They were employees of the government. They were censors, and they read all the mail going to and from. They were just nice people.

PC: Were they Nisei?

AS: I heard they were citizens. I'm sure they were born here. Yoto was older than Clarence was. I guess there were just two of them, but maybe there were more. They'd always read the mail and censor it. (laughter) Again, that was part of the Geneva Convention; we were allowed to make a determination of whether there was any flow of information.

To jump around, it would be from a standpoint of a news blackout where we didn't make available the security aspect of the camp. It would be silly to have a prison POW camp and have a general knowledge as to where every guard was and when the sentries passed and so on and so forth. That certainly was not available.

PC: Could you tell me something about Mr. Williams? You seemed to have a good rapport with him.

AS: Oh, yes, I had a good rapport with everybody that I know of in the camp. We had an enjoyable esprit de corps. I don't want to leave you with an impression that we didn't get along. We lived together, you might say, worked together and we, I think, enjoyed one another, all of us. Ivan Williams, as I say, was a real good friend, just as Jensen was and the other guys that I worked with such as Monroe. We see and hear from one another from time to time. I run into the fellows that worked as guards there. We've all been good friends.

PC: Okay. I believe I've pretty well covered what I would like to ask. Is there anything that you would like to reemphasize or go back to?

AS: Well, I guess I just got to talking and there it was. There's no question in my mind but that this hour or so that we've devoted here has only scratched the surface, and I am reasonably certain that from time to time as new areas come up, I would be reminded of it.

What transpired in my own career, if you're interested in it, I'll give you briefly. I liked Santa Fe so darned much as a result of the war years--I mean, my association with the people in Santa Fe--that I was admitted to the bar in New Mexico and when the AEC [Atomic Energy Commission] took over from the Army, they asked if I wouldn't help them set up the security. I did. I got up here as deputy chief in charge of their security operation. They gave me the title of major. Then they found out that I was admitted to the bar, and they asked me to become the district attorney, which I did for free here for a good number of years. At the end of the term, I stayed in the county and practiced law.

I want you to preface anything you do with this that this is from memory. I have no recollection of having said anything derogatory about anyone, and certainly I have nothing derogatory to say about the people with whom I worked, and I don't have much if anything of a derogatory nature to say in regard to the prisoners. They were just prisoners--internees, I guess, is a better word--and as I say, nice people.

PC: Well, on that note, let me thank you on behalf of the Japanese American Project of the Oral History Program at California State University, Fullerton.

AS: You're welcome. I enjoyed talking with you.

END OF INTERVIEW

NOTES

1. For a popular history of the U.S. Border Patrol, See John M. Myers, The Border Wardens (Englewood Cliffs, N.J.: Prentice-Hall, Inc., 1971).

2. The German liner Columbus was scuttled in the Atlantic Ocean in December 1939 to prevent capture. Its crew, which was rescued by United States warships, was interned in early 1941 at Fort Stanton Internment Camp in New Mexico. Schreiber is perhaps referring to other German seamen brought from Latin American states and held under similar circumstances.

3. These French diplomatic detainees remained at Hershey, Pennsylvania, awaiting exchange until the fall of 1943 when they were moved to the Cascades Inn in Hot Springs, Virginia. Their American counterparts were apprehended in France and taken to detention facilities at Baden-Baden, Germany.

4. For more information on the Japanese diplomats detained for exchange, see Gwen H. Terasaki, Bridge to the Sun (Chapel Hill: University of North Carolina Press, 1957).

5. See, elsewhere in this volume, the March 18, 1977 interview with Richard Dockum by Paul F. Clark and Mollie M. Pressler for the Japanese American Project of the Oral History Program, California State University, Fullerton.

6. Lloyd H. Jensen served as Santa Fe's officer-in-charge from 19 April 1943 to 26 October 1944. He later became Chief of Detention, Deportation and Parole Division, Immigration and Naturalization Service.

7. See the transcript of the May 22, 1975 interview with Katsuma Mukaeda by Paul F. Clark for the Japanese American Project, California State University, Fullerton in Clark's unpublished study, "Those Other Camps: An Oral History Analysis of Japanese Alien Enemy Internment During World War II" (M.A. thesis, California State University, Fullerton, 1980).

8. For the use of the term "barrack lawyers," see Mollie M. Pressler's unpublished 1976 manuscript "The Lordsburg Internment/POW Camp." For information on Pressler, see the introduction to the interview with Richard Dockum in this volume.

9. See Jerre Mangione, An Ethnic at Large (New York: G.P. Putnam's Sons, 1978).

10. Fort Stanton held such individuals as the leader of the German American Bund, Fritz Julius Kuhn. According to the Immigration and Naturalization Service, Fort Stanton "was operated in accordance with the Geneva Convention, its internees received stricter treatment than that given to other interned alien enemies." See Monthly Review (October 1945): 212.

11. In September 1943, one of the ten relocation centers managed by the War Relocation Authority, the Tule Lake Relocation Center in northern California, was converted to the Tule Lake Segregation Center to hold those interned in the relocation centers who, on the basis of an extremely ambiguous and controversial questionnaire, were deemed "disloyal." On October 10, 1945, the Tule Lake center came under the jurisdiction of the Immigration and Naturalization Service and the center's military police were replaced by the border patrol.

12. The group referred to here, successively, as "these people," "them," and "they" were "kibei," Americans of Japanese ancestry who were educated during their formative years in Japan before returning to their native United States.

13. On the morning of the Santa Fe Riot, March 12, 1945, twenty-five internees left the camp for the golf course, but they were quickly returned to their quarters. See "Activity Report of Tour 1, 4:00 AM to 12:00 N, March 12, 1945," tour logs, Santa Fe, Records of the Alien Enemy Internment Camps, Records of the Immigration and Naturalization Service, Record Group 85, General Archives Division, Washington National Records Center, Suitland, Maryland.

14. According to Will Harrison, a reporter for the Santa Fe New Mexican, a "wartime curtain of censorship" shrouded the activities at the Santa Fe camp so well that no contemporary mention of the March 1945 riot was made in his paper. See Will Harrison, "Nobody Will Mourn End of Camp Where Thousands of Japs Held, Santa Fe New Mexican," 21 March 1946. The Immigration and Naturalization Service later reprinted this article as "The Santa Fe Internment Camp"; see Monthly Review (April 1946): 298-300. For a recent overview of the Santa Fe camp and the 1945 riot there, see John J. Culley, "The Santa Fe Internment Camp and the Justice Department Program for Enemy Aliens," in Japanese Americans: From Relocation to Redress, ed. Roger Daniels, Sandra C. Taylor, and Harry H. L. Kitano (Salt Lake City: University of Utah Press, 1986), 57-71.

15. Harrison, "Nobody Will Mourn."

Index

An Interview with
DR. AMY N. STANNARD
Conducted by Paul F. Clark
on November 30, 1978
for the
California State University, Fullerton
Oral History Program
Japanese American Project

(Department of Justice Internment Camps
Administrative Experience , O. H. 1615)

This is a slightly edited transcription of an interview conducted for the Oral History Program, sponsored by the California State University, Fullerton. The reader should realize that an oral history document is spontaneous in nature, and portrays information and impressions as recalled by the interviewee.

Scholars are welcome to utilize short excerpts from any of the transcriptions without obtaining permission as long as proper credit is given to the interviewee, the interviewer, and the University. Scholars must, however, obtain permission from California State University, Fullerton, before making more extensive use of the transcriptions and related materials. None of these materials may be duplicated or reproduced by any party without permission from the Oral History Program, California State University, Fullerton, California, 92634.

Interview Introduction

Dr. Amy N. Stannard was the only woman to command a United States civilian internment compound during World War II. As the officer-in-charge of the Immigration and Naturalization camp at Seagoville, Texas, Stannard offers a view of that facility from its beginning as a prison through its tenure as a unique link in the U.S. Justice Department's chain of alien enemy camps.

Stannard was born in Appleton, Wisconsin, in 1894. Upon graduating from college, she taught school in Oregon before beginning medical studies at the University of San Francisco, where she graduated in 1923. Specializing in psychiatry, Stannard trained thereafter at Saint Elizabeth's Hospital in Washington, D.C., and subsequently practiced in the Washington area.

In 1930, Stannard became both the first woman and the first psychiatrist to be appointed to the newly formed Board of Parole in the U.S. Department of Justice. She left this position after five years for further professional training and private practice. In 1940, she returned to the U.S. Justice Department to serve as the assistant warden at the Federal Reformatory for Women at Seagoville. As her interview relates, Stannard successively became the reformatory's warden, and then its assistant and sole officer-in-charge under the Immigration and Naturalization Service.

Finishing her wartime service, Stannard came back to California in 1946 to practice on the staff of the Palo Alto Veterans Hospital, retiring in 1956. In 1972, after suffering a heart attack, she left Palo Alto and settled in the Rossmoor retirement community outside of Walnut Creek, California.

The interview with Dr. Stannard was conducted by Paul Clark on November 30, 1978 at her Rossmoor home. While she possessed prepared notes and an alert mind, her advanced age and debilitative heart condition required two, approximately one-hour taping sessions. Six weeks afterward, Stannard, sadly, passed away.

Fortunately, Stannard's interview transcript was systematically and thoroughly reviewed by her executrix, Dr. Dorothy G. Sproul, who served with Stannard at Seagoville as its chief medical officer. A psychiatrist by profession, Sproul received her B.A. degree from Boston University, College of Liberal Arts, in 1924. By 1934, she had graduated with a medical degree from the University of Maryland, and thereafter trained at Butler Hospital in Providence, Rhode Island. While at Seagoville from April to December 1942, she served in the capacity of a United States Public Health Service officer. Her additional comments, included in the notes following the interview, enrich this oral document and often derive from firsthand experience. Dr. Sproul was not present during the interview.

CALIFORNIA STATE UNIVERSITY, FULLERTON

ORAL HISTORY PROGRAM

Japanese American Project

INTERVIEWEE: DR. AMY N. STANNARD

INTERVIEWER: Paul F. Clark

SUBJECT: Department of Justice Internment Camps
                           Administrative Experience

DATE: November 30, 1978

PC: This is an interview with Dr. Amy N. Stannard in her home at 2664 Ptarmigan Drive, Number 1, Walnut Creek, California, for the Japanese American Project of the California State University, Fullerton, Oral History Program.   Today's date is November 30, 1978, and the time is a little before eleven in the morning.   The interviewer is Paul F. Clark.

Good morning, Dr. Stannard.   Perhaps we can begin by you telling me a little about your early life and education as background to your experiences during World War II.

AS: My pre-World War II years were devoted first to getting an education.   I received an A.B. from the University of California, Berkeley in 1918.   In 1923, I graduated with an M.D. from the University of California, San Francisco, School of Medicine.   I, thereafter, obtained special training and experience in psychiatry at Saint Elizabeth's Hospital in Washington, D.C.   Then, in 1930, I was appointed to the newly formed Board of Parole in the Department of Justice when they were looking for one member to be a woman psychiatrist.   After five years, I left to take further professional training and to engage in student health work and private practice.

In 1940, I accepted an appointment to the Bureau of Prisons to join in the development and staffing of a rehabilitation program at the newly built Federal Reformatory for Women at Seagoville, near Dallas, Texas.   I was associate warden and became warden shortly before the outbreak of World War II.   Our institution had received only a small number of prisoners up to that time.[1]   It was known by the planners in Washington, D.C., to be adaptable to the minimum security detention of certain aliens of enemy nationality.   But it was quite a surprise to us to learn suddenly, in the spring of 1942, that the Bureau of Prisons and the Immigration and Naturalization Service would jointly administer our institution as an "Alien Enemy Detention Station."   That was its first title.[2]

PC: When did you say you learned this?

AS: It was in the spring of 1942.   We admitted the first detainees early in April, about April 5, 1942.   We didn't have very much advance notice.   (laughter)   We did have the organization that was, in general, suitable for this purpose. My title at first was superintendent, and in 1943 it was changed to officer-in-charge.[3] We tried to instruct the staff about the change in administration and tell them about the international Geneva Convention. They had to be well-rounded in their knowledge of that in order to be sure their attitudes were proper.

A memorandum of agreement was drawn up and signed by officials of the respective bureaus. Roughly, it provided that the admissions and releases of aliens and their surveillance while in custody would be the responsibility of the Immigration and Naturalization Service, and the housing, feeding, health care, and other activities would be the responsibility of the Bureau of Prisons staff which was already operating in these functions. As I intimated, it was strictly emphasized that all policies and management were to be in accord with the Geneva Convention of 1929; the watchword being "reciprocity" to insure that no grounds were given for Americans confined under comparable conditions [in enemy areas] to be maltreated. For approximately one year, Mr. Joseph O'Rourke, a career man in the border patrol, was assigned to represent the Immigration and Naturalization Service as supervisor of internment [at Seagoville]. He was transferred in the spring of 1943 to Crystal City as officer-in-charge of that internment camp.[4] Crystal City became principally a family camp, although it had facilities for taking care of troublemakers removed from other camps. In fact, we sent them a few.

The physical setup at Seagoville comprised a reservation of some 830 acres, most of which was farm and pasture land, including a small wooded section used by internees only in the latter part of the duration. They used it for picnic outings. These areas were enclosed only with the ordinary type of farm fencing. The internment area proper was about 80 acres, and it was surrounded by a six-foot, chain-link fence topped by barbed wire. There was a gatehouse at the entrance manned at all times by members of the border patrol[5] They also patrolled the perimeter of the enclave, sometimes on horseback, but were under orders not to enter buildings housing internees, except on special orders in an emergency. Near the gate, facing each other across the flagpole plaza, were 2 two-story, red-brick buildings of identical outward appearance. One was the administration building with offices for our key staff. The other was living quarters for staff who did not choose to live elsewhere. There were also two frame buildings outside the fence occupied by staff members. The internee living quarters were divided into two parts. One included 6 two-story brick buildings facing a quadrangle, each having from 40 to 75 single sleeping rooms, dining rooms, recreation rooms, and a kitchen. The second type of housing was about 60 prefabricated, temporary, wooden "victory huts," which were sixteen by sixteen feet each. These, together with a mess hall, made up the "colony."

PC: I see. The colony was not a special compound for family members. Was it just a temporary affair?

AS: No. Some of the couples occupying them had children with them, while other huts were occupied only by a couple. Having been manufactured in Dallas for various wartime needs, these huts were readily available and were put up speedily when a large influx of Japanese was expected. I should say here that the internees in each house organized their own kitchen and dining room crews, and prepared and served provisions delivered from the central storehouse. The menus were planned by our professional staff dietician and her assistants and could be altered by request, provided the total daily ration as required by the Geneva Convention was not disturbed. For example, we found that they didn't want the traditional American turkey and fixings for Thanksgiving. (laughter) So they had other things: the Germans wanted roast beef and whatnot and the Japanese wanted cherry pie.

PC: Cherry pie for Thanksgiving?

AS: Yes, this was incorporated into their menu for the day. That was part of the function of the dietician. She adapted the menus to the ethnic values of the internees. The Japanese, for example, had a great many things that were never used by the Germans. They had special rice and vegetables that they prepared and used in certain different ways. The dietician was able to analyze their particular menus and see that they didn't deviate from the daily ration prescribed by the Geneva Convention. There had to be so much protein, so much carbohydrate, and on down the line. The dining room tables were square, seating four at a table and, like the other furniture in the houses, were of maple. The table service was stainless steel cutlery--knives, forks and spoons--and lightweight Syracuse china of a pattern seen in tearooms. It was not that fancy stuff Mr. [Herbert V.] Nicholson mentioned [in <u>Treasure in Earthen Vessels</u>].

PC: I think he mentioned dainty chinaware or something to that effect.[6] It was not dainty?

AS: He really went off the deep end.

I should add, there was no large general mess hall serving the whole population such as you see in prisons and other institutions. There was a separate staff dining room and kitchen, of course.

Other buildings of the brick construction were the auditorium and educational building containing classroom facilities including a beauty shop, a barbershop, on the second floor a well-stocked library, a storehouse where perishable and nonperishable items were kept and issued to the housing units, a power plant, maintenance shop, and last, but far from least, a fully equipped and staffed hospital operated by the United States Public Health Service.

It must be made clear that these internees were civilians, not to be confused with POWs [prisoners of war] who were under the jurisdiction of the Army, nor with the special group of Pacific Coast Japanese confined in the camps set up for them and administered independently by the War Relocation Authority. The internees in our custody, with the exception of the voluntary ones, were interned because they were aliens of enemy nationality, and investigation had shown them to be potentially dangerous to the security of the United States. The "voluntary internees" were the wives of the above who had signed petitions to be interned because of hardships at home resulting from the enforced absence of the head of the family. Some of these "voluntary internees" were even citizens of the United States. Each one had signed a specific petition to be interned.[7]

PC: Were these voluntary internees at Seagoville before Crystal City was organized? Did you have this type of a situation before Crystal City?

AS: We`, it stemmed from an order from the central office of the Immigration and Naturalization Service, that got out that voluntary internee petition. I suppose there may also have been voluntary internees in various other internment facilities.[8]

We began admitting women and children from Central and South America. They were the families of male aliens of enemy nationality--Germans, Japanese, and a few Italians who had been interned in other camps in the states. They had been caught up in a sort of dragnet because they were thought to be potentially dangerous to the security of the United States. It isn't clear to me just why the State Department and Immigration came to work that out. Apparently, it was the result of some fear that Japanese, Germans, and Italians in Central and South America might rise up in some way to endanger the United States. I know of no episodes where that ever happened, however.

Many of these women and children were very primitive and confused; very few of them spoke English. Sometimes Spanish was the language most commonly spoken in the camp.[9] Fortunately, we had a few staff members who served as interpreters and one or two young girls among the internees helped in this respect. Later, staff members of German and Italian descent were very helpful in communicating with the Germans and Italians from Latin American countries, and we were able to recruit an American missionary teacher who had not been able to get back to her post in Hiroshima after Pearl Harbor. She was an excellent interpreter of the Japanese language and culture and served as a highly satisfactory liaison between the Japanese group and the American administration.

PC: Do you recall her name?

AS: Yes, her name was Myra Anderson. She went back to Japan just as soon as she possibly could after the war. She was so devoted to the Japanese people. She was required to take a whole year's supply of provisions with her before they [occupied Japan] would let her come back.[10]

Our staff at Seagoville was a well-qualified group selected only recently through nationwide civil service recruitment and experienced in duties not too different from their new assignment. Special mention should be made of the dietician who, before Seagoville, worked in a large state hospital in a Western state, and of the librarian who happened to have had experience in storytelling for children and fluent in Spanish. Our chief liaison officer [Annette MacDonald] had supervision of general housekeeping and clothing supplied to the internees. She spoke both German and Spanish. We also employed extra people temporarily, mostly unskilled, from the nearby community. The men supplemented guards and laborers, the women did housekeeping chores for the offices and staff quarters and assisted in the staff kitchen and dining rooms, and in the hospital. These were all functions which formerly we had trained women prisoners to perform.

The people of the surrounding community were mildly curious but not troublesome. I think the local people we employed spread the word about keeping away from the fence. Some were satisfied to get sight of a Japanese for the first time in their lives. In hiring local people, I always inquired if they had relatives serving in the armed forces and gave them a simple explanation for the purposes of the Geneva Convention. No hostile act ever occurred.

The internees did their own housekeeping and took care of the classrooms and hobby shops organized by them with the assistance of equipment and materials furnished by the administration. I cannot remember the details, but there was an internee-managed employment service under which certain internees were assigned to assist in various departments. One of those was the library, and there were others in the hospital, maintenance shops, and on the farm. These helpers were paid ten cents an hour.

Soon after the husbands were permitted to join their families, the internee government was organized through the election of spokesmen for each house, a council made up of the respective spokesmen with a speaker chosen to represent each, the German and the Japanese groups. The council met from time to time with staff advisers to work out plans for a variety of events and activities. For example, a style show, an arts and crafts exhibit, and amateur theatricals. One very active committee frequently met with the librarian and planned for internee-taught classes for the children. They also suggested movies to be shown. The internees were fond of cowboy and Indian films, and liked the Western flavor of their setting. They liked to sing "Home on the Range" and "Deep in the Heart of Texas."

PC: This is both the Japanese and the Germans?

AS: Yes, especially the children.

Aside from those who came from the Immigration and Naturalization Service, visitors were representatives from the Swiss Delegation and the Spanish Embassy, the former being the protective power for the Germans and the Italians, and the latter for the Japanese, as required by the Geneva Convention. Others were the International Red Cross, YWCA [Young Women's Christian Association], and the Quakers. All met with the internees' speaker and council. I should make that speakers "plural" because the Japanese had their speaker and the Germans spoke for everybody else.

PC: The Germans, you say, would speak for the Italians as well as for themselves?

AS: To the Swiss, yes, I think so. Although there were so few Italians, and they didn't stay long because the war with Italy was over sometime in 1943, I think. The Quakers arranged a few musical and lecture events which were well-received.

I want to say that I hope you're not putting much credence into what Mr. Nicholson said about his visit. I don't believe he was a genuine, qualified representative for the American Friends Service Committee.[11] I never met anybody that was an itinerant wayfarer accepting money as he went along, like he says those Japanese women collected for him. He just fictionalized a great deal of his account of his visit. Was that in an official Quaker report?

PC: No, it was in an oral history interview similar to what we're doing now. When you mention fictionalizations, how extensive do you think they are?

AS: I don't believe his judgment was good and his observations reliable. It just sounds like he looked upon himself as an itinerant wayfarer going about. From the little I have read about him, he seems to have traveled by foot a great deal of the time and hitched rides. That wasn't the way the other Quaker people did. They had travel orders and their expenses were paid. They were not dependent on handouts. I think he just volunteered and they maybe played along with him. I never heard of him before.

PC: You had never heard of him before?

AS: No. If you want to look up somebody's report in the Quaker files, if they'll open them to you, see Mr. Howard Elkington's. I'm sure he made a report which was of a different style at least from Mr. Nicholson's. He [Elkington] seemed to be a man who worked for the Quakers for years in different situations, quite stable.

PC: But don't you remember anything happening such as what Mr. Nicholson recounts in his oral history interview?

AS: I doubt very much whether Mr. O'Rourke would have permitted him to go over to the ladies' quarters and be entertained at tea by them. Most visits took place in the administration building and were conducted with a staff member present.

PC: This is even with the regular Quakers coming in, such as Mr. Elkington and others?

AS: I know the Swiss didn't have any members of the administration with them. They met privately with the internee counsel and so on. Probably the YWCA people and the Quakers did, too. I truly can't remember particularly about that.

PC: But it would be quite extraordinary for a visitor to actually go into the quarters, such as Mr. Nicholson says he did?

AS: Yes.

PC: To your memory.

AS: I think he made up a very fine story about all that.[12]

PC: Your first detainees arrived on April 5, 1942?

AS: Yes, that's when women and children came from Panama.

PC: So your first internees were from Panama?

AS: Yes.

PC: Not from the United States?

AS: No. As I say, the first ones were from Central America and South America, and the prevailing language was Spanish. We needed interpreters very badly. Fortunately, we had a few people that could fill in. These graphs show you how the population fluctuated from time to time.[13] There were never any more than about 654 people, but there were ups and downs due to the repatriation movements of, maybe, hundreds of people at a time.

PC: On the Gripsholm.

AS: Yes.

PC: Most, if not all, of the internees at Seagoville then are from Latin America?

AS: No, later we admitted Germans, Japanese, and Italians from the United States.

PC: I must have missed it.

AS: These graphs aren't broken down by ethnic groups, but they show that there was movement out and in. You mentioned the Gripsholm which reminded me that one of the songs the internees sang in New York when they were about to board the Gripsholm was, "Oh Give Me a Home on the Old Gripsholm." (laughter) I don't remember the other words to it.

PC: These were Japanese?

AS: No, these were the Europeans who were being repatriated.[14] A great many people left to be paroled back into their own community or some other community than in the United States. That's where our social worker came in, and there was correspondence with local agencies and so on. Also, the border patrol made their investigations before people would be released on parole.[15]

PC: Could you tell me a little bit about Joseph O'Rourke.

AS: Well, he was really a jolly Irishman. I think Mr. Jerre Mangione gives about the best picture of him in his remarks about how he was the Pied Piper of Crystal City; children liked him so well.[16] He did warm up to the children at Seagoville, too. He was like other Irishmen; he had his moments of irritation and blowing up. I think some of it was because of this overwhelming number of female staff that he had to work with. Every once in awhile he would cuss out some real gentle person in a most surprising way. (laughter) He drank quite a bit, too, as Jerre Mangione says.

PC: Did that seem to affect his work?

AS: Well, I can recall one or two episodes that were definitely related to a hangover or, on another occasion, drinking too much. Not drinking right then and there on duty, but socially.

        I think he made a very good administrator down there at Crystal City. I don't know a thing about the staff that he had or where they came from. We did transfer some to go there temporarily. I believe our dietician, Miss [Marian] Brooks, went down in an advisory capacity for awhile and possibly the weaving instructor [Mrs. Kelsey], an elderly person who was very well-liked by everybody. I think she might have gone down to help in establishing their weaving crafts. The librarian [Miss Sara Lewis] was not sent.

PC: Can you recall any other interesting or colorful members of the staff? Did the other members of the staff get along well, or were there some problems, perhaps, because of the sudden influx of internees?

AS: Well, a teacher that we had originally as a member of the reformatory staff did not get along well with internees, especially after the men came. They wanted to take a more active part in the education of their children, and they objected very much to the way the American school was being handled. They apparently didn't want to be tainted by American educational methods.

PC: This is both the Japanese and Germans?

AS: Yes. They wanted to find teachers among their own groups that would convey the Japanese or German cultures and languages; so it was set up that way.[17] The librarian was the consultant to the education committee and, of course, she had a lot to do with gathering materials for them. We had quite a lot of recordings, such as records of stories and musical things.

PC: Was Seagoville strictly for women, or was it for families, too?

AS: Yes, it was for women and children first and then the husbands were added. (chuckle) Miss Lewis told a story about a little boy who got so excited and dashed into a story hour one time and said, "Our husbands are coming, our husbands are coming!" (laughter) I guess he didn't know his father very well, but he knew the husbands were coming.

PC: Was this a German or Japanese boy?

AS: I think he was a German. Do you want me to talk about the characteristics of the Japanese as a group and the Germans as a group?

PC: Yes, I'd be very interested in that.

AS: The Japanese, as a group, were quite self-contained and generally very cooperative. I don't remember any incident of their registering any strong wishes, except over that matter of the teaching of the children. They raised wonderful vegetable gardens, and they saved scrap metal for our war effort.

PC: Our war effort?

AS: Yes, it was for our war effort. They would bring it to the administration and say, "This is for your war effort." It's hard to understand that quirk they had of being so polite under all circumstances. Another time a man had raised a tremendous cucumber in his garden and he brought it to the office and said, "this is from my 'victory garden'."

      You know, Jerre Mangione described the scene when the husbands and fathers came. There was quite a difference in the way the Japanese greeted their spouses. They lined up quite some distance from each other in two lines--the women on one side and the men on the other--and they spent some time bowing. Then a signal must have been given, and the men marched off to the Japanese mess hall of the colony and the women stayed in the background pointing out to each other whose husband was which and giggling during it all. We never saw any of them get close to each other at all. That was reserved for later when they got in their quarters. The German women were wildly enthusiastic in greeting their husbands. They put their arms around them and went and carried on joyfully, and then went to their lunch in separate buildings.[18]

      Another story occurs to me. The Japanese and the Germans each had a sort of cooperative canteen that was managed by themselves. They used scrip money that was issued by the administration against money they had on deposit in the safe in the chief clerk's office.

PC: This was the only money they had in their possession? They did not have actual money?

AS: No, they didn't have dollar bills to throw around.

      As far as I'm concerned, they ran a very successful operation, and didn't require very much help from the administration, although there was a staff member who helped to purchase supplies for the canteens in Dallas. She made many trips, and she carried out special orders for things that the internees wanted. After the surrender of Germany in 1945, when it came to closing the respective canteens, the Germans worked it all out in their typically methodical way down to the very last penny to be credited to every German internee. Whereas, the Japanese added up their profits and brought them to the front office and asked that the money be turned over to the International Red Cross!

PC: I'll be darned!

AS: Yes.

PC: So there were Japanese still in the Seagoville camp when it closed?

AS: Yes. They knew they were going to Crystal City. Of course, the war wasn't over for them yet, so many of them stayed out the duration in Crystal City.[19]

PC: Did the Japanese ever celebrate the emperor's birthday?

AS: If they did, they did it so quietly and discreetly that I don't think we knew about it.

PC: They did not engage in any other political, what you would consider, well, political or semipolitical activity then either?

AS: No. They didn't march. The Germans were apt to march to mark anything important.

PC: The Germans did?

AS: Yes.

The Germans would celebrate Hitler's birthday for one thing, and display big, blown up pictures of him in their quarters. Undoubtedly, they had some meetings that the administration didn't participate in which gave honor to the German heroes. I don't remember anything very specific, but there were such meetings. There were factions among the Germans. The Japanese were too proud to show if they had any cliques or any splinter groups. The Germans brought a lot of their prejudices against each other with them when they came. Some were known to be extremely pro-Nazi Bundists and things like that. There were troublemakers among the Germans, but not among the Japanese. The principal troublemakers were the extreme-oriented people. They wanted to take over the management of things more than the majority would put up with. They fostered a lot of mean gossip and felt that they had a mission to continually complain to the American authorities about a great variety of things that were wrong. (chuckle) Oh, they got into big arguments among themselves. They were dissatisfied with their spokesman, you know, from time to time and made threats, so that they were a very disturbing element. We had to ask that about ten or a dozen couples be removed from our camp to go to Crystal City. They had enough room and facilities to take them over.

PC: Were there conflicts between the Germans and the Japanese?

AS: No, I don't believe there was. There was a standoffishness. They didn't understand each other and each other's cultures, and they didn't try.

PC: Did they mix at all, or did they stay in separate compounds?

AS: I don't think they mixed at all except when there was entertainment, like the movies twice a week. We had quite good movies of current issues, but they liked the Westerns most of all. In one film, I remember, I was apprehensive about a scene where the American cavalry came riding up the hill, you know, saving the day. I as afraid that might cause some stir or negative reaction on the part of the internees, but they just enjoyed it all. (chuckle)

I should have said that in this auditorium where they showed the movies, it seated about three hundred people. There was a Hammond electric organ which was played by one of the German internees who was a musician. The auditorium also had a piano, a standard quality projection room, and a stage that was used for meetings and theatricals. Some musical entertainment was put on, too.

PC: Did the Germans and the Japanese have their own sections when they went to the theater?

AS: I think they just sat in their own self-segregated sections. There wasn't any official attempt to keep them apart.

PC: So the so-called Axis allies really didn't . . .

AS: No, they didn't go at each other that way. The conflicts the Germans had were with their own people and, of course, against the American authorities. They always had bizarre tales to tell to the protective power when they came to visit, so that all of those things had to be looked into by the Swiss. I don't remember that the Japanese protective power [Spain] ever asked us questions at all.

PC: I see. So the Japanese were much easier to handle than the Germans?

AS: Yes, yes they were. And a lot of that, I think, was due to this Myra Anderson who was such a wonderful go-between between the Japanese and the Americans. Maybe that's a good place to end.

PC: For the time being.

PC: Okay, this is our second session of the interview with Dr. Amy Stannard.

What I'd be interested in talking to you about now is the alien enemy control program. I understand, Dr. Stannard, that you were probably the only woman who was in charge of an internment camp, or any type of POW, or similar camp, during the war.

AS: Well, yes, I think I was. Of course, I was busy with my own work, so I didn't know very much about others. (laughter) I went to some conferences of officers-in-charge and different officials in Philadelphia, but I never met any woman, except Miss [Evelyn] Hersey, the chief social work adviser to Mr. [Earl] Harrison, the commissioner [of the Immigration and Naturalization Service].[20] She was a very capable and experienced social worker, especially experienced in looking after foreign born. She'd worked with the International Institute for many years.[21]

PC: When you attended these conferences, or just in your general work as the officer-in-charge, did your being a woman in what to my mind appears to have been mostly a male-oriented world present any problems for you? Did you feel under any unusual pressure?

AS: Well, yes. There were people that were sort of suspicious of a woman, or were dubious as to whether a woman had what it takes to be the head of an internment camp. Some were resentful because they thought they could do a better job, I guess, but the criticism, as far as I know, didn't go very far. We felt that to some extent, with the border patrol, who were not really under my orders at all. We had a chief of surveillance who was acting officer-in-charge when I was away. He was a career man in the border patrol, and he had charge of all the guard duty people, the immigration male employees. I think they were somewhat estranged from having to work with women because they never had before, and they probably thought we were over fussy about a few things. I don't know exactly what. I think one was about fire regulations. When I was a little concerned one time about something in the auditorium that I thought was a fire hazard, the man on the post of duty there indicated that he thought I was worrying unnecessarily.

PC: Were you appointed officer-in-charge right away after Mr. O'Rourke left or was there a delay in there?

AS: Yes, that was concurrent with his going to Crystal City.

PC: Were you appointed directly by Mr. Harrison from Philadelphia?

AS: Yes.

PC: Did you have an opportunity to meet Mr. Edward Ennis[22] while you were at Seagoville?

AS: Yes. I knew him quite well. He was the legal representative, I guess. I've forgotten what his title wa·

PC: He was in charge of the Alien Enemy Control Unit.[23]

AS: Well, he must have been associated very closely with Mr. [Willard F.] Kelly who was [the INS's] Assistant Commissioner for Alien Control. Yes, Ennis visited us several times. I remember him very agreeably.

PC: In what way, may I ask?

AS: Well, he was very pleasant. He went out to dinner in Dallas with several of us, and we had an enjoyable time. I remember he didn't drink. Most of us took a cocktail or something or other, but he didn't. Did he sign his name in any other connection?

PC: Normally he would come up in connection with the hearings; if the internees were to be given a hearing.

AS: Oh, yes.

PC: Was this primarily why he came to Seagoville, as you recall?

AS: I don't remember specifically that, but probably he and Mr. [William S.] Southerland, the chief of surveillance, would have worked together on that.

PC: Southerland was in Philadelphia?

AS: No, he was at Seagoville. He was the chief of surveillance and a border patrol career man who lost an arm in the line of duty, by the way. He was acting officer-in-charge when I was away.

PC: He didn't lose his arm while at Seagoville, did he?

AS: Oh, no, this was some years back. He wore an artificial appliance. It was probably due to some border skirmish, I don't know.

PC: Would you like to tell me what you did after the war?

AS: I went to Washington to work in the Bureau of Prisons as an adviser in connection with the classification of inmates. I worked mostly with records of inmates from the various penal institutions, and surveyed court records, particularly of patients with medical and psychiatric problems, for about a year.

Then I decided that I didn't want to stay with prisons indefinitely, and I heard that the Veterans' Administration was revamping itself after the war and recruiting medical officers. So on inquiring about that, I found there was an opening at Palo Alto, California, in the veterans' hospital. I was appointed to work on the staff there, which I did until I retired in 1956. That was about the longest stretch I had in one placement in the government service. I retired with about twenty-eight years service all told. I lived in Palo Alto afterward until I came here to Rossmoor. I had my home there in Palo Alto. Dr. [Dorothy] Sproul, [a former medical officer at the Seagoville camp], in the meantime came to town and was about ready to retire. She had her home in another part of the city. I had a serious heart attack in 1971 which set me back to the point that I wasn't able to live alone entirely anymore, and she helped me out a great deal. We both decided to sell our homes and came to Rossmoor in 1972.

PC: Is there anything that you would like to say in conclusion about your experiences at Seagoville that you haven't covered?

AS: No, except to say it was entirely out of the blue that I got involved with the internment program. On the whole, I'm very glad to have had the experience and enjoyed the associations and knowing people who visited.

I have enjoyed the aftermath of corresponding to some extent with ex-internees. I have met with one of them, a man and his wife, when I was touring Europe in 1960. This was the man who had played the organ in the auditorium. They came from quite some distance in order to see me. I was very sorry I had such little time because our bus had been rambling around the country in a rainstorm trying to find where it was going. By the time we got to Baden-Baden, which was the place we were to stay the night and have dinner, Mr. and Mrs. [Fritz] Wirz had been waiting for hours for us. I appreciated their coming and enjoyed their visit. The Wirz family had been repatriated. I don't know what else I could say.

PC: Looking back on the type of internees that you had at Seagoville, particularly the Japanese, but also the Germans, do you feel that most of them were indeed potentially dangerous?

AS: I didn't see the official records on which their internment was based, so I don't know. It was hard to believe in some cases that they had been disloyal to the United States government. Of course, among the Japanese, there were people picked up on very flimsy circumstantial evidence. Dr. Sproul reminded me the other day about one man and his wife who were interned with us. We learned that he had been interned because it was habit to take walks along the coast and take pictures. That seemed to be about the only thing they had against him, but they may have had correspondence and other things that showed that he was in communication with enemy agents. Among the Germans, I think those rabid Bundists were potentially dangerous if opportunity had afforded and if Germany had invaded the United States, as many of them fully expected would happen. They would have aided the enemy. But then, many of them were just ordinary people going along in their trades and businesses. As far as we knew, they didn't bother anybody. They may have had some associations or joined some German American society or something or other that made them suspect. I really don't know for sure.

I don't know that I should go into the business about some of the people who were troublemakers just because of their nature.

PC: They appear to be rather a distinct minority.

AS: Yes, they were. Some of them, though, were very smart, and very vocal and had quite a hold on the other German population, so that the others were afraid to speak out in opposition. For quite awhile, we had the notorious "Princess" [Stephanie] Hohenlohe [Waldenburg Schillingsfurst] with us. You've read about her, I guess.

PC: You mean in Jerre Mangione's book?[24]

AS: Yes. He gives quite a number of paragraphs to her when she was with us. She was a complainer and finagler of the first order. (laughter) She was trying to wind somebody around her finger to get what she wanted. She did succeed with one of the men who was in a high position in the Philadelphia offices, as is shown in by Jerre Mangione's book. I don't know what became of her eventually. She was great on physical complaints, exaggerating them and using them to the nth degree to get sleeping pills and other special considerations that the medical department didn't think she really needed. On the whole, the other internees suspected her and did not like her. They knew she had a Jewish background and that was one of the reasons. Her marriage and her title was accomplished by a shotgun marriage. She'd been connected with some minor princeling.

PC: So she was a colorful person.

AS: She was to some people, if you could put up with it. (chuckle) All the time you knew in the back of the head she was trying to work some scheme out of you.[25]

PC: Well, that seems to conclude the questioning that I have. I would like to thank you very much, Dr. Stannard, on behalf of the Japanese American Oral History Project at California State University, Fullerton for taking your time today to talk with me about your experiences at the Seagoville Internment Camp.

AS: Yes. You're welcome.

END OF INTERVIEW

NOTES

1. The new institution, Federal Reformatory for Women, Seagoville, known as "a prison without walls," opened in 1941 and received women prisoners convicted of federal offenses; none were illegal aliens. Their sentences ranged from one year and a day to life. All of the prison inmates were transferred to other federal facilities when Seagoville was converted to an alien enemy detention station in April 1942. This notation was supplied by Dorothy G. Sproul. Hereafter notations deriving from Sproul will be indicated by the initials D.G.S.

2. The first title, "Alien Enemy Detention Station," originated in 1942 after the federal prisoners had been moved out and the alien enemy detainees began to arrive. In 1943, the title was changed to "Seagoville Internment Camp," and the detainees thereafter were known as "internees." D.G.S.

3. In 1943, Joseph O'Rourke was transferred to the Crystal City Internment Camp as its officer-in-charge. At the same time, Dr. Stannard became the officer-in-charge at Seagoville. William S. Southerland, a career man in the border patrol, became Seagoville's chief of surveillance, in charge of the Immigration and Naturalization Service's male employees on guard duty. Southerland served as acting officer-in-charge when Dr. Stannard was away. D.G.S.

4. Until 1943, Stannard's title was "superintendent," and O'Rourke's was "supervisor of internment." Neither was subordinate to the other. Each had responsibilities and duties defined in the "memorandum of understanding" signed jointly by officials of the Bureau of Prisons and the Immigration and Naturalization Service. D.G.S.

5. There were no watchtowers at Seagoville; nor did the border patrol carry firearms at this camp. D.G.S.

6. Herbert Nicholson recounts that while visiting Seagoville during the war he enjoyed lunch with the internees "on a table with linen cloth and napkins and dainty china and silverware." See Herbert V. Nicholson, Treasure in Earthen Vessels (Whittier, Calif.: Penn Lithographics, 1974), 69.

7. One Japanese couple, who had two sons serving in the United States armed services, requested voluntary internment because they were the only people of Japanese ancestry living in a small midwestern city and they feared for their safety in that hostile atmosphere. D.G.S.

8. Crystal City, Texas.

9. Among the Panamanians, Spanish was the native language spoken by the women and children. Later, staff members of German and Italian descent were very helpful in communicating with the Germans and Italians from South American countries. D.G.S.

10. Myra Anderson died in 1955. D.G.S.

11. The American Friends Service Committee is a welfare organization founded in 1917 by the Religious Society of Friends (Quakers). Early in the war, Nicholson was employed with the committee. However, due to a falling out, he came to break off his employment with it. See Betty E. Mitson, "Friend Herbert: Concern in Action within America's Concentration Camps" (1980), 45-47. The sole copy of this valuable, unpublished manuscript, consisting chiefly of in-depth interviews conducted by Mitson with Nicholson and originally intended

as an M.A. thesis in the Department of History at California State University, Fullerton, remains in the possession of its author.

12. If Herbert Nicholson was not received by Joseph O'Rourke as an official representative of the Quakers, Nicholson's story of his visit, alone, with the Japanese women is incredible. Furthermore, no United States currency was available to the internees. Any private funds they had were on deposit in the chief clerk's office. Scrip was issued monthly to the internees to spend in the canteen. They could request to order items from outside sources. If approved, payment was made from funds on deposit with the chief clerk. The $43 Nicholson alleges he found in his pocket after leaving the detention station could not have been placed there by the Japanese women. Might the donor have been the kind person who is alleged to have driven Nicholson, "the wayfarer," to Dallas after leaving the station? D.G.S. The comments by Dr. Stannard and Sproul relative to Herbert Nicholson's visit to Seagoville are based exclusively upon his comments as found in "A Friend of the American Way: An Interview with Herbert V. Nicholson," Voices Long Silent: An Oral Inquiry into the Japanese American Evacuation, ed. Arthur A. Hansen and Betty E. Mitson (Fullerton, Calif.: Japanese American Project of the Oral History Program at California State University, Fullerton, 1974): 127-28.

13. These are hand-drawn graphs covering the entire period of Seagoville's use as an internment station. The originals are on deposit in the Japanese American Collection of the California State University, Fullerton, Special Collections.

14. The first exchange of Europeans was in May and June 1942 when the S.S. Drottningholm sailed between New York and Lisbon, Portugal, on two round trips. The M.S. Gripsholm was utilized later that same year and again in 1943 for the exchange of American and Japanese personnel.

15. The border patrol served only to provide security to the various INS internment camps. Other arms of the Justice Department, such as the Federal Bureau of Investigation and the Attorney General's Alien Enemy Control Unit, were the agencies responsible for parole investigations.

16. Jerre Mangione, in Ethnic at Large (New York: G. P. Putnam's Sons, 1978), 331-32, comments that O'Rourke "exuded more charisma than any government employee I had ever met. The prisoners considered him the most popular man in the camp [Crystal City], and their children responded to him as though he were the Pied Piper reincarnated."

17. The internment experience among the Japanese at Seagoville was later described in the volume Japanese in Southern California (Los Angeles: Japanese Chamber of Commerce in Southern California, 1960), 576, as mostly peaceful. However, the issue of education stands out as the one incident of disagreement with the camp authorities. According to this source, in late 1942 there were three teachers assigned to 2,590 students, with the Japanese internees deemed insufficient. Also, there existed questions over school texts. Accordingly, the Japanese speaker, a Mr. Sugimachi, proposed a change in operation. Within three weeks, eight new teachers had been recruited and new textbooks were ordered, thereby resolving the issue. This volume also notes that in 1942 there were from thirty to forty Japanese internees from North America, with the remainder originating from Latin America. Thus, the need for Spanish language texts was also felt.

18. Early 1942, the first group of several hundred women and children arrived late one morning, many non-English speaking, exhausted from a long train ride from New Orleans where they had been held in the immigration station. The administration had prepared a hot noontime meal that was served at long tables in the hospital's quarantine quarters. It was pathetic to see how frightened they were, and so hungry. They ate ravenously, and at the same time snatching food to hide inside their clothing, as though they expected to be

starved later on. In late 1942, as described by Dr. Stannard, the husbands arrived and joined their families. On the following day a small delegation of German men came to the hospital. After brief, formal introductions, they were invited to visit their sick children. The fathers insisted, instead, upon removing the children immediately to the family quarters. None of the children were critically ill, but in need of bed rest and nursing care. The men ignored the questioning as to whether the mothers wanted this relocation and indicated that they would take the responsibility of caring for the children. This response was accepted without arguing. In a day or so, the sickest children were returned to the hospital. Raw potato poultices and home remedies had not cured boils and other illnesses. In contrast to the apprehensive German fathers, when the delegation of Japanese fathers appeared at the hospital, they were courteous and effusive in expressing appreciation of the medical care available. When asked if they wished to see their sick children, their reply was apologetic, "only if the doctor approves." After visiting the children briefly, they departed with expressions of satisfaction and gratitude for the medical care of their children. D.G.S.

19. Seagoville reverted entirely to the United States Bureau of Prisons and became a federal prison for male offenders only. D.G.S.

20. Earl G. Harrison was the INS commissioner from 1942 until 1944. A Republican, he had impressed Francis Biddle, the liberal attorney general, by an outstandingly humanistic 1940 campaign to register resident aliens. Harrison was succeeded by Ugo Carusi.

21. The International Institute stems from a desire in 1910 of the Young Women's Christian Association (YWCA) to provide social services to immigrants in large industrial cities. In 1933, due to diverging interests, the institute became an independent organization.

22. Edward J. Ennis was the director of the Justice Department's Alien Enemy Control Unit from December 1941 to March 1946. For more information on Ennis, see "Edward J. Ennis Resigns from Justice Department," [Immigration and Naturalization Service] Monthly Review (April 1946): 300.

23. The Alien Enemy Control Unit originally operated out of the Office of the Assistant to the Attorney General. Later, in the summer of 1943, the unit was transferred to the Assistant Attorney General, War Division, where it remained until after the war when both the unit and the division were abolished.

24. See Mangione, 206-98.

25. On arrival at Seagoville, the "Princess" was brought to the hospital on a stretcher, advance notice having been received that she was very ill. A pleasant, single room was prepared for her. Examination revealed no medical problems of a physical nature. She received attentive, reassuring care from the nursing staff and two days later requested to be released to the German internee group. We learned later that she was not warmly received by many of the internees. Shortly, the "Princess" came to the hospital to request sleeping pills. When refused, she reported the incident to Joseph O'Rourke. He then called the medical officer to insist that her request be granted. He would not agree with medical opinion that such medication was contra-indicated under the circumstances of her situation, and announced that he himself would go to town and buy sleeping pills for the Princess out of his own funds. Whether he did never became known to me. D.G.S. O'Rourke's proclivity to make out-of-pocket donations to the internees under his supervision was not limited to [Stephanie] Hohenlohe. In the spring of 1944 he personally provided the Japanese at Crystal City with a $15 trophy to be awarded to the winner of athletic events connected with a Japanese celebration. See O'Rourke to Kelly, 30 May 1944, file 103/036, box, 4, Crystal City, Records of the Alien Enemy Internment Camps, Records of the Immigration and

Naturalization Service, Record Group 85, General Archives Division, Washington National Records Center, Suitland, Maryland.

Index

An Interview with
ROBERT L. BROWN
Conducted by Arthur A. Hansen
on December 13, 1973 and February 20, 1974
for the
California State University, Fullerton
Oral History Program
Japanese American Project

(Manzanar War Relocation Center, O.H. 1375)

This is a slightly edited transcription of an interview conducted for the Oral History Program, sponsored
by California State University, Fullerton. The reader
should be aware that an oral history document portrays
information as recalled by the interviewee. Because
of the spontaneous nature of this kind of document,
it may contain statements and impressions which are
not factual.

Scholars are welcome to utilize short excerpts from
any of the transcriptions without obtaining permission
as long as proper credit is given to the interviewee,
the interviewer, and the University. Scholars must,
however, obtain permission from California State
University, Fullerton before making more extensive use
of the transcription and related materials. None of
these materials may be duplicated or reproduced by any
party without permission from the Oral History Program,
California State University, Fullerton, California,
92634.

ROBERT L. BROWN

CALIFORNIA STATE UNIVERSITY, FULLERTON

ORAL HISTORY PROGRAM

Japanese American Project

INTERVIEWEE: ROBERT L. BROWN

INTERVIEWER: Arthur A. Hansen

SUBJECT: Manzanar War Relocation Center

DATE: December 13, 1973; February 20, 1974

H: This is an interview with Robert L. Brown, formerly reports officer
    and assistant project director of the Manzanar War Relocation
    Center, by Arthur A. Hansen, for the California State University,
    Fullerton, Japanese American Oral History Project, at 2321 D Via
    Puerta, Laguna Hills, California, on December 13, 1973, at 3:00
    p.m. /The interview is continued on February 20, 1974 at 2:00 p.m./

    Let me begin the interview, Mr. Brown, by finding out a little bit
    about your background: your age, where you were born, and where you
    were raised.

B: Well, I'm sixty-five, believe it or not! I can't believe it. I
    was born in South Pasadena on March 11, 1908. I was brought up in
    Los Angeles and went to high school in Modesto, California; so
    I'm a Californian. I went to the University of Southern California
    from 1927 to 1931 and got a B.A. degree in English, but I special-
    ized in journalism. Then in 1935 I went back and got a general
    secondary credential in education and taught high school, first
    in Big Pine, California, which is in the Owens Valley, for two
    years, and later in Sanger, California. I really enjoyed teaching.
    But as you know, there wasn't very much money in the teaching
    business in those days.

H: What did you teach?

B: In Big Pine I taught pretty near everything. I taught English, his-
    tory, some mathematics, and music--we gathered a choir together; we
    couldn't quite make it with an orchestra. I even taught Latin for
    one year, for one student.

H: Big Pine is located in Inyo County between . . .

B: Between Independence and Bishop. We had a high school that had
     thirty-seven students and six teachers. We had a grammar school
     that had about a hundred students, and I think they had about seven
     or eight teachers there.

H: How did people in Big Pine make a living at that time?

B: They were mainly cattlemen and ranchers. In those days, they were
     still leasing property from the Los Angeles Department of Water and
     Power, which owned most of the Owens Valley. We had a big Indian
     population; about half of our students were Indian.

H: Were Indians integrated into the town life pretty much, or did they
     keep to themselves?

B: They pretty much kept to themselves. The Indian Bureau had come up
     there and built some very nice small houses for them. But there
     was another group of Indians there who called themselves the Free and
     Independent American Indians and they lived on their own land, which
     was sort of taken over from the Department of Water and Power.
     They were squatters, but nobody paid too much attention to them.
     Most of the Indians were fairly well employed by the cattlemen and
     sheepmen around the country. We didn't have any poverty problem or
     anything like that. They all went to school; nearly all of them
     graduated from high school and quite a few of them went on to
     colleges. They were pretty well-educated for the Indian culture
     in those days; they were pretty well-to-do Indians and, by and
     large, a lot more intelligent than some of the other Indians that
     I've known in my life.

H: What was your life like in Big Pine? Did you find yourself bored?

B: No, it was a very interesting little town. It had all of five
     hundred people. At that time it had a gas station, a general store,
     a post office, a telegraph office, a two-story hotel--but no motels--
     and a Chinese restaurant that was open in the summertime. In the
     wintertime the Chinaman went prospecting.

H: Was there a large Chinese population?

B: Just the one Chinaman who went prospecting.

H: I've talked to some people up there in the Valley and apparently there
     used to be some Chinese communities there.

B: Yes, that's true.

H: Was there one in Bishop at the time?

B: No, I think the Chinese population was in Independence and Lone Pine.
     After the main gold rush in California, the Mexicans came up into
     that country--out of Mexico, Mexican nationals--and they pretty well

picked the country clean of whatever gold or silver there was. Then following them the Chinese came in, and the Chinese did pretty well in a lot of the canyons over in the White Mountains. So this started the Chinese community, but by the time I'd gotten there most of them had gone except Wing Foo. He was the town's best cook in the summertime--he was also one of the best hunters, so he used to take people hunting--and then he'd go prospecting in the wintertime.

H: Then the Chinese didn't come into the Owens Valley as a result of the railroad so much as because of silver prospecting?

B: No, they were all prospecting. No, I don't think they had any Chinese workers on the railroad at all.

H: I'm sure that while you were teaching in Big Pine you got around to Lone Pine, Independence and Bishop at one time or another. Do you remember any Asians in those areas?

B: Not that I know of. There weren't any. There was quite a Basque population because it was sheep country and . . . There were one or two Basque in Big Pine, but most of them lived in Bishop. There is still quite a Basque population there, but no Orientals.

H: You mentioned before about the Indian Bureau, and its contact with the Piutes, and I know that a lot of the relocation authorities came from an Indian Bureau background.

B: That's right, I'd say that maybe 50 percent of all the administrators came from the Bureau of Indian Affairs.

H: Did you have any contact with the Indian Bureau yourself?

B: No, not at that time, not a bit. I didn't know anything about the bureau.

H: How do you think that situation came about, that about 50 percent of the administrators in the WRA /War Relocation Authority7 were recruited from the Indian Bureau program?

B: I know. Let's see, let me reconstruct that. I'd have to go and look that up to really . . . I can tell you that Si Fryer, /E. R. Fryer7, who was the superintendent of the Navajo Reservation in Arizona, was one of the men picked by the administration in Washington to come out to San Francisco and actually run the ten camps from there. I forget who did that in Washington. So, I would say that most of the people who were hired by Fryer were hired from the Bureau of Indian Affairs. I think he had a great deal to do with that.

H: Do you think it was reasoned that, since they had been dealing with concentrated people on the reservation, they might have expertise in dealing with another concentrated minority group?

B: I would think so, yes. At the time I wasn't conscious of it, actually, because we didn't have that philosophy thrown at us at Manzanar--at least to start with. But I noticed that as they picked administrators for the other camps, they picked either people from the Department of Agriculture or people from the Bureau of Indian Affairs.

H: I guess the upper-echelon positions were staffed somewhat heavily by Department of Agriculture people?

B: Yes. That was when Dillon Myer was made the director of the War Relocation Authority; I think that was almost at the start of the WRA. Dillon Myer was from the Department of Agriculture, and I think that's where some of the agriculture people got into the act. I know Ray Best, who ran the Tule Lake camp, was a Department of Agriculture man and pretty well up in it. A lot of the people who came to us . . . well, our man that ran all our agriculture, all our farms at Manzanar, he was a Department of Agriculture man, and the chief engineer at Manzanar, a man named Sandridge, was also from the Department of Agriculture as I remember. It was kind of split between Bureau of Indian Affairs and Department of Agriculture people.

H: You had contact with neither?

B: I had had no contact with any of them, that is correct.

H: Did you, then, go straight from teaching to the position at Manzanar?

B: Well, after my third year of teaching. In the summertime I used to work at Yosemite National Park for the operating company, in the transportation end of it. But I had made some friends over at Big Pine and Bishop and all the people in the Owens Valley were having a very difficult time existing in those days--it was the Depression-- and the Department of Water and Power of the City of Los Angeles had come up in the twenties and purchased most all the land--they owned at least 90 percent of the land in the whole valley. But people still had businesses, they had grocery stores and gas stations and clothing shops, and they were living off what little summer traffic came up to go fishing in the High Sierra and that type of thing.

H: They didn't have much skiing?

B: Didn't have any skiing at that time, there wasn't any skiing at all. There were two or three very interesting people then living in the Owens Valley who have had national publicity, both at the time and since. One of them was a man named Ralph P. Merritt, who had been president of the Sun Maid Raisin Growers' Association and had started that deal. Prior to that he'd been head of the Rice Growers' Association in California. Ralph Merritt was a University of California man; in fact, he was on the Board of Regents at the University of California at one time.

H: He's not originally from Inyo County, though, is he?

B: No, he's not from Inyo County, although he knew it well. One of the things that he was always interested in was mining, and he was an expert on the mineral deposits of Inyo County and Mono County. And another man was Father John J. Crowley, who was the Catholic priest in Lone Pine who, when he was alive, had the byline of the "Desert Padre,"--Padre was a very interesting . . . well, he was just sort of a brilliant guy. He had a little trouble with the church. He was a monsignor. He had a little trouble with church politics and so he elected to take this desert missionary region, and he covered the area from Death Valley to Bishop every Sunday. He'd say mass in Death Valley about five o'clock, drive over the mountains to Lone Pine, say mass there about nine-thirty or ten, and then go up to Bishop and say mass there at eleven o'clock. So he knew everybody.

And they, Ralph Merritt and Father Crowley, along with two or three other people in the valley, decided that it was time that the valley had some kind of chamber of commerce representation or publicity representation or something. For some reason or other, they remembered me and the fact that I was a journalism major and had taught school in Big Pine. One of the men came over to Yosemite, I believe it was during the summer of 1937, and wanted to know if I'd take on the job of running a sort of two-county publicity bureau. And they said, "You'd have to start it from scratch, but we have the newspaper behind you." They had one newspaper in the area. "But you're going to have to sell yourself and raise your own money to pay yourself a salary." And I said, "Well, all right, I'll try it." So I did. I came over, and we raised enough money to get started the first year. That was the start of the Inyo-Mono Association, which was, in effect, a publicity bureau. We were trying to get the newspapers in Los Angeles and San Francisco to give us space on the sports pages about the great hunting and fishing, in order to get people to come up into the area and bolster the economy.

We were quite successful. We started out with a budget of $2,500 which I raised by calling on pretty near every business in the two counties and asking for anything from five to ten dollars. I got about half the people to give me about half of what I asked for. When the war broke out, we had a budget of around $20,000 a year, which today doesn't seem like much, but it was very good then. We had lots of help from the newspapers in southern California and those in the Bay Area. We had lots of friends and the publicity really began to take hold--witness what the area is today. So I suppose how I got into it was that I knew all the major business people in Inyo County and Mono County, as well as all the political people--the judges, the district attorneys, the sheriffs--and all the newspapermen.

H: You were a salesman whom they were indebted to, then, in the sense that you were selling publicity.

B: Well, I was selling the area through publicity, that's what I was doing.

H: For the benefit of their economy.

B: Yes. And in doing it, of course, we had to work very closely with the city of Los Angeles, not only the city council but with the Department of Water and Power officials who were "dead set" against having any more people coming into the valley.

H: Because of the shortage of the water?

B: No, because they just didn't want the issue to come up of people saying, "Well, now we need to have another gas station but we don't have any land to build a gas station on, so please, Mr. City of Los Angeles, won't you either lease us or sell us a corner lot?" And they didn't want to get back into this, at least that administration didn't. Our largest problem was getting the Department of Water and Power people and the Los Angeles City Council people to recognize that this was a new day and that Los Angeles was growing and the Los Angeles people had to have recreational areas and that there wasn't any reason why they couldn't have it in the towns in the Owens Valley, except the city of Los Angeles wouldn't release any of the land. And there were lots of lands that were not agricultural lands, just city lots that, you know . . .

H: So there was still room for expansion?

B: Yes, there was still room for expansion. And we finally got that program put across and we got the city of Los Angeles to sell back a lot of the property within the towns for private ownership. So the organization itself was pretty well-known in the press. There were some very influential people in Los Angeles who were watching this struggle between the tiny community of people fighting for their life and the big outfits trying to hold onto the status quo. One of our big friends, finally, was the Los Angeles Times. We finally got the Los Angeles Times and Harry Chandler, who was then editor and publisher of the paper, to get on our side and start needling the city a little bit.

H: Was there a lot of antagonism toward Los Angeles in Inyo County as a result of, first, their major landlord position, and secondly, their diverting of Owens Valley water?

B: Yes, yes. Yes, lots of antagonism--still is today, to the old-timers. They thought that they had had their land stolen from them. It's a long argument, but it's been written up two or three times, and it's quite an interesting story and quite an interesting fight.

One of our friends was the publisher of the Los Angeles Daily News,

a man named Manchester Boddy. The Los Angeles Daily News was the
only Democractic paper in Los Angeles--if you would consider the
Times a Republican paper then, as well as the Examiner. Boddy was
quite aware of what was going on up there. In fact, I had met him
earlier in the business and he turned out to be a pretty good
personal friend of mine. The director of public relations for the
Department of Water and Power in those days was a man named Glenn
Desmond, who was also personally, I'm sure, sympathetic to the
people of the Owens Valley, but who had a job to do to maintain the
position that the department took. But Glenn and I got to be real
good personal friends. So when it appeared that war was imminent,
or actually when war was declared, and the great hue and cry went
up about the Japanese Americans and those few Japanese who were
Issei--who were born in Japan--being a threat to the Pacific Coast,
we began to get rumbles that something was going to be done with
the Japanese. At first we thought maybe Inyo County, because of all
the metal minerals that were there, would probably get in on a war
boom of extraction of minerals. That's what we actually thought.

H: Did you push this in your publicity at all?

B: Yes, we pushed it in our publicity and we showed all the stuff that
was available. Inyo County has the largest tungsten mine in the
world--still, to this day--right out of Bishop.

H: Was the tungsten then being extracted?

B: Tungsten was in short supply, so we knew that was going to go.

H: But were they already mining it?

B: Oh, yes, they were mining it. But there was a lot of tungsten all
through both the Sierra Nevada Mountains and the White Mountains,
so there were a lot of tungsten deposits that had maybe been marginal
earlier but now as the price of tungsten was going . . . see, China
had most of the tungsten and we couldn't get into China to get the
tungsten. That was a very necessary metal. So there was a big boom
in tungsten.

But to get on with the story, I was up at Minden, Nevada, early in
March, 1942, making a standard publicity speech about "let's get
skiing going." We were by that time trying to get skiing operating,
although we had not yet done it.

H: Where were you trying to get skiing going?

B: In and around Mammoth, where it is now, where it's so heavy, and
around June Lake. And I got a call from Glenn Desmond of the
Department of Water and Power saying that there was a big emergency
meeting he wanted me to attend with Manchester Boddy, the publisher
of the Los Angeles Daily News. He asked me if I could come down to
Los Angeles, and I replied that I could.

H: In what capacity were you going to be serving?

B: As the executive secretary of the Inyo-Mono Association. This was
     like a chamber of commerce. We didn't call it a chamber of commerce,
     but it was an association backed by the businessmen in the two
     counties, and I was the official voice of it. I did all the public-
     ity work for it.   So that's why Glenn asked if I would come down;
     in other words, I would sort of be representing the feeling of
     people in Inyo County and Mono County.

H: Who was president of the Inyo-Mono Association?

B: Well, the first president was Father Crowley. And the second presi-
     dent was a Bridgeport man named Slick Bryant. I think he's still
     alive.

H: Is Bridgeport in Mono County?

B: Yes. Bridgeport is the capital of Mono County. And the third presi-
     dent was a man named Doug Joseph, who was the grocery store king of
     Bishop. Doug's still alive. But anyway, Glenn asked me to come
     down and have a meeting with Manchester Boddy. So I did. In fact,
     we went out to Boddy's house for lunch, as I remember, and he said,
     "I've just gotten word from Attorney General Biddle"--who evidently
     was a personal friend--"that the president is going to sign pro-
     clamation number so-and-so which will, in effect, take all the per-
     sons of Japanese ancestry out of the coastal states"--that's
     California, Oregon, Washington, and I guess Nevada and Arizona, too.
     I kind of forget the pronouncement, but it covered the eleven
     Western states.

H: This meeting was probably a little bit earlier, wasn't it? I think
     you're probably talking about Executive Order 9066, which came out
     in February of 1942, so . . .

B: You're right. You're right. You've done more research recently
     than I have. You're right. The executive order had already been
     signed. Nobody gave it too much attention in the Owens Valley; I
     suppose on the coast they did. I remember thinking, "When I go
     down to this meeting, I wonder what Boddy will want us to talk
     about, tungsten or roads or land or air forces or possibly the
     Japanese?" But we didn't give it too much thought. So then Boddy
     said, "I've just been in touch with Attorney General Biddle and the
     Army is going to move all the Japanese off the West Coast and they're
     going to do it real fast." "I suggested to Biddle," said Boddy,
     "that a good place to put them would be up in the Owens Valley."

     And both Desmond and I were sort of aghast. We said, "How many
     Japanese are there?" And they said, "Well, about a hundred thousand."
     I said, "Good Lord! We can't take care of a hundred thousand
     people. What are we going to do about our own people? No, that
     won't work." And Boddy said, "I've arranged for the two of you"--

this was Glenn Desmond of the Department of Water and Power and me, representing the Inyo-Mono community--"to meet a man named Tom Clark, who is an assistant attorney general"--who later, as you know, served as a Supreme Court judge--"and he's been sent out here by Biddle and the president to make all the arrangements to get this thing underway and to move all the people." "Well," he said, "right now we've got an appointment this afternoon." So Tom Clark had an office set up for him in the city hall of Los Angeles. We went down there and met with Tom Clark. And he told us the same thing: Yes, the Army was going to move and they were going to move fast; he'd been giving a lot of thought to the Owens Valley as a place to put all of the people of Japanese ancestry, but he thought maybe we were right, it wasn't quite big enough for that, but he also had some ideas about Death Valley and he had some ideas about the upper Mojave Desert and he had a lot of ideas that he was kicking around.

H: Had they even mentioned Manzanar yet?

B: Oh, they never mentioned Manzanar. They didn't even know there was such a place. They were just thinking in terms of the whole area. So we listened more than we talked, and Clark said, "You people could help, both of you--you, Mr. Department of Water and Power, and you, Mr. County Representative--by sitting down and thinking about this and maybe coming up with some ideas of what we could do."

So Glenn and I went back to his office and we thought about it a couple of days and we came up with kind of an outline. There were a lot of things that needed to be done if we had that many able-bodied people who were going to be removed from the coast. There were trails to fix and all sorts of make-work projects that you could get where you could keep at least the male population busy. And I came up with the idea that it would be a good idea if we got some of the leaders of the community into a committee that would be appointed by the government to give it some executive impulse, some feeling of: "Well, we're working for the government." You know. At least the original members of the committee would have a letter from the attorney general saying, "Would you be on a committee to study this problem?"

So we went back and talked to Clark again, and he said, "That's a good idea. Give me a list of the names that you'd recommend, and I'll check them out." Which he subsequently did. I kind of forget the exact route, but we put Ralph Merritt on the committee. By the time this all came about, Father Crowley had been killed in an automobile accident, so he wasn't available. We put on the committee a man named Roy Booth, who was head of the Forest Service, and Spence Loudon, who was head of the Highway Division, and four or five of the other good citizens of the valley. We put the newspaperman George Savage on it, also.

H: Do you remember what the name of the committee was? Was it the Owens Valley Citizens' League?

B: It was the Owens Valley something or other Committee. There's probably some documentation on it somewhere. I noticed someplace here a couple of years ago some mention to it; I think it was in the Eastern California Museum at Independence. Yes. So there's a list of that. So that went on for two or three days. It seemed to happen awfully fast. Tom Clark went to San Francisco where he employed a large public relations firm to sort of guide him in planning the story and in getting notices out through the Army to the Japanese people in the community and whatnot. The next I remember—this was all just in a matter of two or three days—I got a telephone call from Tom Clark's secretary in Los Angeles saying that she had a reservation for me and for George Savage, the editor of the Bishop paper, to fly to San Francisco and talk to Clark and to this public relations firm—which we subsequently did. Clark said, "I need either you, Savage, the newspaperman, or you, Brown, the publicity man, to go to work for me in this whole program." And Savage said, "Well, I've got my own business and I've got to think about that."

H: Was this the Chalfant Press?

B: The Chalfant Press, yes. "And I don't think I'd better do it, but I think Brown will do it." And I said, "I don't know whether I ought to do it or not. There's a lot of things about this that are going to upset the whole community." And Clark turned and he kind of smiled and he said, "I didn't ask you, I'm telling you. You went to work for me yesterday." So that's the way I got hired. And I represented what was first set up as WCCA /Wartime Civil Control Administration7, which was temporarily controlled by a man named Nicholson. The man they sent over to Manzanar to run it right from the beginning was a man named Clayton Triggs, who was an old CCC /Civilian Conservation Corps7 camp administrator.

H: Now, Karl Bendetson was the head of the WCCA, wasn't he?

B: Bendetson was the head of the WCCA, and evidently he picked up Triggs some place through the Army and through the CCC. Triggs was a fine administrator, a tremendous administrator. A hell of a guy! But that WCCA thing only lasted four, five, or six months, something like that.

H: I don't even think it lasted that long, did it?

B: Maybe not even that long.

H: I think from about the middle of March to the first of June. Then the WRA took over.

B: Yes, you've got a better handle on this because you've been studying it lately. I'm so rusty in my mind. At the same time this was going on—the San Francisco meetings and whatnot—the Army Corps of Engineers came up into the valley without telling anybody or without anybody paving the way for them and started talking around

Lone Pine and saying they were going to bring a hundred thousand "Japs" up to Lone Pine. And this just threw the town into a panic, you know? No forewarning, no working through the committee, no working through Savage the newspaperman or anything else. They did it all independently.

H: They had no publicity whatsoever on it yet?

B: No publicity on it whatsoever. I was able to get that stopped through Tom Clark.

H: What, the talk?

B: I was able to get the Army, when they came up there, to quit talking, and when they did come up, to come up under the auspices of the committee and, say, the Forest Service man, you know, so that when we were going around in all these Army jeeps looking at property, everybody wasn't following us around saying, "What's the Army going to do now?" This sort of thing had been taken care of.

H: They still hadn't picked Manzanar yet.

B: They still hadn't picked the site, no. They had four or five sites in mind, one down by Olancha, one up in the Bishop area, and one over on the east side of the valley where they would have had a water problem--they would have had to take it out of the Owens River. But they finally settled on the site of Manzanar, which was an old, abandoned, very large apple orchard at one time, and had a very fine stream coming right down through the middle of it.

H: I think they still had the water pipes there, too, didn't they?

B: I think so. So they had plenty of water. So anyway, that's how I got into the act.

H: Okay. Can I backtrack just a second and find out a little more about your activities in the Owens Valley during the prewar years?

B: Yes.

H: So you taught school in Big Pine and Sanger during the middle part of the thirties and then you took this job as secretary of the Inyo-Mono Association. And during this time that you had this job, between 1937 and 1942, you traveled a lot and you met almost all of the businessmen in your community. So you knew the area and its people very well. I want to find out a little bit about each of the communities in the valley to see if we can't pinpoint something of the nature of their economy and their leadership. Let's begin with Lone Pine and continue north from there. What kind of economy did Lone Pine have then?

B: It had a cattleman's and tourist economy. That's about all. You had the stores that hired the people that waited on the summer trade, and you had about, oh, I'd say twenty or thirty pretty fair-sized cattle ranches, and one or two very large cattle outfits. They used to run their cattle up in the High Sierra in the summertime and bring them down into the Owens Valley and feed them in the wintertime. And eventually they got a little more water for raising alfalfa and that type of stuff so that they could raise their own feed. You had miners. You had quite a bit of mining still going on in those days-- more dreamer's mining, I would say, but there was a lot of prospecting. Oh, they had big sulphur fields over in one of the valleys west of Lone Pine. The town of Darwin was still going with a big lead mill and had about a hundred to two hundred people working there. That kept some of the economy coming into Lone Pine.

H: Where's Darwin located?

B: Darwin is southwest of Lone Pine on the road to Death Valley.

H: When you wanted in your role as publicist to put something over to the Lone Pine people, who were the major people in the town that you went to see? In other words, who within Lone Pine possessed the power to effect action?

B: Well, let's see. John Lubken was the largest cattleman in the country and also chairman of the board of supervisors. At that time John didn't like what we were trying to do in bringing the transients in, because people would cut his fences and all that. He was not particularly for the program, although he was a smart and very able supervisor and realized that the economy had to be kept up by the merchants in the main streets of the town. So he wasn't too bitter, too vociferous in his antagonism, but he was one of the ones that I personally worked on for a long time. Finally we got to be real close friends. One of the major store owners in Lone Pine was one of the Joseph boys, Douglas Joseph's brother Irving. There were two drugstores; they were both active because they naturally got all the tourist business. There were also three or four restaurant owners, but I've sort of forgotten their names. One man who was very helpful was Jack Hopkins. He's still there in Lone Pine in the hardware business and has been on the board of supervisors. You might have run into Jack during your interviewing trips up to the Owens Valley. Well, he knows a lot about things in the valley, and was very close to it. There were four or five small hotel operators. Lone Pine was a very small town. I think it had eighteen hundred, maybe two thousand, people in the town. It had once been a larger town but by this time it was pretty well run-down.

H: How would you describe the outlook of the townspeople? Were they pretty provincial people? I'm getting at this because I've been in Independence. As the county seat, and perhaps it is because they have government employees there, it seems to have more of a cultural tradition than Lone Pine.

B: Well, they're very proud of the history of the Owens Valley. All the old-timers in the valley are. I found them really quite intelligent people, the people that I dealt with--and I dealt with practically every businessman in all the towns. You would find a few businessmen who were soured and who didn't like life in general, who didn't think we were doing any good, who thought things were all going to hell in a handbasket and that it was all the city of Los Angeles' fault, and this and that and the other, but really not very many. Of the major businesses in Lone Pine, we had good support, like I say, from the drugstore people, the grocery people, the hotel people, and anybody who would profit by getting more tourists into the county. They could see the results of what we were doing with the newspapers in Los Angeles because tourist travel picked up right away, just right away. There was a noticeable change in the cash register and that's the thing that . . .

H: That spoke rather powerfully?

B: It spoke very powerfully, yes. We were quite pleased at the way things went because we didn't have any split-off splinter groups, for example, trying to undermine us. Everybody was all for the program.

H: What about Independence? What kind of a town was that?

B: Well, Independence was the county seat, of course, and that's where the judge was and where the district attorney was, and all the county clerks and all the school officials were. And I think you're right about Independence. There's a pretty intelligent group of people there in Independence, and there always has been. In teaching school, for example, I had all kinds of help out of the county school super-intendent's office.

H: Who was the county superintendent at that time?

B: Ada Robinson to start with and then Dorothy Cragen.

H: Dorothy Cragen?

B: Yes, she's still alive and she serves as the county historian. She's been a real close friend of ours. When I moved into the San Joaquin Valley in 1936 and went to teach in the little town of Sanger, which was about ten thousand people as against five hundred in Big Pine, I found very provincial attitudes in Sanger and very negative attitudes, as far as I was concerned. I was a young man and a young teacher and interested in seeing that the kids got the right kind of education, but I had all sorts of opposition from everything from the American Legion boys to certain ethnic groups they were against--they didn't like the "damn Japs" and they didn't like the "damn Mexicans," you know, this type of thing.

H: You didn't find that so much in Independence, though.

B: There was none of that in Independence, none whatsoever.

H: How about the town's political orientation?

B: They were mainly Republicans, but I would say theirs was an enlightened Republicanism. Speaking in today's terms, they were progressive Republicans. There were very few die-hard negativists, very,
very few.

H: What did the people in Independence do to make a living? Were the
government offices the main basis of the economy?

B: Yes, the government offices and its branches, also the division
office of the Department of Water and Power. That's about all.
And there was a grocery store and a couple of motels and that in
town as well.

H: Was there farming there?

B: No. Not anymore.

H: Was there a lot of ranching then?

B: No, there weren't any ranches.

H: Let's proceed north to the first town you taught at, Big Pine. You
said earlier that the economy there was largely cattle and tourism.

B: Cattle and a little tourist trade. One man that I forgot to mention
in Lone Pine who was a very big help to us was a man named Walter
Dow. The Dow Hotel is named after him. Walter was a man of considerable means. He had made his fortune someplace else and then moved
to Lone Pine--even though it was decaying--and tried to put it back
on the map. He started a lumberyard and he started to build the
hotel and he was very active in community development type of
things. I would say that he was sort of the pillar of Lone Pine in
those days.

H: What about Independence, the county seat, which we were talking about
before? Here you had a lot of officials. Who was powerful in
Independence? It seems to me if they were powerful there, their voice
would also carry weight beyond the confines of Independence; in
other words, they must have been influential in the country at large.

B: The superior court judge was the most respected of all of the county
officials. He was a highly respected man and a very fine judge. He
used to be called into Los Angeles, San Francisco, and other places
because his calendar wasn't too tight in the valley.

H: Do you recall his name?

B: William Dehy.

H: There's now a park named after him in Independence, isn't there?

B: Yes, Dehy Park. William Dehy. And George Francis was the district
attorney when I was there, and George later became a superior court

judge and he's operating here in southern California. I still see
news of him in the paper. He is quite an unconventional judge in
that he makes an attempt to get to the bottom of the problem, whatever it is, himself, and get the litigants to settle between themselves, out of court and this type of thing. And he's had some very
fine write-ups . . . just recently in the Los Angeles Times, for example, there was a nice piece on him. I think George is past retirement age but he's still working. We had . . . I forget the fellow's
name right now that followed him, but he ended up being a judge in
Inyo County. Anyway, he had a fine reputation, still has. I'll
think of his name in a minute. So there were some interesting
people. Well, you know. Mary Austen, who wrote The Land of Little
Rain, lived in Independence, and her husband was the county surveyor.
This was before my time, back in 1900 to 1918, something like that.
And she turned out to be a real, real top thought-of writer.

H: What about Bishop? That was a much bigger town than Lone Pine,
     Independence, and Big Pine.

B: Yes, Bishop was the largest town in the area and, interestingly
     enough, it hasn't changed very much. That's where our headquarters
     were for the Inyo-Mono Association. When I was living there, I think
     Bishop's population was about four thousand; now it's only about
     five thousand. It was really the hub of the valley. You had access
     to more lakes out of Bishop than you did any of the other towns for
     fishing. And even in the old days it was only about an hour and a
     half or two hours from the Mammoth country, which was only open in
     the summertime. But even then, it was quite a recreational area.
     During World War I, somebody had discovered this tungsten mine up in
     Pine Creek Canyon, which is out of Bishop, and had worked it in those
     days, and then for some reason or another the price of tungsten fell
     and the mining company abandoned it or went broke or something.
     Ralph Merritt and two or three other people managed to get it going
     again and got a big tungsten outfit, the United States Vanadium
     Corporation—largest tungsten mining outfit in the world—to buy it
     up and go in and spend a lot of money in it. This was a few years
     before the war. I think they could smell the war coming, you know.
     And they spent millions of dollars up there and put in a huge mill,
     and the mine itself. The tunnels were at about ten or eleven thou-
     sand feet elevation, so they had to go in and winterproof all that
     work so they could work it at ten thousand feet, you know, at twenty
     or thirty below temperature all the time. And they ran a full crew,
     and still are running a full crew, I think, for twenty-four hours a
     day. It's the largest producing tungsten mine in the world.

H: So in Bishop there's basically an economy built around mining and to
     some degree, I suppose, cattle ranching?

B: Yes, to some degree cattle ranching.

H: And tourists?

B: I think the biggest thing was tourists. I know it is today and I think even in those days the tourist trade was the biggest thing, because the minute it began to pick up--when I first moved into Bishop, oh, there'd be one or two stores in each block empty and it wasn't a year after the Inyo-Mono Association was going that they started building up and people came in, and you could see it. You could see it immediately. You go out and talk to some of the fellows there now that have been there since then, and they'll tell you the same story. The minute the Inyo-Mono Association started going, they saw immediately a noticeable business increase. We didn't get skiing going prior to the war because the war kind of stopped us. But Dave McCoy and I are old personal friends. Dave and I--he's the guy who owns the big chair lift complex at Mammoth--Dave used to work for the Department of Water and Power. He was a snow-measurer in the wintertime. He went out and measured the snow and that's how the Department of Water and Power figured out how much moisture was in the content of the snow pack and regulated their water intake and this kind of stuff. I think Dave was chief hydro-grapher. Dave and I used to go up to Crestview, which is just past the turnoff to Mammoth. You couldn't get into Mammoth in those days because they didn't keep the road open. We'd go up to Crestview on a weekend and take my old Model A Ford and take the wheel off and put just a rim on, you know, and jack the thing up and put a rope tow around that and tie it up to a tree, and that was the very first start of any rope tows in the country. And we didn't have sense enough to charge anybody in those days. We were just doing it for ourselves, you know? And Dave one time said, "Hey, I think there ought to be money in this thing. We ought to get paid for it." And I said, "Yes, that's a good idea." Subsequently, he went out and built all that complex at Mammoth, as you know--or probably don't. Are you a skier?

H: No, I'm not, but I know a little about Mammoth.

B: Well, he's internationally known. He really is. I mean, he . . .

H: He's Mr. Mammoth, right?

B: He's Mr. Mammoth and he probably has got invested, without any exaggeration at all, ten million dollars. Just one of those things, you know. And he's still old Dave. He isn't any different than he was when we were putting the rope tow up to haul ourselves up to the tree.

H: Can we now talk about preparing the people in the Owens Valley for the coming of a large influx of Japanese Americans at the Manzanar camp? I'm wondering what your position was like as a publicist. On the one hand, in a sagging economy during Depression years, certainly there was money in having a relocation center built in the area. Yet, at the same time, there was probably a certain amount of fear or resistance to having enemy aliens and their children being confined in areas proximate to towns like Independence and Lone Pine. This would seem to present a paradox. How did the people react to this paradoxical situation? Did you try to emphasize the . . .

B: Yes. In the first place, we had the support of George Savage and the Inyo newspapers. He published them all at one plant but one had a dateline of Bishop and one Independence and one Lone Pine--and later on one in Bridgeport. We had George behind us 100 percent, and he kept the positive things going; you know, that it was good for the community so don't listen to the hate-mongers, and this type of stuff. He did a nice job, a very nice job. Then we got the members of this committee who were appointed by Tom Clark, and we had people from WCCA and the Army and the attorney general's office come out and brief them very thoroughly, and then most of the members of the Owens Valley Citizens Committee would go out and talk to the Rotary clubs and women's clubs and PTA people and whatnot. We did this fast--within the first four, five, six or seven days-- when we had to get this thing all through. Looking back on it, we had firm support from everybody who was on the original citizens' committee. We had sort of a "let's wait and see" kind of support from most of the people. And we had 10 /percent/ or 15 or 20 per-cent of the people who were violently against it.

H: Ten or 15 percent of the people?

B: Yes, violently opposed to it.

H: Do you recall any leaders of this opposition group?

B: Yes. I can't remember the guy's name, but there was a guy in Independence who formed his own militia of trained people and they were going to march . . . they were going to "save the women and children of Independence when the Japs broke loose!" (laughter) I forget his name.

H: But he had only very little support?

B: Yes. And, oh, my boy was nine or ten in those days and would come home and say, "Daddy, are you a Jap-lover?" And I'd say, "Where did you get that?" "Well, all the kids at school said, 'Your dad's a Jap-lover.'"

H: Was your son going to school in Bishop?

B: Yes.

H: So in Bishop there was also some opposition?

B: Yes, there was an amount of opposition in Bishop. But it pretty well got straightened out. I'll tell you what straightened it out. It didn't take it long to change, although I'm sure we still had 10 or 15 percent of the people who thought we were doing the wrong thing. But the minute the camp got operating, we had to have local supplies. So this meant everything from hardware that some-body had forgot to buy in San Francisco to groceries that somebody didn't order and drugs and printing and newspapers. Well, it just affected almost everybody in the community, especially those in

Lone Pine. Bishop didn't get it so much as Lone Pine. Lone Pine suddenly found itself just rolling in Uncle Sam's money, and the situation stayed that way all during the four years the Japanese were there.

H: How about Independence? Was it affected?

B: Not very much. There wasn't anybody in Independence that had anything, you know? There was a little tiny grocery store and there wasn't even a drugstore in Independence. There were law offices for ex-district attorneys and other attorneys who lived there because they were going to defend somebody in the county and this type of thing. And so Independence didn't get anything.

H: Well, did you find that--insofar as Lone Pine was profiting from it-- that the attitude of the people in Lone Pine was more receptive than that of the people in Independence?

B: Yes, I would say so.

H: And as you went up north in the Owens Valley would you say that it got less receptive?

B: No, I wouldn't say so. People sort of understood. There was never too much rivalry. You know, small towns in a little valley like that are sometimes highly competitive. The grocery store guy in Bishop hates the grocery store guy in Lone Pine, and like that. We didn't have any of that, as I remember, or at least we didn't seem to. And one of the things that helped the nonrivalry attitude was the Inyo Associates that Father Crowley and Ralph Merritt and Ray Goodman put together. It met once a month and it was a sort of a "get it off your chest" meeting: "What's going on, and where are we going?" We had the Forest Service people who'd come and say what was going on in the Forest Service and the highway guy would tell us what was going on in the Division of Highways and the newspaperman would say what was going on in his place and the grocery store people would get together and sit down at the same table and, you know, that kind of thing. So there wasn't the kind of rivalry that you see between so many small towns where one town is fighting another one. We didn't have that. We were a pretty cohesive group. When asked, "Where are you from?" most people would say, "I'm from the Owens Valley." "Well, what part of the Owens Valley?" "Well, I happen to live in Lone Pine." You know?

H: So their primary identification was with the region rather than with an individual town in the Owens Valley?

B: Yes. That's how everybody would answer you--most everybody.

H: Is there a lot of status connected with being a pioneer family in the Owens Valley?

B: Oh, I don't think anymore—gosh, yes, I suppose. There was in those days, yes.

H: Was there resistance to either Ralph Merritt, who later became Manzanar's director, or yourself? Although both of you had lived in the area, in some small towns they continue to regard people as outsiders fifteen or twenty years after their arrival.

B: Yes. It's a hard thing to say. I don't know. I suppose I had people that didn't like me, people who I didn't know anything about. But by and large, I think everybody that I know of there, or knew then, were quite friendly. Ralph had a few more people against him. Ralph was sort of a controversial man. He was a big man—big in his thinking, big in his ideas.

H: What sort of controversies surrounded Merritt?

B: He was always a man of some controversy. You know, after Manzanar, he went to work for the War Assets Board. He was a disposal guy; he went around getting rid of air bases and that kind of stuff. Then he drifted into this rapid transit deal in Los Angeles. He's the guy that put the rapid transit together, there's no doubt about it. And he was controversial in that. But he had the Los Angeles City Council on his side for a long time and then they got some new members in the city council and they didn't like some of the things he was doing and whatnot. But he actually put the thing together, which I know very personally. I'm almost like a son to Ralph Merritt. We were very close together. And I know all the struggles he went through.

H: What were the controversies that he was embroiled in before the war, with respect to the people in Inyo County? What made him albeit a respected person, a controversial figure to them?

B: Well, Ralph went broke in the Depression, you know. Ralph had made a lot of money, and, of course, the Depression came along and the Sun Maid Raisin Growers' organization went bankrupt. This personally bankrupted Ralph. And he had old, old friends from Independence, the Gunn family—anyway, Jack Gunn discovered the Minietta mine, which is over toward Death Valley. And he took a lot of money out of it. It was a silver and lead property. He took a lot of money out of it and used it. He'd mine it for a year or so and then he'd take his family and bundle them up and spend a year in Europe, this kind of thing. Well, he finally died. Mrs. Gunn was somehow or other an old friend of Ralph's father, who was a judge in Berkeley and also had come from that territory. He had something to do with mining laws and that. Now Ralph got polio right when he was about broke, and Mrs. Gunn took him in and he lived there with the Gunns for two or three years and actually opened up the Minietta again, opened it up and got it going; got a loan from the government, the Metals Reserve Corporation.

H: He wasn't married then?

B: Yes, he was married, but his wife didn't particularly like the
    desert and she had some kind of a feeling about the Gunn family. So
    she stayed in Oakland. So I think probably that people didn't know
    Ralph too well over there and the fact that he went into mining when
    he'd been a food man all his life . . . they got the idea that maybe
    he was sort of a promoter, which, you know, he wasn't. But they would
    always come to him for advice, even though they didn't like him.
    It's one of those things, you know? You've seen that in your own
    life. And then he and Father Crowley and Ray Goodman of Death Valley
    and Roy Booth, who was head of the Forest Service, and guys like
    Doug Joseph who were then getting to be financially well-off, sort of
    got together. I think the feeling toward Ralph on the part of some
    people dissipated. And I didn't feel any of that at the end of the
    Manzanar program. I think the whole valley was really very proud of
    Ralph Merritt and the way things were run in the camp. I don't think
    you'd find now in the old-timers anybody, outside of a guy like
    Arleigh Brierly of Independence, who would have anything bad to say
    about Ralph Merritt. I don't think so. I hope not, anyway.

H: There's a strange situation in that here was an area that was, as
    we've pointed out before, profiting, at least in Lone Pine, consi-
    derably from the camp being there, and yet, as studies that have
    been done on the various communities surrounding the various reloca-
    tion centers reveal, there was a special sort of hostility in the
    Owens Valley that you didn't find in most of the other areas. Now
    part of that could be due to lack of real scholarship concerning those
    other areas and the greater focusing on the California area because
    it was closest to the Japanese American population center. But it
    does seem that Manzanar and Tule Lake were the only two camps where
    the people in the surrounding areas would not allow the internees
    to come into their towns. In the other areas, after a short while,
    the towns were opened up to the internees. Although there was re-
    sistance and certain businessmen refused to serve internees when
    they went into restaurants or refused to sell them clothes in depart-
    ment stores, there was much more of an integration between town,
    on the one hand, and camp, on the other. And you never found this
    true with respect to Lone Pine or Independence. Do you think the
    reason was because Manzanar happened to be closest to the coast
    and therefore people were more anxious owing to this proximity? How
    do you account for this situation?

B: It's a good question. I don't know. Let me think about that for a
    minute. It never bothered us at the camp. We made two or three
    efforts early in the camp's history--this was before Ralph got there
    when Roy Nash was running the place and actually when Clayt Triggs
    was right there. One thing we suggested--you know where . . . Is
    it Tinemeha Lake? Anyhow, one of the lakes that is a storage thing
    for the city of Los Angeles for the aqueduct there--oh, it's not
    Tinemeha, it's the one below that.

H: Little Lake?

B: Between Little Lake and Tinemeha. . . I'll think of the name. Anyway,
    that was all full of carp. And the Japanese love carp, you know,
    so we suggested that why don't we--in those days we had the Army
    with us. I guess we had the Army with us all the time, didn't we?
    Anyway, we'd take the Army and a couple of launch-loads of these
    Japanese fishermen, go down there, and clean out Haiwee Reservoir.
    And I recall that we got a lot of back talk about that. "Oh,
    Christ, no! Don't let those bastards out of the camp." So we just
    said, "Well, the hell with it, we'd give it up, too." I think really
    the Japanese didn't want to go into town. I think that's probably
    the main reason. We never tried it after that. We finally, after
    Ralph arrived, got the camp so quiet and so well-organized that
    everybody seemed to us to be so happy that nobody wanted to go
    anyplace.

H: Well, I found out from two sources in Independence that one of the
    store owners, I think his name was Alex Krater, was perfectly willing
    and had in fact started a movement to allow internees to come into
    town. But apparently there was then a countermovement, which easily
    squelched the permissive policy.

B: Yes, that's this guy who worked for the city of Los Angeles and was an
    American Legion nut. (laughter) Really, he was crazy, a screwball.
    We used to just sort of chuckle about him and say, "Well, the hell
    with it." We had all the territory we needed; I mean, we had water-
    falls and we had great big picnic areas and we had . . .

H: Well, the camp was actually much more cosmopolitan than the sur-
    rounding towns. I mean, after all, there were ten thousand people
    living in Manzanar.

B: Oh, sure. We had everything we wanted; we had a really good school
    built, had a big auditorium, had all kinds of music deals going . . .
    oh, it was just amazing what went on in there.

H: So you didn't feel a lot of hostility coming from the townspeople.

B: Not at all. I never got any hostility from them.

H: You went to town, too, quite a bit, didn't you?

B: Oh, yes. I lived in Bishop. I'd go home on weekends and sometimes
    I'd go home during the middle of the week. I had a place to stay
    there at Manzanar, after I got to be assistant director. There was a
    gal that was assistant director who had all the welfare--the schools
    and that kind of stuff--and then the hospitalization end of it, and
    then Ed Hooper who was the head of accounting and that kind of
    stuff, and I had charge of all of the, oh, agriculture, engineering,
    police, manufacturing, and that type of stuff. We were pretty self-
    sufficient. We raised practically all our own stuff there, raised
    all our own cows and raised all our own sheep and raised all our own
    pigs and raised all our own vegetables and had everything but a

canning plant. We dried and packed a lot of stuff. One year we got
ambitious. We planted forty acres of tomatoes. My God, I never saw
so many tomatoes in my life! I didn't know how much forty acres of
tomatoes were. We had to ship them into Hunt's in Los Angeles and
have them canned.

H: You actually raised some produce for other camps, too, didn't you?

B: Yes.

H: Did you ever sell any of your produce in the towns?

B: We sold some of the tomatoes.

H: In Lone Pine?

B: No, just to a cannery. No, we didn't sell any of it to the Owens
Valley towns.

H: I want to backtrack again to the time when the camp was just starting.
What was your official capacity when you got hired?

B: I was what they called the reports officer. That's the public relations department.

H: So you were there when the camp was still unbuilt?

B: Yes.

H: What was your responsibility as reports officer?

B: Just like a press officer, keeping the press informed. We used to
have newspapermen by the droves coming in there. So then when they
finally got the camp going, we all knew that there had to be some
means of communication. So that's when I got the newspaper, the
Manzanar Free Press, started. We did it first just on mimeographed
sheets, so that we had daily communication going with the people, and
that's why they hired this tremendous crew of kids. They just ran
the damned newspaper. I didn't. We never did hire another reports
man. When I got to be assistant director, Roy Takeno was then the
editor, and Roy just ran the whole damned thing. He was the public
relations man for fifteen bucks a month. (laughter) He was a
graduate of USC, too. He was one of Roy French's boys and a very
capable newspaperman. French was director of USC's school of
journalism. Takeno later went to work for The Denver Post. Now he's
head of the JACL /Japanese American Citizens League/ in the Denver
area; a very capable guy.

H: Bill Hosokawa was with The Denver Post, too.

B: Yes, that's right.

H: Who built the camp? To what extent were local people involved, just as hired carpenters or painters or what have you?

B: I don't remember too many local people being involved in the actual building of the camp. The contractor came in to build it and I think he brought a big crew with him. He undoubtedly hired some local people, but there weren't too many craftsmen around at that time. We later hired a number of people in maintenance jobs. The guy that took care of all the electrical wires was a guy named Ralph Feil, who worked for the local telephone company. And the fellow that was in charge of all property was a man that used to work for the power company up there. We hired quite a few local people later. But I think in the building of it, as I remember . . . that was a hectic time. I was traveling between San Francisco and Reno and Los Angeles and Manzanar doing newspaper chores and getting other things set up so it would flow, you know, and I wasn't around there too much when they were just starting to build it. I was there at a time--you know, we had the first and the only voluntary exodus. A thousand Japanese made up their minds that they'd drive up there, and so they were escorted up by the Army. And these were the key people that really started the camp. We got doctors and we got nurses and we got cooks.

H: Were they handpicked?

B: I think they were kind of picked and I think the WCCA boys did that out of the Pomona center and whatnot. But I know that all of a sudden here we got all these people up there. Actually it was just lucky that we had a place for them to bed down that night when they came in, and they were kind of the start of the crew that took over and ran things. Highly capable people. Dr. James Goto, for example, a doctor, was a real top specialist. He was really something.

H: Is he still alive?

B: I think so. I think probably a guy like Togo Tanaka could tell you where he is.

H: He was a heart surgeon, wasn't he?

B: I think so. I think that's what he is. He was a young man. God, he put that hospital together in nothing flat. And he did a hell of a job.

H: Can you think of some of the other people who were prominent at the beginning?

B: Well, yes, Togo Tanaka was one of the guys who came up as a volunteer.

H: I think he came a little bit later, actually.

B: Did he? I thought he came with that original thousand.

H: No. One of the things he points out in a report he's written is that

there was a group of people in camp whom he calls "anti-JACL."
The designation doesn't mean that they weren't in sympathy with the
JACL's position vis-à-vis the war but that these individuals had
some reservations about the JACL and tended to be even more progressive politically than the JACL people. Tanaka says that when he
arrived, most of the positions in the camp were pretty well occupied,
and that both he and Joe Masaoka got jobs as newspaper delivery boys
for the Manzanar Free Press because the editorship of the Free Press
and most of the positions in the camp had already been staffed.
Later the JACL, partially through a camp group called the Manzanar
Citizens Federation, managed to start taking over certain of the key
positions in the camp.

B: Could have been, could have been. Togo wasn't there very long, you know.
He went over with that group to Death Valley after the Manzanar
Riot in December of 1942. And they got him out of there and sent him
back to Chicago. Togo was there in Manzanar only four or five months.

H: There's a man who worked for you that I'm somewhat interested in, a
man by the name of David Itami. He served, I think, as your assistant for awhile with the Manzanar Free Press.

B: Well, Dave did all the translation for the Japanese section of the
Free Press. He ended up in the Army. He was in the conference with
General MacArthur. He did all the translating for the Army for
MacArthur.

H: Is that right?

B: Yes.

H: He was the first one to leave Manzanar. He volunteered to go teach
Japanese at a military language school, I think, even before the
riot.

B: Dave was, oh, yes, Dave was a tremendous . . . he was a Kibei, which
means he was born in the United States and educated in Japan. Yes,
we found very soon after we started the newspaper that we had to have
a Japanese section, and so I found Dave someplace somewhere, and he
did all the calligraphy by hand. He would do all that scratching
on a stencil and we'd mimeograph it. That went out to all the Issei
who couldn't read English. Oh, Dave really went high up in the
Army. Golly, I haven't thought of old Dave for so long, isn't that
funny?

H: Who were some of the administrators who came to the camp about the
same time you did? You were reports officer. Can you recall some
of the other people? Triggs was running the camp?

B: Clayton Triggs was running the camp. He's dead now. Did a hell of
a job in the war afterwards, survived seven days in the Atlantic, in
sub-zero weather in a lifeboat, that kind of stuff. Man! Oh, there
was a guy named Kidwell. I forget his first name.

H: Was Ned Campbell assistant project director from the beginning?

B: No, Si Fryer sent him over when the WRA took over and Roy Nash came in as director.

I don't remember too many of the first staff members. I really don't remember. I was so damn busy keeping the press off our backs that I had a full-time job of that, you know. We used to have, oh, I remember sometimes we'd have a briefing every day of fifteen or twenty guys. They even came from England and Australia and every-place else, because it was the first camp, you see.

H: Right, right.

B: Oh, I got some help. I got some tremendous stories about some of those briefings!

H: Why don't you save those stories for our next session?

B: That will be fine with me. This interviewing business can be really tiring.

H: /February 20, 1974. Throughout this portion of the interview, Mr. Brown will read excerpts from the diary he kept during the year of 1942./ Mr. Brown, at the close of our last session we were discussing your arrival at Manzanar as reports officer in March, 1942. You were about to relate some of the events which occurred during those opening days of the camp. So, let's pick up the story at this point.

B: My notes are from a diary that I was keeping at that time. It shows that on Saturday, March 21, 1942, the first Japanese, or Japanese Americans, came into the camp. I think they started construction on the camp two or three weeks before that, so some of the buildings were built, but not very many. There were three busloads, and they contained, among other things, twenty-four girl stenographers and some kitchen help. We were very happy to have the twenty-four steno-graphers because we didn't have any help at all. And newspapermen from the Los Angeles Daily News and the Los Angeles Examiner came with them. My notes indicate that we seemed to handle everything very well and everybody had food, including, I suppose, the two newspaper-men. I remember that Joe Winchester, who was in charge of all the food, kitchen preparations and whatnot, was driving around in sort of a van-like pickup truck, and he had enough food in the back of that to feed everybody for the first two or three weeks. In fact, the bread got so stale that, when we really started to feed it to the people in camp, we had to toast it; otherwise nobody could have eaten it.

Then on Monday, March 23, the caravan of 140 automobiles driven and owned by the Japanese was escorted, I suppose, by the military. And about twenty newsmen and newsreel people came with them. My notes show that a man named Lee--Bob Lee, I think--of the Los Angeles

Examiner and a freelance writer were the only people there looking for a yellow journalism angle. At that time, Clayton Triggs was the director of the camp under the WCCA. We were having a lot of problems as to how much the Japanese were going to get paid: that is, if they were going to get paid, or if they were to have money allowances so they could buy little items like toothbrushes and toothpaste, and that type of thing. And at that time, it seems to me, somebody suggested that they get paid what the Army privates got paid. Am I right? You probably know more about that than I do.

H: Yes, but this suggestion was later spurned--for reasons both of a political and a public relations nature.

B: And in just discussing all this with the newspapermen, we said that's what they were going to get paid. So, Lee of the Los Angeles Examiner broke a story wherein the headlines came out, "Japs To Get As Much As Soldiers," which didn't do us any good, particularly in the camp.

H: Now, was this when the camp was known as the Owens Valley Reception Center?

B: No. To my knowledge it was never known as the Owens Valley Reception Center. Manzanar was always a permanent camp. At first it was operated by the WCCA. But we were never going to make Manzanar like Pomona, for example, or Santa Anita, where they just temporarily put the people, and then sent them off to various camps. No, Manzanar was always intended to be a permanent camp right from the beginning.

H: Where were you drawing your salary from while the camp was still under the aegis of the WCCA?

B: I forget whether it was from the Department of the Interior or whether it was from the Army. I think it was the Army, but I'm not sure. I don't think I say in my diary, either. I remember it took me two to three months to get a paycheck and I had to finally go over to San Francisco and get it. I think I went to the General Accounting Office-- the people who made out paychecks for all government employees--to find out where mine was.

H: In any event, it was a GS /Government Service7 rating that you had.

B: Yes, it was a GS rating. I was still, of course, part of the Inyo-Mono Association, and I was trying to resign and have somebody else take care of that. We didn't know whether to still keep plugging the beauties of the High Sierra so that the fishermen and skiers would come up there, or whether because of the Japanese program and the war, we should stop it. And I have a note here in the diary that we had a meeting of the Inyo-Mono Association on March 23 wherein they allowed me to resign and actually gave me one month's bonus pay.

H: Did that terminate the organization?

B: I had a secretary, a young woman, and she stayed and carried it on for

two or three or four more months, and that stopped all that. That
terminated the organization. On Tuesday, March 24, 1942, my notes
show that I spent all morning with the newspaper people, and Clayton
Triggs, who was the director, spoke for an hour. Then George Savage,
the editor of the local newspaper, the Inyo Independent--I think they
called it that then; it's the Inyo Register now--spoke. The paper
was published by the Chalfant Press. At that time George Savage owned
it. George Savage and I gave them a background of the country. I
spent a great deal of time with Don Eddy of the American magazine and
Larry Davies of the New York Times, both of whom were doing features
on the whole Owens Valley country. A man named Lee McCirdle of the
Baltimore Sun was also there and was fascinated with the country. Then
Norris Harback, one of our local employees who we all knew, came in
with a story by a man named Fred Ferguson. It was a story done for
the NEA Service on me, saying that I was the guy that asked for the
Japs for the whole Owens Valley. This turned out to be quite a controversial story--in many ways--for several weeks.

H: So it appeared then?

B: Yes, it did appear. It was very poor publicity and it wasn't a help
at all in the Owens Valley.

H: Did that cause you a lot of personal grief?

B: That caused me quite a lot of personal grief with the local people.
With all those newspapermen, I told the story of Inyo County, and
the fight between the people and the city of Los Angeles and the
Department of Water and Power, so many times that I was pretty worn
out. I noted that in my diary on March 24, 1942.

H: Do you recall any specific response to that story? Were you called
into any meeting with the chamber of commerce in Lone Pine, or were
you held accountable to the Inyo-Mono Association?

B: I don't think they had a chamber of commerce in Lone Pine at that
time. The Inyo-Mono Association acted as the Chamber of commerce for
all the towns.

H: They had a chamber of commerce of sorts, because one of the people,
and I can't recall his name--you suggested that I interview him, and
I subsequently did--but he's still there in the town, and I think he
owned, at that time, a hardware store . . .

B: Oh, that's Jack Hopkins.

H: Yes, Jack Hopkins. He informed me that he served for a while as the
president of the chamber of commerce.

B: Even in those days?

H: Yes.

B: It could be. I don't remember. It's interesting to note that all this
     time the people of Mono County, which is north of Inyo County, sort of
     felt left out in this thing. They could see the fact that all these
     Japanese were going to move to the lower part of the Owens Valley and
     that businesses in Lone Pine and Independence were going to get some
     business from all these people. So the next day, on March 25, a
     delegation from Mono County came to visit with me and Ralph Merritt
     in Independence. This committee was led by Walter Evans, who at
     that time, I think, was Mono County district attorney. Later he was
     superior court judge in Mono County.

H: Is Bishop in Inyo or Mono County?

B: Bishop is in Inyo County, and Bridgeport is in Mono County. This was
     a group of people led by the man who was the district attorney in
     Mono County. Mono County is just a little, tiny county even today.
     I think at that time, it might have had two thousand in the whole
     county. Bridgeport was the county seat, and has been for a long
     time. Walter said that a mass meeting of Mono County people the
     night before had authorized them to offer Mono County as a place to
     put Japanese and take the pressure off the West Coast, as well as
     Mono County. I suppose that they wanted the Japanese so that they'd
     have a little better economy in their county. And I make a note on
     March 25, "This is the first good break in a bad situation." The
     story on me had the people in Inyo County, which includes Bishop and
     Lone Pine, sort of thinking that I was the guy who brought in the
     Japanese. Then when the people from Mono County came down and said,
     "Well, we'll take some of them," this sort of helped. And I'm sure I
     got George Savage to get this on the front page of the next weekly
     edition of the Inyo Independent. By that time we began taking pic-
     tures for the press, and I went back to Manzanar--I kept going be-
     tween Bishop and Manzanar--in the afternoon to take more pictures.

H: I think you mentioned during our previous session that you were then
     living in Bishop. Is this correct?

B: Yes. I maintained my residence in Bishop, and although I lived at the
     camp quite a lot, I'd go home on weekends.

H: You mentioned Clayton Triggs. Maybe before proceeding you could
     render a profile of him.

B: Clayt was quite a guy. He came from WPA /Works Projects Administration/.
     He had worked for the WPA, so he had run big camps. I suppose he had
     had camps in the woods at one time or he had had camps of people
     working on roads or this type of thing, so he knew camp administration.

H: Was that as a civilian?

B: Yes, as a civilian. And a lot of the people that came to Manzanar to
     start with were fellows that he picked up from his WPA experience, and
     were people he knew. For example, Joe Winchester, who was in charge

of all the mess halls . . .

H: He was chief steward, right?

B: Yes, he was chief steward. Joe had worked for Clayt in a WPA camp
someplace, and a man named Kidwell that Clayt brought in had been a
social worker in a WPA situation. What a social worker in a WPA
situation did, I haven't any idea, but that was his background.
Another one of the staff came from the Red Cross and he subsequently
went with the Red Cross after the WCCA days were over.

H: Can you identify anybody from the Red Cross that was on the original
staff, or that later joined the staff?

B: No, I can't right offhand. I think Kidwell was a Red Cross man, too.

H: Was Lucy Adams, perhaps . . .

B: Lucy Adams didn't come until the WRA took over the camp. No, she was
never with the Red Cross. Lucy had been with the Bureau of Indian
Affairs for many years; that was her background. She came at the
request of Si Fryer.

H: And Mrs. D'Ille? I can't recall her first name. What about her
background?

B: Lucy dug up Mrs. D'Ille. She came to us because, originally, she
had been married to a missionary who had lived many years in Japan
and China. I don't think Mrs. D'Ille spoke Japanese, but I'm pretty
sure she spoke Chinese. She had a lot of experience. Her husband
died early in their married life and she stayed on in China as a
missionary, so she knew the Oriental phase of the thing. Besides
that, she was a very good organizer and a very good social worker.

H: Wasn't Lucy Adams in charge of community activities?

B: Lucy Adams was an assistant director in charge of what I think we
called, in those days, community affairs. There was the director
Ralph Merritt, and I was the assistant director in charge of the
reports office. As an assistant director. I was also in charge of the
agricultural department, and any industrial stuff--we had some
factories. I was in charge of all the engineering people, the people
that kept up the roads, and the people that kept the water and sewer
systems going. In other words, I ran the physical part of the camp.
Then there was Lucy, who was in charge of education and welfare and
the hospitals. That was the division of labor. In addition to that,
we had a project attorney.

H: Was that Robert Throckmorton?

B: It was Bob Throckmorton to start with, yes. Then we had a man named
Hooper, who was the accountant in charge of the budget, personnel,
payroll, et cetera.

H: This was Ed Hooper, I guess.

B: Ed Hooper, yes. He's living in Sacramento now. That was the general setup of the administration.

H: Let's get back to Triggs for just a moment; you were drawing a profile of him, so continue.

B: Well, Clayt was a doer. He'd make a decision right now. He'd have a problem, and one side of the problem would be presented and the other side of the problem would be presented, and Clayt would say, "Let's do this." That was one thing we always liked about him. You never had to worry about him making a decision. He'd make it right now. He was used to doing that because he was used to directing people and he was a very, very fine director.

H: Did he hold an Army commission at the time? Was he a colonel or a . . .

B: No, he was a civilian, and I . . . that's a good question. Who did we work for? We worked for WCCA, and who was behind that?

H: That's the Army, I think. The WCCA . . .

B: I think it was a civilian branch of General DeWitt's staff out of San Francisco. It was just a civilian group that was put together in a hurry.

H: So then Triggs wasn't a military man?

B: He was not a military man, no.

H: Was he well liked by the staff?

B: Yes, very much. We just hated to see him go. When WRA took over, and they sent in another director, Roy Nash, everybody was sick about it.

You were asking about the people. Oh, different kinds of people kept coming into camp all the time. Harry Brandeis of the London Sunday _Times_ came in and wanted to do a feature on the camp and a man named French from _Liberty_ magazine came. Milton Silverman was a man first hired by WRA. Milton Eisenhower, as you probably know, originally headed up the WRA in Washington, D.C., and Milton Silverman was one of the first people he hired. Milton had a long background of working with monthly magazines, and he came out with a photographer. My notes say that he was doing a job for the War Department, and how that tied in, I don't know.

H: Was there, then, a conscious attempt to sell the relocation centers to the American public?

B: I think there was a conscious attempt to sell the way it was going and what we were doing with them, yes. I really think so. My notes show that George Savage, local editor-publisher, and I talked to Milt Silverman till about one o'clock in the morning, and the next day, on April 2, we were also with Silverman, and then I went back up to Bishop. Silverman covered Independence, Lone Pine, and Bishop, talking with everybody that he could so as to get the local people's reactions to all of this.

H: Do you recall what the local reaction was?

B: I don't seem to say here in my diary.

H: Do you recollect any hostile feelings?

B: I don't recollect any hostile feelings then. I've got some entries in here later on regarding the hostility that came up. About this time we were getting ready to get the Manzanar Free Press together. There was a man by the name of Benedict in the early days, hired by either Tom Clark or Karl Bendetson, in San Francisco. Benedict worked for a public relations firm. I've forgotten the name of it now, but it was a good public relations firm in those days; a very large one. Benedict was a public relations man rather than an advertising man.

H: What's Benedict's first name, do you recall?

B: I forget his first name. I don't know what his first name was . . . oh, yes, Larry. Lawrence Benedict. He ended up sort of being the man I reported to, even though he was in San Francisco. I've got a note here that he called me and wanted me to meet him in Reno the next day. So the next day I went up to Reno and picked him up at the airport at 10:00. This was on April 6. See how much running around we had to do? I drove through a snowstorm both ways to get there. The local people were kind of worried about what was going to happen. Here are all these people living on sort of a reservation. And the district attorney of Inyo County--in those days, a man named George Francis, who is now a very famous judge here in southern California-- he wanted to talk to someone in authority instead of me. So I brought Benedict down to talk to him. This is in Independence, the county seat of Inyo County. We talked to him about the legal status of the area, not the people. Francis said it had to be federal authority. Benedict asked him to prepare a statement on the legal moves necessary, and he did that. And as far as the county was concerned, he wanted to know about taxation, who would be responsible for police protection, and who would take care of the sewer and fire departments. That all then became a federal job, and that's where WRA came in. We set up the business of the police department and the fire department and that type of thing.

H: Were the people of the Owens Valley afraid that they were going to have to handle that responsibility?

B: Yes. That was when the people in the valley thought that maybe we had just brought all these people in here, and had a small crew of local people working for the government. They wondered about who was going to protect them, who was going to keep order in the camp, and who was going to put the fires out and whatnot. I have another note in here that Charlie Brown, who was a state senator and a very famous guy in the desert area, came over and talked to us about fires. He was concerned with who was going to take care of the fire department and so on. On Thursday, April 7, Benedict was still there, and the supervisors of Inyo County passed a resolution stating that the federal authority must hold at the camp, and they also passed a resolution against letting any of the Japanese out of the camp. It seems that the supervisors and the local people were worried about the defense of the area. So, my notes here show that Benedict and I sent a wire to Tom Clark back in Washington asking him to help with this.

H: Was there, by this time, a considerable Japanese American movement into the towns to buy supplies?

B: No, we never did let any of them out of the camp. In my memory, I don't think we let them out at all, at anytime. I know they did in some of the other camps—at Minidoka and at Tule Lake and some of the other places—but I don't think we ever let any of them go into Lone Pine or Independence. Oh, I remember we took a couple in one time for a wedding. We had them escorted in by the military police, but that was before we had some ministers at camp, so we had to go ahead and have the judge marry them. Anyway, at the end of Benedict's stay, which was April 8, he suggested that we get going immediately on a newspaper for the camp. We knew we had to have some kind of communication, and we'd set up the information offices. Now that I read that account that you gave me /Morris Opler, "A History of Internal Government at Manzanar March 1942 to December 6, 1942," U.S. War Relocation Archive, Relocation Center, Manzanar, California, Collection 122, Box 12, Folder 1, Special Collections, University of California, Los Angeles Research Library_7, I remember setting up the information offices and having the information officers report for work. And there was a conflict when we set up the newspaper. The information guys said, "Well, what are we going to do?" We said, "Well, sorry, we're going to have to do it all with the newspaper." And I remember that Benedict himself suggested the name Free Press sort of tongue-in-cheek, you know? And there was some problem of publishing a newspaper without getting permission from General DeWitt's office. Benedict said, "I don't want to ask, because I know the old general won't let us do a newspaper, so why don't you just print a newspaper anyway? And on the front page, in a little editorial, why don't you put a little article thanking the general for allowing you to do it or not, and that will make him feel good." So we did that. We put a little box and thanked General DeWitt for permission to print the paper, because it was such a necessary item. And I remember the old general was tickled to death; he said, "That's fine. That's fine. That's what they need to do over there; they have to have communication."

H: I've seen that item in the course of my research, but now I understand the strategy behind it. I had taken it somewhat more literally at the time I encountered it. At the end, it says, "Thank you, General."

B: Have you seen that? You've done more research on this stuff than I have. I went back and wrote the general history of the camp, after I left UNRRA /United Nations Relief and Rehabilitation Administration7 in Washington, D.C., and came back to California. Do you have a copy of that? Have you seen the general history of Manzanar, the Final Report?

H: Yes, it's available in the Special Collections at UCLA /University of California, Los Angeles7. That's where I read it.

B: I've got a copy, and I think it's out in the garage. We can look through it later.

H: Who did you get to run that newspaper and how did you . . .

B: Well, that's kind of interesting. I say here--this is on Friday, April 10--now, remember at the time, the camp had only been open about a month, right?

H: Well, you were actually hired on March 15, and the camp started on March 21.

B: Yes, March 21, well, this is April 10, so they're moving pretty fast. On April 10, 1942, I write, "Back in camp, I interviewed boys and girls for the newspaper, sending them out on assignments, and I had great enthusiastic responses. I inherited a boy named Joe Blamey."

H: Now, he was a British Japanese, wasn't he?

B: Joe Blamey was half Irish, a quarter Japanese, and a quarter Spanish, I think. Blamey was his Irish name. On April 10, I also write, "The boy seems to sense the situation of factions, and appears to be getting all groups to participate. I got Miyo Kikuchi as a secretary." Miyo was a great gal. Still get Christmas cards from her. Miyo's father is a dentist. The last time I saw him was about four years ago, and he was in his late eighties, and he was still a dentist. They came all the way to Phoenix to see me. We were still down in Phoenix. Isn't that interesting?

H: She lives down there now?

B: No, she lives in Los Angeles, and Dr. and Mrs. Kikuchi are in the Japanese section of Los Angeles, over in Boyle Heights. They traveled a great deal, and they were coming to Phoenix, and they knew I was there someplace. So they came over to the office and spent half an hour.

I note on April 10, "Sam Hohri appeared on the scene--another fine, intelligent boy. Again, I am finding myself agreeing with Glenn Frank on his theory of intelligence vs. ignorance." I don't remember what Glenn Frank said about that. "The copy was coming into the paper, and fast. I told them this was their paper. Later, they would elect an editor, et cetera. At first, just the staff. Some excellent stuff was coming in. I called Benedict, stating that Bishop and Tecopa had been recommended for defense areas. Asked more dope on the other towns and suggested going to Bishop with this news."

H: What does that mean, "defense areas"?

B: Oh, they were setting up defense areas where people couldn't go into town, so that meant that no Japanese could go into Bishop. And Tecopa was way out in the desert; I don't know where it was. They made that a defense area because the China Lake United States Naval Reserve, I think, was just starting down there.

H: So nobody could go in there?

B: Nobody could go in there.

On first edition day, April 11, 1942, I write, "I left Bishop at 7:30 a.m. for camp. Stopped at Independence for suggestions on defense area and also talked to Ralph Merritt." Ralph was not the camp director at that time. He was still running a ranch right outside of Independence. That was before he went to Nevada. "Got into the business of putting out the paper. The boys had lined up copy all night. Joe Blamey said they had talked about it until 1 a.m. and Chiye . . . " She was a translator. She was a friend of Togo Tanaka's, too.

H: Is this Chiye Mori?

B: Chiye Mori. Yes, she was quite a gal. She came to work on the staff. She was accepted . . .

H: She became the editor, didn't she? Wasn't she your first editor for the Free Press?

B: I don't know; it'll say in here someplace. Continuing on April 11, I write, "She is accepted on the same level as men; here again is proof of Americanization of these people. Sam did a real job on our rumor editorial. Tom Hashimoto will make a good city desk man; he's a top-trained newspaper man. Staff meeting at 10 p.m., and they elected an editorial board. Everybody was enthused."

H: Did you realize at the time that many of the people that affiliated themselves with the Manzanar Free Press were leftists, that several of them were Communists? They had taken very much of a pro-American position on the war, since they were very anxious to do everything possible to . . .

B: No, I never thought of them as being left-wing. I thought of them as being progressive. I suppose I was the same way at the time. Yes, they were pro-American, and they all were pitching in to get . . . they understood that you had to get information going back and forth, you know. And most of them felt that this was a big chance to make a name for themselves. They'd been under the thumbs of their elders for so long and here they had a chance to run a newspaper, and they had a chance to say what they thought. But it never dawned on me that they were anything more than just progressives.

H: Well, some of the people that you've been mentioning, like Chiye Mori and Joe Blamey, were actually somewhat ideologically different, from say, the JACL /Japanese American Citizens League7 people like Togo Tanaka, Joe Masaoka, Fred Tayama, and people like that. There was quite a cleavage between the two groups, although they ideologically shared the same point of view with respect to the necessity of the camps and support for the war effort. Did you at all sense this division?

B: I don't remember. I might have been insensitive to it because I was working so hard, and I was so sold on these youngsters. They were a smart bunch of kids, really a very, very smart bunch of kids.

H: So they were all just people working on a paper as far as you were concerned?

B: Yes, they were just working on a paper.

I write on April 11, "We put the paper to bed at 8:30, and it came off the press, which was a mimeograph, by 10:00. The Manzanar Free Press." Here are some of my other comments, "This day made history: a newspaper in English by Japanese American citizens, placed in a concentration center by public opinion and the Army and directed by a Caucasian. I went home at midnight." Some of the things I tell about in my editorial lines /in the diary7 are sort of interesting. I was reading through them the other day.

H: Was there censorship of the paper's contents?

B: Not a bit; none whatsoever.

H: Could the staff writers have been critical, say, of American policy or of camp policy?

B: Sure, they were. If they didn't like something, I said, "It's your paper, you edit it. You do whatever you want to do. If you don't like what's going on, say so." They asked me, "Do you mean it, Mr. Brown?" I told them, "Yes, I mean it." So they did. I guess there's a complete file of the Free Press there at UCLA, isn't there?

H: Yes. So you weren't afraid, then, that DeWitt, in light of his cautiousness about even the fact of having a paper, might have closed the whole operation down if the Free Press journalists said something that was critical in nature.

B: No. The Army left us alone, after getting it set up and whatnot. They had guards, and they were not too bright. We had one good lieutenant, who was a commander. I remember that we had one who was a stinker, and we got him out of there pretty soon by putting the pressure on. Hall, I think, is the man's name who was a good one. He was fine. No, they left us alone. Anyway, I say on April 15, "Left for Manzanar to get out the second issue of the Manzanar Free Press. The staff was growing. Joe Blamey, Tommy, and Chiye were developing into leaders."

H: Tommy Yamazaki?

B: Tommy Hashimoto. He's the one I said would make a good city desk man, because he was a trained newspaperman. I think before the evacuation he worked on that Shimpo thing that you brought over.

H: The Rafu Shimpo?

B: Yes, I think so. On April 15, I say, "The Associated Press wants a story from inside. I've asked Tommy's wife to write it. I received a letter about the paper from a seventeen year old Japanese girl that was astounding for its perception." Anyway, that's how we got the newspaper started. And it was an instant success.

H: Did you get any grumbles about the statement in the Free Press thanking DeWitt?

B: No. Benedict called me back and said that the old man was tickled to death. So we did it right.

H: But you didn't get any community response on that?

B: No. Well, actually, the paper never did get out into the community. We kept it right there in the camp. We kept to ourselves pretty much, after we felt that there was a feeling against us.

H: I meant the Japanese American community in camp, the camp community. Did you get any response from the internees?

B: On the editorial?

H: Yes. In the sense that, here they are, put into a camp and all of a sudden a statement appears thanking the government officials for carrying this out so efficiently?

B: Yes, I know. I don't remember.

H: Did you have any restrictions as to who could be on the paper's staff? Did you just have citizens, let's say?

B: No.

H: Why was it that most of the staffers were citizens?

B: Well, I suppose it was because they could write. And most of them had some kind of training, either on a high school newspaper or a college newspaper or sometimes on a regular paper. I think that's why. When we started doing the translation of the Free Press in Japanese, Dave Itami did that. Dave Itami was a Kibei who was pretty controversial even in the early days of the camp. But he went on to be a top guy in intelligence.

H: Do you know why he was controversial?

B: Yes, because he was a Kibei.

H: He was accused by a lot of those other people you've been mentioning-- the leftists on the Free Press--as being a pro-Fascist before he came to Manzanar. And there was a Communist newspaper named Doho, which Karl Yoneda and James Oda, among others, had worked for prior to the war. A contingent from Doho took an inspection tour of Manzanar during its first days, and the last issue of Doho reported their findings. One thing that disturbed them was that Roy Takeno and Dave Itami were heading up the information center. Both were criticized by Doho as pro-Japan because of their affiliation with the Kashu Mainichi, another venacular newspaper in Los Angeles. Everything else about the camp Doho seemed to approve of. Things seemed to be under control, but the one disturbing factor was that there was this vestige of pro-Japan sentiment. Now as it turned out, Itami was one of the first guys--in fact, I think--to volunteer to go off to Fort Savage to serve as an interpreter in the United States Army. But you say that he was controversial from the beginning, right?

B: Yes, he was controversial. I'd forgotten those points of the issue. Actually, I'm trying to remember, but we didn't pay any attention to the ideological phases of the Japanese. There were so many different factions, and we had a job to do and my job at the moment was to keep everybody happy in the Owens Valley and get a newspaper out, and to get some communication going inside the camp. I suppose we had a lot of discussions about it, and all through this diary you'll probably find . . . and you'll probably find more of it in my final report because I had time to . . .

H: Be a historian?

B: Yes, to be a historian. It's very interesting. Well, I think that's how we got the paper going, and it went very well. What else do you want to know now?

H: In the camp, when did you first start to sense--maybe it was from the beginning--that there was some hostility, some sort of organization forming among internees which resisted both the very existence of the camp and the direction in which it was being run--when resistance started to coalesce around a number of grievances, of one sort or another? Do you recall early problems with either pro-Japan sentiment or just plain dissidence, or resistance, or anything of that sort? I know, for instance, that by the summer of 1942 there were threats against and attempted beatings of some of the people working with the Manzanar Free Press.

B: I honestly don't remember this, Art.

Well, we had all kinds of people coming in there. I went to Los Angeles on May 26, and made a speech to Sigma Delta Chi. Sigma Delta Chi is the journalism fraternity for working journalists. On May 26, 1942, I write, "Spoke to Sigma Delta Chi and Institute of Journalists. There were 125 people present, including Norman Chandler, Lee Shipley, and others. Flannery of CBS, who was the ex-Berlin representative of CBS spoke also." I was always going off, making speeches about Manzanar, telling about what we were doing, and that kind of stuff.

H: You were gone, then, from the camp quite a bit?

B: Yes, in checking this diary, I'd be in camp for two or three days and then I'd be out making speeches. I'd either be making speeches in Bishop, Independence, and Lone Pine to their Rotary clubs and those kind of organizations, or I was going to Los Angeles, speaking to people. It was quite an interesting deal.

H: Were you encountering much hostility? Were you finding outside that a lot of people were greatly disturbed as to what was going on inside the camp?

B: No, I never did feel that people were disturbed. I didn't feel any hostility in the audiences. I remember one time I went to San Bernardino, and I spoke to a great big bunch of people. I forget who they were, maybe a chamber of commerce group or something. They were more interested in what was going on and they asked a lot of interesting questions. Another time I remember I spoke at the prison camp at Chino to a great big gathering of people from Ontario, Pomona, and everyplace else. I don't know what group was behind it.

H: Were the prisoners also in the audience?

B: No, they were just waiting on tables and that kind of stuff. I got a lot of interesting questions from that group, too. The time I spoke to the Sigma Delta Chi people, the only guy that was kind of bitter about it was Ed Ainsworth. His name probably doesn't mean anything to you, but Ed Ainsworth was the top columnist of the Los Angeles Times back in those days, and he has since written several books. I saw Ed eight or nine years ago out at Death Valley, and he was still kind of bitter about the whole thing. He said, "Yes, I remember you; you're the guy who worked in that damned Jap camp."

H: You said that there were interesting questions; exactly what kind of interesting questions?

B: Oh, they would ask, "What about the Japanese, what are their attitudes and what do they think about being put in a camp? Do they think it's helpful for them or harmful? How do you control them? What do you do about your internal police?"

H: Those were kind of sticky questions to have to answer, weren't they?

B: No, not really.

H: At the time, how were you feeling about your own involvement in the camp?

B: Oh, I was tickled to death; I thought it was the best job I ever had. I was really enthused about it.

Frank J. Taylor of the Reader's Digest came into camp. Frank and I got to be real close friends. He was going to do a big story on the camp for the Reader's Digest; but I don't think he ever did it. What we were trying to do was tell the general public how the camps were working and tie it in with publicity for Inyo County. I made this note on May 30, 1942, "Frank Taylor and Mrs. Taylor arrived about 2 p.m. Frank had a go-ahead signal from Reader's Digest to do a story on Father Crowley and Owens Valley and the Japanese. This is the break we've been waiting for."

H: You wanted to get a little national publicity?

B: Yes, we wanted to get national publicity on it. Everybody, including Dillon Myer, the WRA director, wanted all the good national publicity we could get.

H: Did there, after a while, set in on the administrative staff, in any sense, a reluctance to be identified with the camp? Were there any internal discussions that you recall within the camp wherein certain staff personnel found that they could no longer in good conscience affiliate themselves with the camp, that it was too illiberal in its tendencies, or in its thrust?

B: Felt it was what?

H: Illiberal. Were there discussions, informal or formal, among you and other people on the staff as to perhaps the soundness of the internment policy?

B: Oh. After Ralph Merritt arrived at Manzanar, in November of 1942, there was no feeling that this wasn't being done right. Up to the time he got there, I think we were divided amongst ourselves--that is, the Caucasian personnel--about whether the camp was being run right or whether the right stories were coming up.

H: This wasn't quite so true during Clayton Triggs' administration?

B: Oh, no. Triggs was fine. But after Roy Nash got there, and during the stints of the two acting directors, we kind of came apart.

H: Let's talk a little bit about Roy Nash.

B: I have this note on June 1, 1942, "Morale at the camp was very low.

None of the administrative staff knows where he is going. It's all confusion."

H: Can you recall what the confusion was at that point?

B: Yes, we didn't like the way Roy Nash was running the thing, and . . .

H: He wasn't there yet, was he?

B: Yes, Roy Nash came in right after Clayt Triggs.

H: I thought he came in on June 1, when the WRA took over.

B: Here, on May 13, 1942 I write, "Triggs came in saying that the WRA was taking over immediately. Roy Nash, from the Indian Service, was to be the new man. Triggs feels very bad. Says this is the first job he's had where he really wanted to stay. We knew this was coming, however. Triggs said Eisenhower asked for him, but Nicholson wanted him for other work." He was working for a guy named Rex Nicholson who had something to do in the early days with the WPA. "Held a staff meeting and told the bad news. Harry Black and Flugstad are going also." Harry Black was the assistant. "Any maybe Kidwell is going to go."

H: Were those staff members popular in the camp?

B: Yes. Kidwell was a nice guy. Harry Black was a very fine administrator. We had a good staff, compared with . . . So Roy Nash came in. "Roy Nash arrived in Lone Pine this evening, " I note on May 14, 1942.

H: I guess the WRA took over officially on June 1. Nash probably came early to get acquainted with his duties.

B: Yes, he came early.

H: What was your immediate reaction to Nash upon meeting him?

B: Oh, he was a little guy, and he was quite pompous. He didn't discuss things; he gave orders. I didn't like him at all, but I got along with him.

H: What do you think his strong points were, as an administrator?

B: Well, I say here on May 16, 1942, "Nash seems to have the idea of doing something for the lasting good of the community. He says he will ride over the /Inyo County7 Supervisors if necessary. He wants to give the Japanese a better break than they have ever had."

H: So he was advertising himself as a humanist?

B: Yes.

H: Did you think that was deceptive, as it turned out? Or did you feel that he did, in fact, live up to that reputation?

B: No, he didn't do a damned thing. He just didn't do a thing.

H: Who was shouldering most of the responsibility when Nash took over, if he wasn't doing a thing? Who was the assistant project director under Nash?

B: Well, there wasn't an assistant director. When Nash came in, both Harry Black and Triggs left, and then Si Fryer sent Ned Campbell over. I forget when Campbell arrived. It's in here somewhere. Hicks, a guy named Hicks was Nash's assistant to start with.

H: Do you recall him?

B: Not very well. He was only there about two or three weeks. He got into trouble with a beautiful Japanese secretary.

H: So that was the end of Hicks. Then about how old was Nash at the time?

B: Nash? It seems to me that he was in his forties. I was in my thirties and he was in his forties.

H: Was he married?

B: No. Oh, I don't know. I guess he was; his wife was back East some-place.

H: What was his background, do you remember?

B: He was an Indian Services man. He'd been a superintendent for one of the reservations someplace.

On May 24, 1942, I note, "Nash made a speech to the American Legion in Bishop. It seemed to kick back. People thought there was too much freedom for the Japanese. Evidently, faulty thinking on the whole subject."

H: So Nash upset the Owens Valley community a little bit? Did you feel he was being a little too sensationalistic?

B: Yes, he was going to turn the Japanese loose.

"I was stopped this morning," I write on May 25, 1942, "by several people in Bishop protesting about the freedom to be given the Japanese on account of Nash's speech."

H: When you went home to Bishop on the weekend?

B: Yes. Phil Sinnot was working for the Army. He was an old friend of mine and George Savage, and was kind of in charge of gathering information on all the centers. Then the WRA hired Ed Bates as public relations director out of San Francisco public relations. He came over and he said that I was to be the assistant in charge of project reports. Then he added an old gag that I was not going to qualify for civil service.

H: Well, what were you before that?

B: I was just sort of working for the WCCA as a public relations man. I don't know; I didn't have any title.

H: So you didn't become Manzanar's reports officer until the WRA took over the camp.

B: No. On June 3, 1942, I write, "A fellow from the WRA by the name of Dean came in to do a report, and he said some of the old reports that we had done were too emotional. So I told him I'd help on a factual one, but not another one." And I underline this: "I got my appointment today by phone, via Nash." So I was appointed reports officer on June 3.

Here's something interesting from June 5, 1942, "Hicks and Kidwell and the others have told the Japanese to take their troubles to me, and this is happening. George Akahori and Oko came over, both with troubles. No one seems to trust the new administration. I had a long talk with Oko about Tanaka and the Japanese American Citizens League. She tells me that these boys were out to run a racket on the older Japanese before the evacuation order and that they helped put the finger on older aliens to get their business. Told of a fifty dollar 'fee' deal for filling out travel orders for the older men who could not write English."

H: Who told you that?

B: Oko Murata was her name. She was the secretary to the doctor in the hospital.

H: So she was a Nisei, too?

B: She was a Nisei. I saw some of this in the report that you had me read, so this fills it in. On May 5, 1942 I also write, "She said she got mad and did it for nothing, thereby incurring the enmity of this group. She does not know about Tokie Slocum and where he stands." I wonder who Tokie Slocum was?

H: Well, Tokie Slocum was the self-styled patriot of the camp. He was, in effect, orphaned, and he was brought up by a family in Minot, North Dakota, and he got his citizenship by dint of his service in World War I.

B: Oh, yes, I remember him.

H: And he helped to secure citizenship for all WWI vets of Oriental ancestry, because the government had taken it away after initially

granting it to them. He helped to restore citizenship for all those
Asian American aliens who had fought in World War I. He had been
affiliated during the evacuation crisis with the Anti-Axis League of
the Los Angeles JACL. He was perhaps the number one "devil" in the
minds of the Issei, because he was the one who was accused of fingering
all these people, of turning their names into the FBI, et cetera.
He is the one who is usually associated with selling names to the
authorities for set fees. When he came into the camp, he was unpopular
virtually with all the evacuee elements. Togo Tanaka has suggested
that although he agreed with Slocum's position, he didn't agree with
his style at all. He was very contentious, and it alienated a lot
of people, including Tanaka. In fact, he got along so poorly that he
was one of the people they had to pull out of the camp after the riot.
But they couldn't even send him to Death Valley with the rest of the
"pro-American group" because he didn't get along with the other people
they were going to send there. So, he had to be sent alone to New
Mexico.

B: Oh, there were a lot of politics going on inside the camp at that time.

I see here in my diary that I was finally invited to go to the staff
meetings.

H: As reports officer? And this was when, in June?

B: June 8, 1942.

H: Did you feel more "inside" as a result of this?

B: Yes, I suppose I felt more inside. I didn't say anything about it
here. Here's an editorial comment I wrote on June 9, 1942, "I am
becoming more and more convinced that there is a certain Japanese
element, perhaps the majority, who will do everything possible to
make this movement a failure, hoping thereby to gain sympathy or
at least legal status at the end of the war. They know that they
must be clever in their activities, but must hamper the administration and at the same time not work a hardship on their own people.
For this reason, we must have enlightened leadership in the camp
management through the whole program. We must get the best men
available, no matter what the cost. We can't treat these people
as if they were Indians or Negroes. I do not frankly believe that
/Milton/ Eisenhower or anyone else in the present top setup understands
the scope of the problem as things stand. I hope I'm wrong, but I
don't believe I am."

H: So at this point, you were thinking that it might possibly even be a
majority of the internees who were taking a pro-Japan position?

B: Yes. That changed, of course. It all changed after Ralph Merritt got
there.

H: You alluded to politicking going on in camp. Of what sort?

B: Well, between the staff . . . nobody liked Nash and everybody was
    trying to see how they could get him out of there.

H: Who was the staff leadership coalescing around, then? What were the
    factions within the administration? Can you think of a close circle
    around Roy Nash, for instance, that tended to support his position?

B: On June 3, 1942, I note, "It finally dawned on me that maybe the
    insidious propaganda of some is taking place. Some Japanese might
    well be sitting back, laughing about this confusion of the white
    people, and we must stop this."

H: This is entered in your diary for what day?

B: June 3.

H: And that other entry was on June 8, wasn't it?

B: Yes, June 8. Isn't that something? So evidently we were having quite
    a few little problems inside our . . . I think the administrative
    people were thinking at that time that we could take these people,
    these Japanese, and do something in the county to aid the county--
    build trails, or help on the roads, or this type of thing. And all
    this labor could be put to work, and nobody was doing anything about
    it.

H: There was internee resistance to working, then?

B: I don't think there was any resistance from the people in the camp; they
    would've liked to have done it. But there was resistance on the outside
    to letting them out. That was the resistance on the thing.

H: So some around the community benefited economically, but they didn't
    want to benefit if it involved having internees go outside the camp.

B: Yes, that's right.

H: Have you run across anything in your diary yet on the administrative
    factions?

B: Well, just this; it has to do with people in government, I suppose
    you'd say today. I have a note from June 7, 1942, that Hicks, who
    was the assistant director, " . . . got back in the evening with as
    pretty a tale of knifing in the back by Ed Bates as you would want
    to hear. It's all tied up with politics and old deals in Washington,
    when Hicks got Bates thrown out of the Senate press gallery. Hicks
    came out on top in this round, but it shows that there is some pretty
    bad political messing around here." Ed Bates was head information
    officer in the San Francisco office of WRA.

H: That was when?

B: This was June 7. This shows . . . it's still going on today. It's no different. I was a young man, and I was learning a lot about in-fighting in the political administrative jobs.

On Monday, June 15, 1942, I write, "Went to Manzanar early. All morning taken up by the Japanese. Dave Itami was very worried about conditions. Says the pay has lots to do with it. He suggested today one wage scale of fifteen dollars, to do away with class distinctions which the other scale is causing." Evidently some internees got fifteen and some got seventeen, I think.

H: And some got twelve?

B: Yes, some got twelve. "I suggested that this come from the Japanese."

I also say here, "Ned Campbell is back." I don't remember when Ned Campbell came to start with, but he evidently went back to San Francisco and then came back. On June 15, 1942, I also write, "He is a bull in a china closet, but a hard worker. We discussed problems until past midnight. Ned wants to throw the whole responsibility of camp on the Japanese. I told him I didn't think it would work, as they couldn't get along with themselves and would not accept respon-sibility. I feel there is a conflict in the philosophy of running the camp, and there can only be one boss. That boss has to be a Caucasian, not a Japanese, and then a second man, who is white. Often, a Japanese will skirt another Japanese to get to the white man. Perhaps I'm wrong. I don't know. I think if it fails under Japanese policy makers, the public will blame us for giving them so much authority. I could be wrong here, too. Let's wait and see." So it shows how our minds were working back and forth there. We were fighting with a problem that nobody had had, up to that time.

H: So Campbell was suggesting that perhaps you turn the responsibility of camp management over to the Japanese?

B: Yes, turn it over to the Japanese and let them run it.

H: Nash was moving in this direction in any case, wasn't he?

B: Yes, he was kind of moving in that direction.

On June 18, 1942, I note, "Went to camp for breakfast. Block leaders will reorganize. My information boys will scatter through the camp with these men. Question of who is to be boss—the block leaders or Dave Itami." That's right. I remember. Dave was head of the whole thing, wasn't he?

H: The Information Office?

B: Yes. On June 18, I also write, "My boys are skeptical of it working. They feel they have done a good job and why change? They want a reelection of leaders. Feel it is a political deal." Here again is demonstrated the Japanese suspicion of each other. "I had a talk with Togo and Joe." Whether that's Joe Blamey or Joe . . .

H: Masaoka.

B: Masaoka, probably. Also on June 18, "Told them to quit knifing in
     the back and do some constructive suggesting. Hit at the taxpayer and
     offer to take care of themselves if the United States will give them
     some land. Togo said the boys were going to tell me they were
     through hitting at me. I think we understand each other."

H: What were they doing when you say they were "hitting at you"?

B: Oh, I don't know. I forget; it wasn't important. Continuing on June
     18, I write "Togo's talents could be turned to constructive efforts.
     He could be a real leader. He needs to be less for Togo and more for
     other people. It might be impossible, but we'll try it. I'll work
     on him in that way."

H: You don't recall anything in connection with Tanaka that stands out?

B: No.

H: He indicated in his interview that he had had problems with you but he
     didn't spell them out. He said that there was some tension. I
     suppose it came from the fact that he came late to camp and he ended
     up working as a paperboy with Masaoka on the Manzanar Free Press. And
     here he had been an editor for the Rafu Shimpo, the biggest vernacular
     newspaper in Little Tokyo. I suppose he felt tension because of this.

B: Yes, he was probably let down a little bit, though I don't remember
     the "paperboy" incident specifically.

H: So eventually, he got a job as a documentary historian along with
     Masaoka, and I suppose they went around the camp and they wrote up
     reports as to what was going on within the camp. And that, of course,
     made him pretty visible; it gave him a rather high profile, which got
     him into quite a bit of trouble with other internees.

B: I gave Togo and Masaoka the documentary historian jobs, which they
     did well, in my estimation. Yes, Togo was a real smart guy. But we
     always got along, I always thought. Maybe he thinks differently.

     The trouble at camp really didn't straighten out until Ralph Merritt
     got there. At one point--I've got it in my notes--he said if I'd
     take on the Japanese, he'd take on the staff, and we'd see if we
     could get it straightened out. So, I took on the Japanese and he
     took on the staff, and we got it straightened out. After the riot,
     well, the camp ran real smoothly from that time on.

H: What about the riot itself? Maybe we could get into it a little bit.
     Do you feel up to it?

B: Yes, sure.

H: Let's deal briefly with the long-range problems before we focus on the immediate problems.   There were apparently a lot of beatings, and there was also a lot of unchecked gang activity in Manzanar during the months preceding the so-called eruption on December 6, 1942. Recalling your perspective, from where you were sitting at the time, what kinds of discontents did you see starting to arise? You've looked at this report /"A History of Internal Government at Manzanar, March 1942 to December 6, 1942"/ by Morris Opler, the Manzanar community analyst, and he indicates a number of things going on within community government with respect to rumors concerning misappropriation of certain internee food supplies, et cetera. What about some of these things? Did you feel something was going haywire in the camp?

B: I never had a feeling that anything was going haywire. I think I'll have to read this report again to see how . . . because I see I'm at the opposite end of the deal with the Opler report about Harry Ueno and the Kitchen Workers Union. He seems to give a great deal of credence to the fact that Harry Ueno got it started because he was accusing people of stealing sugar and selling it outside on the black market, and I say it never happened.

H: Did you know Harry Ueno?

B: Oh, only just to see him; I don't think I ever talked to him at all.

H: Did he ever emerge in your mind, prior to the riot, as either a troublemaker or as a dissident leader?

B: No.

H: So he was a virtual unknown to you?

B: He was just a cook as far as I was concerned.

H: Did most people in the camp think of Ueno in this way?

B: I would think so. I didn't think . . . he might have had a following amongst the cooks and maybe in his own block--that type of thing--but he was just another cook.

H: So in no sense was he a person who stood out as either a bete noire or as any kind of . . .

B: No, he was never a leader of any kind, to my recollection.

H: What about the Kitchen Workers Union itself? Was that identified in the administration's mind as a potentially troublesome group?

B: I think at the time we thought, "Well, here we've got a bunch of cooks and if they want to go on strike we're in trouble because somebody's got to feed these people. What are we going to do if all the cooks quit?" And so you've got a real problem there, just a physical problem of feeding people. And I think we were taking maybe some of the things that Ueno was saying, listening to them and saying, "Oh, we've got to

do something about this character." I think that's why Ned Campbell
had him thrown in jail in the first place.

H: Maybe we ought to discuss Campbell for a second. Now, he was a very
controversial figure. He's usually pointed to by almost all people
involved in the episode, from whatever point of view, as a person
who made enemies. You alluded to him earlier in your diary as a "bull
in a china closet." What was Ned Campbell's background. What, in
general, was his political style?

B: He was a Texan; that's why he learned to speak Spanish, because he
was born close to the border. I think he went to work probably for
the Bureau of Indian Affairs and I think he'd been with them a long
time. He ended up on a Navajo reservation with Si Fryer, as one of
Si's assistants, when Si was the superintendent of the Navajos.

H: Had you known Campbell before Manzanar?

B: No.

H: What was your impression of him?

B: Oh, personally, I liked him very much. He was quite a guy, but he
didn't think. And he was, as I say, a bull in a china closet. He'd
go off and do this and do that, and make decisions that somebody that
was thinking a little bit more would shudder at.

H: Do you think he had an authoritarian personality?

B: Yes, very.

H: Could you tell that he was widely disliked by the Japanese?

B: I think I say so in my diary here someplace. Yes, I think that, as
a whole, he made a lot of bad mistakes in the administration of
the camp, and I think he would admit it now that he's older. He
was trying to do a job, and we were all trying to do a job, and he'd
make a decision, and that's what it was going to be, and nobody could
change his mind.

H: Even other members of the staff?

B: Yes, even other members of the staff. He and I used to sit up until
almost midnight every night and talk about what was going on and where
we could change it and how we could make it better, and whatnot.

H: You say in your final report that the accusation that was leveled
against Ned Campbell and Joe Winchester as to misappropriating certain
supplies--sugar namely, but also meat and things--was totally
groundless?

B: I say it in the report, and I think I say it in my diary here, too,
that it's absolutely groundless. Who would steal sugar and meat and

try to sell it on the outside? That's silly. They had the same trouble at Tule Lake, and they actually caught some people in the warehouse department who were stealing meat and selling it on the outside.

H: Hired personnel?

B: Yes, hired Caucasian personnel. So, maybe that story got switched down to Manzanar. I imagine if you'd read Dillon Myer's book, Uprooted Americans, which I haven't read yet myself, you'd find that this was probably true in all the camps. You have a shortage of stuff and here was a great big camp and truckloads of stuff coming in, and who is to know whether the people in the warehouse would slide some of it out and try to pick up a buck on the side, you know?

H: They did discover that there was a sugar shortage at Manzanar, but as to how this came about, well, that was the thing that was left in the air.

B: Did we discover that?

H: There was a shortage of some nature, but whether it was in the warehouse where it happened or whether it was someplace else is still unfounded.

B: Somebody was slipping something out someplace? It could be.

H: But you would be willing, more or less, to attest to the fact that Campbell or Winchester had nothing to do with it?

B: Yes, neither one of them.

H: Why do you think the story achieved currency among the internees, and why would a guy like Ueno be believed? You do think people in the camp believed it, and that, as a rumor, it had some credibility?

B: Yes, I think so, probably, reflecting on it after these years. I don't know how. I think I would have noted it in my diary at the time, however.

H: Do you think there was any concerted pro-Japan movement within the camp?

B: No, I never did feel that there was any concerted pro-Japan movement within the camp, never. I might have been isolated by the kids I had working on the newspaper, and the people that were around me: the girls in the office, the block leaders, the guy we finally made "mayor"--he was an old Issei; Amzi was his name.

H: You felt, then, that you might have been isolated maybe from what was going on in the population at large, so you couldn't account for, say, the people who were in the Kitchen Workers Union; they wouldn't have been people you were in contact with within the camp?

B: No, I wasn't in contact with that group; I didn't know a damned thing about them. The food and mess department was in Lucy Adams' division.

H: Well, did you get feedback which led you to believe that there might have been trouble? For instance, weren't there organizations springing up, such as Blood Brothers of Southern California and the Black Dragon Society?

B: Yes, Blood Brothers and Black Dragon, that's in my diary someplace, too.

H: Do you think these were symbolic groups, or do you think they were actual? Do you think there were members?

B: Yes, I think maybe there were ten or twelve guys who had taken on writing some of those messages that cropped up throughout camp.

H: Could you identify anybody with them?

B: No.

H: What about Joe Kurihara? He was a celebrated pro-Japan spokesman.

B: Is he celebrated all through this thing?

H: Yes. Karl Yoneda, for instance, who was very pro-American and identified with a group that was supportive of the administration, in several instances had his life threatened and his child's life threatened. He says, in talking about the Manzanar Black Dragons, that: "this group was organized by Joe Kurihara, Ben Kishi, Harry Ueno, John Umemoto, several Judoists of Seigo Murakami group, and others. Most of them were Kibei and belonged to a salvage crew except Kurihara, Nisei, who was a foreman of field carpenters, and Harry Ueno, Kibei, cook of Block 4 kitchen. Every day, they drove all over the camp in a salvage truck with a Black Dragon banner, throwing rocks at those who worked on the camouflage net project, trying to run over those whom they considered pro-American--they tried this on Tokie Slocum and me several times--threatening to put those who opposed them on 'death list,' shouting slogans such as 'Don't be Korean dogs! by working on the camouflage nets,' 'Japanese Imperial Army will free us.' etc., and posting 'pro-Japan' handbills. They raided our 'apartment,'--10 coming inside and 14 on the outside-- intimating that my mother in Hiroshima would face dire consequences and I would be machine-gunned along with other 'pro-Americans' unless I retracted my criticism of the Black Dragons which I had made at the Block Leaders Council meeting. Their so-called protest against injustice turned into hooliganism of distorted resistance, while the administration took a 'no-see' attitude." This is what he has to say. What do you feel about that last accusation, that this was going on while the administration looked the other way?

B: This sounds like Karl's imagination, in my estimation. I think Karl let his imagination go "full force." We--the administration--did not take a "no-see" attitude. The garbage crew was a bunch of rough-tough

Kibei who had the hardest job in camp--but the garbage has to be picked up! So, let 'em blow off steam!

What's that from, that you're reading?

H: This appeared in the June 8, 1972 issue of the <u>Nichibei</u>, a vernacular newspaper published in New York, where Yoneda reviews the book <u>Concentration Camps USA</u>, by Roger Daniels, and in it he corrects some of the errors and oversights that he believes Daniels makes in his book. That's what he had to say in that particular section. But you say that the administration did not take a "no-see" attitude while this was going on?

B: We "saw"--but at that time I don't think we had any solution.

H: Here's another thing that Karl Yoneda wrote. It appeared in his Manzanar diary, which he is preparing for publication; maybe you could correlate it with yours for June 27, 1942. "1:30 p.m. camp meeting called by administration of Block 1 kitchen. 200 present. Director Nash and Assistant Director Ned Campbell spoke on importance of camouflage net project. During the question period I ask, 'What do you intend to do about the small group threatening those working on nets?' Campbell replied with an authoritative gesture. 'In this camp you are all Japanese, no difference among Nisei, Kibei, and Issei. We all work together.'" Then Yoneda writes in parentheses, "This from a former administrator in the Bureau of Indian Affairs!" (Brown laughs)

B: This sounds like Campbell all right. But the "net program" was a mistake from the start. This was an Army directive, not something devised by the WRA.

H: Yoneda puts in another thing on July 22: "Very hot, 114 degrees. While Tokie Slocum, World War I vet, and I were talking in front of Block 4 office, a Black Dragon truck suddenly charged us at full speed. We managed to jump onto top step. Truck bus lowers step and speeds away. I report this to the council meeting. Joe Kurihara of Block 28 retorts, 'I don't want to do any favor for U.S. government and that will include Yoneda, Slocum, and rest of that bunch. I am a full-blooded Jap now and nobody will change me.'" In any case, the portrait which is being drawn is more or less that the camp was experiencing some real tension. Now, was the administration apprised of this, or was Ned Campbell responsible for handling most of this and perhaps being somewhat insensitive to what was going on?

B: Well, on December 4, 1942, I have this to say in my diary: "Campbell is becoming more and more hard to handle, in that he doesn't think things through. His conclusions in many things are correct, but his methods of arriving at those conclusions are faulty. He won't listen. He interjects irrelevant things. He has poor judgment--a snap judgment. On top of it, he is such a nice guy and he wants to do the right thing; it's too bad."

H: So it was again a question of just Campbell's style.

B: Yes, I think it was a question of style. Looking back on it with
just general impressions, it took us probably six months to settle
down and get to know everybody, to have lines of communication
working, and to let those people who were considered Japanese instead
of Americans run their course in the groups that they would get
together, like the Black Dragon Society. I think, from the administrative standpoint, that we didn't pay too much attention to it.
We said, "Oh, let these guys be, they'll settle down by themselves.
As long as we've got the Army outside the gate to keep it going . . .
So we've got a good, hard-core group of young fellows here that are
trying to see it the way we want to see it and get it going. The
newspaper's running real well, and the hospital and the schools are
going good. The kids are being taken care of, and everybody's being
fed, so let them settle down and one of these days they'll see the
light of day." And that all culminated, of course, in the riot.
I think the riot had a leveling effect on everybody. Everybody started
to think, "Hell, we can't have this going on, so what are we going to
do to straighten it out?" That's when some of the older men in the
camp, the Issei, came to the forefront and began to be real leaders,
rather than just block leaders who swept up and saw that everybody
got their baths and that kind of stuff. At first they didn't have
very much to do, but then they began to be leaders of sentiment,
and of politics.

H: What do you think about the theory that, during the time following
Pearl Harbor--the preevacuation and evacuation itself--what happened
was that the natural leadership of the Japanese American community
was dumped, and that what occurred at places like Manzanar was that
the administration instituted an artificial Nisei leadership, so that
most of the old Issei, who had been in positions of responsibility,
harbored a lot of resentment because they had been disgraced?

B: I think that was true. I think that after the riot, then the older
men, or let's say the more mature thinking men, came to the forefront,
so that you had a better leadership in the deal.

H: Did you find that the camp worked smoother when you did resort back
to the more established leadership within the community, as opposed
to working with the younger and newer JACL types?

B: Yes, I would think so. This diary quits at the end of the riot, so I
can't document this assertion for you.

I had that wrong when I told you before that Ralph Merritt said to me,
"You take on the Japanese, and I'll take on the Caucasians." Here's
a note from December 26, 1942, "Ralph has given me the job of straighten-
ing out the Caucasian personnel and administrative headaches while he
takes on the Japanese." It's just the opposite from what I said earlier.

H: What do you think caused the riot? I mean, here you have a situation
where you've got maybe three thousand people, all gathered together,

concerned about the incarceration outside of camp in a local jail of a relatively anonymous kitchen worker, a union head. Now what do you think accounts for this outpouring of support for Harry Ueno? I mean, why were the people rallying around Ueno at this time, making him in a sense a cultural hero? He was a virtual unknown to most of the people who were working on the paper, to JACL people like Togo Tanaka, to the administration, and to people like yourself who were in contact with others. What do you think accounts for, all of a sudden, this community-wide support? How did you assess it at the time? The protest might have been manipulated by a small group of trouble-makers, but surely the issue found an audience in a circle outside of that small cadre of Black Dragon activists.

B: Yes, I've been asked that question many times. There was no doubt that there was unrest in the camp; that's the first thing. And there was a group of Japanese who called themselves pro-American, for example. These were mostly those who worked on the newspaper and worked for the administration in the offices, and they were younger people. When Ueno and his kitchen workers got going, that was another group. And there was kind of a middle group. Now, Fred Tayama was an older man; he wasn't a youngster. Fred Tayama was thirty-six or thirty-seven, and he was trying to say, "Look, let's not get fighting among ourselves. Let's do what we're supposed to do, and do our work, and pretty soon we'll get out of here." Remember, the point was that we were relocating people. We were getting them out of camp as fast as we could and we were doing a pretty good job then. So I say here, on December 5, 1942, "I was home in Bishop, and a phone call from Ralph told me this: This evening, Fred Tayama was home alone when six masked men entered his house and beat him badly. He was taken to the hospital. Ralph Merritt and Ned Campbell immediately got on it, and questioned many people including Ben Kishi. Tayama said that Ueno was one of them. Kishi said so too, in telling what he knew. Ueno was head of the Kitchen Workers Union, and had been stirring up trouble for the past two months in the kitchens."

H: So this is what Merritt told you?

B: Yes, I knew this. I knew Ueno had been stirring up trouble. So Ralph, on these statements, had Ueno taken to Independence jail as a suspect in the Tayama case. He called me about 9 a.m. Sunday to tell me all this.

H: Why did he take him outside the camp? That was unprecedented.

B: Yes. I think that maybe he felt that the Japanese were running the police department. He probably could have taken over the military, but we were trying to stay away from the military. And I think he thought the best thing to do was to take him into the county jail.

H: And Merritt really didn't know the lay of the camp too well yet, did he?

B: No, he'd just gotten there. He'd only been there about a week.

H: So he kept in touch with you, then?

B: Yes. So on Sunday, December 6, I was still working around the house;
     we had some friends over for dinner. And about six o'clock Ralph
     called again and he said that a mob had called on him at 1 p.m., de-
     manding the release of Ueno. He talked to the leaders and made a deal
     that there would be no more mobs, no more attempted jail deliveries,
     no meetings, and that they would have to get the six attackers. The
     mob agreed. At 3 p.m., Ralph delivered Ueno to the Manzanar jail.
     He brought him back from Independence and put him in Manzanar. Then
     he called me again about seven saying that a second mob was in the
     process of getting Tayama in the hospital and that I'd better come
     down. So I left then. I got to Manzanar around eight. By the time
     I got to Manzanar, the mob was in front of the jail.

H: So you got there before the shooting?

B: Yes, on December 6, I write, "I got in and went to Campbell's apart-
     ment with Ralph Merritt. There was much . . ." I can't read it.
     Maybe the wind was blowing. "And the military police went after the
     tear gas around nine and let them go. The mob dispersed then, and
     reformed and started back. Then the military fired. We heard two
     bursts of Tommy guns. One killed and eight were wounded. It was
     a bad night." And Monday, December 7, I write, "The schools opened,
     but there wasn't any oil or janitors. Half of my crew showed up
     but went home about noon. Black lists were rumored. Most of the
     pro-American, outspoken people were very frightened. More people
     coming in asking for protective custody. We learned that John Sonoda
     was beaten up badly." I forget who he was. "Took a group over to
     the military police for protective custody. The military police rein-
     forcements arrived. Dillon Myer started Fryer out here; he was in
     San Francisco. Censorship of news and trouble with George Savage.
     Some office help in, but very scared. Tom Ozomoto, head of the Citizens'
     Committee, tried to bargain with the military; demanded release of
     prisoners, and demanded the Spanish counsel to be called in. Captain
     Hall said no. First stories of trouble were in. Quite a jumbled mess.
     Old grudges, mixed emotions. Not all pro-Axis, and much the fault of
     WRA policy. Campbell was blamed for much of it by the Japanese. No
     more trouble. I went to Death Valley to see about a CCC /Civilian
     Conservation Corps_7 camp, and I got it. This is to place the good
     ones in."

H: Well, you got there right away, then?

B: Yes, I went that day. On December 8, I note, "The military came in
     from Bendetson's office." That's Colonel Karl Bendetson, who was
     under DeWitt.

H: This was on December 8?

B: I also note on December 8, "The press was hollering. I'm made press
     officer for the military. I got George Savage straightened out and
     releases rolling. Si Fryer was to arrive tomorrow. By now the

evacuees to the military police numbered about fifty." We were taking them over; I remember Togo Tanaka was in that bunch. "This included Chiye Mori and others. Tom Yamazaki and family, and Togo, etc. Joe Kurihara was one of the original ring leaders. The first committee was put in jail."

H: Did you know Kurihara?

B: Joe Kurihara? Evidently. Who was he?

H: He was the one who was usually singled out as . . . he was the leader of the committee that negotiated with Merritt. He's a Hawaiian Nisei who had fought in World War I and had apparently inflamed the mob on the day of the riot, and he was later sent off to an Owens Valley jail and then went to a temporary isolation center in Moab, Utah.

B: Yes, that's who I mean, I guess. I continue to write on December 8, "Joe Kurihara, one of the original ringleaders of the first committee, was put in jail. Several others were put in jail."

H: You don't recall him very vividly, then?

B: No, I don't. I also note on December 8, "What to do with them was the big problem. I suggested the Death Valley place. Had a long talk with Chiye and Tom and others tonight and got a chronological story." And I continue, "This seemed to help Ralph Merritt. As usual, Yamazaki and Chiye had top ideas. Togo seemed stunned. Joe Karata told the best connected story." So then we got the caravan ready to take all those people and the military police over to Death Valley.

H: You know why Togo seemed so stunned, don't you? They were trying to kill him. He was running for cover.

B: Was he? Were they trying to kill Togo? I didn't think so.

H: Yes. You know what he did? He knew that they were going to try to get him; he was on the death list and he hid in an apartment. When the mob was going to his block, they were all out in their pea coats, and he ran right with the mob when they went to his apartment, and his parents opened the door, and Togo was standing right outside in the back, with the mob. But he was safe because it was dark, and because they were all pretty much dressed alike. They started something; then Ben Kishi, who had led them there, told the mob not to hurt the parents, and they left. But Togo was right with them, oddly enough, in the back of the crowd with a butcher knife right inside his coat. Did you get a chance to see the riot?

B: Yes, I was standing right there when they did the shooting.

H: Maybe you could clear up something. Some reports say that the riot was precipitated, or the firing was precipitated, by a car that was sent into the jail. Is that right?

B: Yes, that's right. Manzanar was on a kind of slope, and up the street from the jail there was a parked car. I don't know yet where it came from, maybe from some of the workers. It was like a truck, or a pickup or something. And in trying to get old Ueno out of jail, a bunch of youngsters said, "Well, let's take the brakes off the car and push it." So they took the brakes off the car and pushed it. It started downhill, and it ran into the corner of the jail, which was just a barracks building, you know. And when it hit the jailhouse, that's when the soldiers started shooting.

H: The tear gas came first, and then the car, and then the firing.

B: When the car made all the noise, then somebody let go with the guns.

H: And you were standing where?

B: I was standing right by the entrance gate.

H: What were you doing there?

B: Well, I had just driven in. The wind was blowing ninety miles an hour.

H: So this happened very shortly after you arrived that night from Bishop?

B: Yes. I had just driven in, and I had just stopped. I saw all these people, so I stopped the car and I got out and was talking to the guys that were in the gatehouse when all this stuff started.

H: Were you accosted by anybody?

B: No. We were all only a very short distance from all this stuff that was going on.

H: Who was with you?

B: Just the two guys in the gate building.

H: So you hadn't been privy to any kind of consultative meetings before-hand, except for the phone calls from Merritt?

B: No.

H: So then what happened after the shooting, as far as your personal situation? What did you do?

B: Well, I think I went to Ned Campbell's apartment. I thought I was standing out front. I'm sure I was, because George Savage was there, too, and I remember that he saw it. Anyway, after that, I went to Campbell's apartment with Ralph Merritt. The military police went after their tear gas; no, I must have gone earlier. I guess I was looking around the corner from where Ned's apartment was, and the mob dispersed then and reformed and started back. On December 6, I write, "Then the military fired. We heard two bursts of Tommy guns. One killed and eight were wounded."

H: Do you remember if you stayed up all night in conference?

B: Yes, I suppose. I said on December 6, "It's a bad night. School was open the next day, but not very many people came."

H: Who wrote the press release on the riot that went out?

B: I wrote it.

Let's see what I say here in my final report. Ah, here it is. "Someone started the fire chief's government car in motion toward the jail. It swerved, knocked the corner off the building, and was fired upon by the machine gun crew and finally came to a stop against a truck."

H: Let's try to review some of the riot's possible causes. You mention in your final report that some of it has to do with pro-Japan sentiment; I think we've covered that portion. And you said awhile ago that some of the causes--the responsibility--derived from poor WRA policy. You're making a distinction between the WRA as an agency outside of the Manzanar administration, aren't you? You're talking about guidelines that were imposed upon you from the top and not ones that were initiated by the Manzanar staff, correct? When you say the WRA, you don't mean the WRA within Manzanar, or do you? Are you thinking back to Nash's administration?

B: I think what I'm trying to say is that the Clayt Triggs and WCCA management team, which was very good, was followed by Roy Nash, who was very weak. At the same time the WRA was getting itself set up in Washington, D.C., and eventually did away with the San Francisco regional office, which was closer to us so that we could call them on the phone and whatnot. And then after Nash left, Harvey Coverley came in and also Sol Kimball. There was just no continuity of leadership. And the guy that was kind of running things in those days was Ned Campbell; he was a stronger-willed man, let's put it that way.

H: He was the actual leader, then, while the . . .

B: Yes, while the different directors were coming and going, he was the actual leader. And all this led up to the riot, because Ralph Merritt didn't get there until about two weeks before the riot. While he'd been interested in what was going on as a citizen of Owens Valley and had been on the Citizens' Committee, and knew pretty well the story of things going on, he wasn't aware of the tensions within the camp. So all of these things sort of combined into this one business: here's a guy in jail that shouldn't be in jail. I thought that Ned Campbell was actually the guy that put Harry Ueno in jail, but I see from my notes that Ralph had him sent over to Independence. Probably Ned said, "Well, let's send the son of a bitch to jail, and get him out of here."

And that's what Ralph did. So that was the pivot on which people could say, "Well, here we've got an injustice, and poor old Harry Ueno, all he is is a cook, and sure he's been stirring up some trouble, but they shouldn't put him in jail." When Ralph brought him back and put him in the jail at Manzanar, that's when the wind started blowing and the mob started gathering around. Maybe they were unhappy at the system and what had been going on. The fact that there was indecision and that they didn't think they were getting a real break, the people themselves in there—and so it all exploded in the face . . . and the wind didn't help it any; let's put it that way.

H: Do you think that there was more internee grievance against: (a) the injustice of being put in camps; (b) Ned Campbell and others associated with him in the administration; or (c) the JACL people who were in positions of nominal internee leadership? After all, it was these people who they were putting on death lists and who they were claiming were dogs and treasonable. And it was Fred Tayama who was beaten the night of December 5, and was identified with the JACL because of being president of the Southern California JACL during the immediate prewar period. Do you see the riot more as an intramural thing or more as something directed toward the administration?

B: I think it was sort of an intramural thing. I have the feeling—many years afterward—that the Japanese weren't getting along among themselves, and I say that several times in my diary, you know. They were having fights between the older generation and the younger genera-tion. And the JACL, I guess, came in for its share of criticism. And if the statement is right that I have in there, if the JACL people were taking advantage of the old folks because they couldn't write English and were charging them fifty dollars for permits and all this kind of thing, well, you can see where that would spread and get bad feeling going, you know. So I always had the feeling that the riot was caused internally by the Japanese themselves, and that WRA person-nel didn't help it any in the form of the things that Ned Campbell and some of the other administrators that they were complaining about were doing.

H: So you would see the internees rioting or rebelling more against some-thing that was happening within their own group?

B; Within their own group, yes, I would think so. I would say so, looking back at it; that was the way of it. I don't know how many people would agree with me, but it seemed that way to me.

H: I have no further questions, Mr. Brown.

You have been most helpful. On behalf of the California State Univer-sity, Fullerton, Japanese American Project, I want to thank you very much for your time and cooperation.

END OF INTERVIEW

Index

An Interview with
NED CAMPBELL
Conducted by Arthur A. Hansen
on August 15, 1974
for the
California State University, Fullerton
Oral History Program
Japanese American Project

(Manzanar War Relocation Center, O.H. 1343)

This is a slightly edited transcription of an interview conducted for the Oral History Program, sponsored
by California State University, Fullerton. The reader
should be aware that an oral history document portrays
information as recalled by the interviewee. Because
of the spontaneous nature of this kind of document,
it may contain statements and impressions which are
not factual.

Scholars are welcome to utilize short excerpts from
any of the transcriptions without obtaining permission
as long as proper credit is given to the interviewee,
the interviewer, and the University. Scholars must,
however, obtain permission from California State
University, Fullerton before making more extensive use
of the transcription and related materials. None of
these materials may be duplicated or reproduced by any
party without permission from the Oral History Program,
California State University, Fullerton, California,
92634.

CALIFORNIA STATE UNIVERSITY, FULLERTON

ORAL HISTORY PROGRAM

Japanese American Project

INTERVIEWEE: NED CAMPBELL

INTERVIEWER: Arthur A. Hansen

SUBJECT: Manzanar War Relocation Center

DATE: August 15, 1974

H: This is an interview with Mr. Ned Campbell, formerly assistant pro-
    ject director of the Manzanar War Relocation Center, by Arthur A.
    Hansen, for the California State University, Fullerton, Japanese
    American Oral History Project. The interview is at Monte Verde Inn
    in Carmel, California, on August 15, 1974, at 1:30 p.m.

    Could you begin the interview, Mr. Campbell, by giving a sketch of
    your background prior to your arrival at Manzanar in 1942: where
    you were born and what you did during that first period of your life?

C: Well, to start with, I was born in 1905 in Brownwood, a town in mid-
    western Texas. I was reared on a ranch in West Texas. When I was
    six years old my father moved the family to Fort Worth. I went
    through grammar school and my first two years of university there.
    The only break during this time was for three years, when my father
    purchased a wholesale grocery house in Sherman, Texas, so I graduated
    from high school in Sherman, Texas. We returned to Fort Worth and I
    spent two years at Texas Christian University /TCU/. Then I went to
    law school out in Tennessee for five years.

    At twenty, I was employed by the American National Red Cross for
    several summers as an exhibition swimmer and lifesaver. I traveled
    seventeen Midwestern states trying to develop interest in swimming
    and lifesaving. After leaving school in Tennessee, I went to law
    school at the University of Colorado, where I continued swimming.

    I graduated from the University of Colorado in 1929 with my Bachelor
    of Laws degree and I foolishly came back to Fort Worth, where my
    father had very good connections. A law office offered me a place
    and indicated that they also would allow me to study for my bar exam-
    ination. I refused, preferring to come to their office with license
    in hand. In the meantime, a little thing known as the Great Depres-
    sion took place. I took the bar examination in November, and got my
    license in March of 1930; but the lawyer who had been a close friend

CAMPBELL

of my father's had died, my father had died, the Depression was on and I couldn't get into a law office even as a client because they knew I didn't have the money.

So I turned back to my swimming and the Red Cross offered me a job. I traveled with the American Red Cross for a number of years and was gradually moved into administrative positions--both in the lifesaving and disaster services--and received some condemnation, as well as commendation, for going into very difficult situations right after disasters had occurred. In fact, I was written up in the Red Cross Journal, for taking over a disaster relief operation--a tornado in Frost, Texas--and I guess I won my stars or wings down there. I stayed with the Red Cross until I had an opportunity to open a dude ranch.

I've always had a desire, as my later life proved, to be in business for myself. I went out and opened a dude ranch, right during the Depression, and made a fair success of it for a couple of years, but the bottom fell out as the Depression deepened.

In desperation I went out to Navajo country, where I met and lived with Sam Day, the very famous white man who was for all purposes a Navajo, and we became very intimate. While out there I tried to do a little bit of writing but was not very successful. I picked up little jobs, like teaching school on the Navajo reservation, and I always tried to pursue my writing career. One thing led to another and I was selected business manager for a section of the Navajo Tribal Industries. Then I went up to Many Farms, in the northeastern corner of Arizona, where I built a packing plant and started the first cooperative store on a Navajo reservation--which still exists, I think.

H: What year was this?

C: Well, I was at Many Farms when I heard of the attack on Pearl Harbor.

I was very proud of my little cooperative store there. Then one day, a man showed up and said, "I'm the new manager of the cooperative." Well, I felt that the cooperative was my baby. Nobody could hire a manager but me, but Si Fryer had sent him.

H: Who is Si Fryer?

C: Si Fryer--his real name is E. Reesman Fryer--was the superintendent of the Navajo reservation, the largest single dependancy of the United States Indian Service. Over the years Si and I had become increasingly close friends and associates. I am a great admirer of his and I suppose that he admired me to a different degree. But I was so infuriated by his sending somebody out that I drove the hundred miles across the mountains with the idea that, if Si said anything, I was going to hit him just as hard as I could.

When I walked into his office, still infuriated, almost speechless,

he looked up and said, "Hi, Ned. Well, I guess we're going to make
it." I said, "Make what?" And he said, "Well, you know how you and
I have talked about getting into the war effort; I've got the chance."
"Well, congratulations," I said. "What are you going to do?" And he
said, "Well, Milton Eisenhower's asked me to come out and help him
organize the relocation of the Japanese," which all of us had read
or heard about on the radio. So I said, "Well, congratulations." And
he added, "Oh, and by the way, you're going with me." That completely
disarmed me. He said, "Didn't my girl call and tell you?" I said,
"Nobody's called and told me anything. The only thing I know is that
a fellow by the name of Garcia showed up a couple of days ago and
said he was taking over the store." (laughter) "Oh God, I forgot to
tell you," he said. Dumbfounded, I started out of the office, and he
says, "I'll keep in touch with you. I'll fly out there in the next
few days and talk with you, and we'll go into the details of the
thing." And as I started out the door he said, "Oh, by the way, aren't
you interested in how much you're going to make?" "Well, yes, I think
it would be of some interest to me." And he said, "Well, it's more
than twice what you're making right now."

H: How much was it?

C: I was making about $1,800 per year, plus a house as the manager for
the tribal enterprises for that area. So, I think they were going
to pay me around $5,000; maybe not that much, I've already forgotten.

H: When was this?

C: Sometime in early 1942. First he took me to San Francisco, where Bob
Petrie, his secretary at the time, Milton Eisenhower and I sat down
and drew up the plans for the takeover from the Army. I was originally
hired to be the organizational man.

H: You mean you were right there on the ground floor of the War Relocation Authority /WRA/?

C: Yes, from the beginning. Si was probably there three or four days
before me. We sat up many nights--a few nights certainly--and worked
on plans.

    In my history with the Red Cross I had done a number of jobs reorga-
nizing Red Cross chapters. It was not that I had any particular
training for it, but maybe I had some natural ability--knew something
about organization and how to set up offices.

H: Did they set up the San Francisco office of WRA before setting up the
Washington office?

C: Well, if I understand it correctly--and again, take into consideration
my shortage of memory--Milton Eisenhower first had the idea of setting
up the office in San Francisco. After his talk with Si, Milton said,
"Si, I don't know a damn thing about this. You know the West, the

western people, and these are all going to be western camps. You stay out here and run this. I know my way around Washington." So he left Si in charge, and he was going to be the Washington director, liaison and string-puller, to get us what we needed or wanted.

H: Could you provide some profiles of the people that we've been discussing? Can you give a biographical sketch of Si Fryer?

C: I really don't know his educational background, but he was certainly educated. He had come to the West, or maybe he was from the West, and became interested in the Navajo reservation when he was with Soil Conservation Service /SCS7. He evidently had shown definite administrative ability--originality, drive and all the other qualities needed to make a good administrator. John Collier, then the director of the Bureau of Indian Affairs, picked Si out of the herd to become superintendent of the Navajo reservation. Si did a fantastic job. It was at the time of cutting back the herds, killing off the horses, and really attempting to reduce the overgrazing. My job with him, when I went to Many Farms, was to further that program. I constructed a cannery and packing plant in which we were going to make a market for all the old ewes the Navajos would otherwise refuse to kill, but which ate as much grass and probably destroyed more because their teeth were worn. The ewes were past the lamb-bearing stage and so thin that they were not attractive for edible purposes. So we made mutton stew of them and canned it. It was a rather successful project, because our products were purchased by the government and given back to many of the Indians as part of their food program. It was a good, edible, high-protein diet.

To get back to Si Fryer, he was really an outstanding man. He was a decisive man. He had great strength of character, an ability to say "no" and make it stick, and the Indians respected him for his decisiveness, great fairness, and logic.

H: How would you characterize his political outlook and affiliation?

C: I think Si would probably at that time have been a little left-of-center, but not a great deal. He was a very logical man; and I think you almost denigrate the word "logic" if you go too far or to an extreme. I don't ever remember having talked about politics with him.

Incidentally, I had dinner with him and his wife only about six months ago. He is now retired. And has led a life almost like mine. He went to the Near East, and he took me with him into the United Nations Relief and Rehabilitation Administration /UNRRA7 after the Manzanar breakup.

H: Where does he live now?

C: He's living on either Saint Simons or Jekyll Island, I believe it's down off the coast of southeastern Georgia.

H: But you don't remember him as being very political?

C: Oh, no, never. He considered himself--he once mentioned to me, now
    that you have mentioned it--a professional civil servant. I'd never
    heard the expression used before.

    I went with him to UNRRA. He quit the WRA before I did, and went with
    UNRRA, and then he recommended me. Governor Lehman had been an early
    selection and I was recruited shortly thereafter. When I came back
    after about twenty-two months, Si had resigned from UNRRA and taken
    a position with the Bolivian government to set up several projects
    similar to those he had created on the Navajo reservation. I was one
    of those people he chose to go with him to Bolivia. So Si was more
    or less my mentor for a number of years, and he has remained a very
    close friend of mine for all these years. A very, very outstanding
    man. It has been my good fortune to work with three men who were
    really outstanding--Si being one of them--and if I have any good
    characteristics or abilities, I can attribute most of them to having
    worked with people having, to an outstanding degree, those abilities.

H: Do you recall his attitude at the time toward getting involved in
    the WRA? Did he have any reservations?

C: I doubt it! At that time both of us were driven with the idea that
    we must get into the war effort. I don't know, I think he had some
    type of eye trouble and I have one bad foot. I desperately tried
    to get into the Army, and was selected and even given a designated
    rank--if I could pass my physical. On my physical examination, every-
    thing was okay except one very flat foot. The same thing happened to
    me with the Navy. But our desire was to get into the war, and we went
    into this thing like a couple of missionaries. We were going in to
    do our job, whatever it might be, as our contribution to the war
    effort. And there was certainly no philosophizing.

    Very early both of us learned how highly undemocratic, what a terrific--
    excuse me using the word in Spanish--mancha /a terrific blemish/,
    this was on America. As I look back upon it, I think it's one of
    the most distasteful, disasterous, horrible things that could ever
    have happened in America.

H: What about Milton Eisenhower? He didn't stay very long with WRA
    before resigning and then somebody from one of his Washington car
    pools--Dillon Myer--succeeded him. Do you recall his attitude toward
    getting involved in this business?

C: As I now recall it, he took the attitude that this was a job to be
    done and let's get along with it. I don't ever remember any philoso-
    phizing going on in any of our discussions. There may have been, but
    they didn't stick in my mind. This was a job to be done on behalf of
    the war effort.

H: Let's get the machinery working, right?

C: Yes. I remember at that time, we were still suffering under the trauma of Pearl Harbor, and there were just one hell of a lot of changes that were going have to take place, and we were part of those changes. It was somewhat later in my life, after being associated with the Japanese at Manzanar, that I began to evaluate this.

H: Wait. Let's take that in order.

C: First, I was in San Francisco and from there I was assigned to Poston.

H: How long were you in San Francisco?

C: Just a week or so, as I recall.

H: Were you just setting up the regional offices?

C: Just talking about how we were going to organize the operation, what we were going to need in the way of personnel and how the thing was going to be done. The Army had already contracted for the physical building of the camps, and they had already selected the sites.

H: Was Manzanar already functioning?

C: Yes, and Poston was being built.

H: Okay, so Manzanar and these other camps were temporarily under the aegis of the Wartime Civil Control Authority /WCCA7.

C: Right, if I remember correctly.

H: And WRA didn't take them over until around June of 1942.

C: Yes.

H: But you were beginning your role with the WRA.

C: Yes. This was prior to the WRA takeover of the camps because I went to Poston and helped set it up. And the young director there, whose name I've now forgotten, wanted me to stay. There was going to be three camps in that archipelago down there, and he wanted me to stay and run one of them. I called Si, and he said, "No, I want you back here, Ned."

My job was to go from camp to camp to help get them functioning, running smoothly, and then move to another. To be more or less a trouble-shooter in the organizational end of it. I would be a warehouseman, director, head of the motor pool--wherever there were some holes that needed to filled, I would have to be flexible enough to do that type of job.

H: Were you a charter staff member of the WRA?

C: Oh, I was there very, very early in the picture.

H: So did you do any of these troubleshooting jobs?

C: Well, no, I didn't. When I got to Poston, Si said, "Come on back here, because I've got a fellow that we can send out to Poston. Our organization is going out there, and you've done your job, come on back."

I went to San Francisco and very soon after, exactly when I can't recall, he had me go to Lone Pine, California.

Meanwhile, I was living the life of a bachelor. My wife was pregnant and expecting the baby any time. I was in Lone Pine when I was told that she was about to have an emergency Caesarean. I went back to Gallup, New Mexico, where she was living at the time, and arrived a little late for the birth of my one and only son. Then I went back to Lone Pine.

H: What were you doing in Lone Pine?

C: We were working out of Lone Pine, in the Owens Valley, as there were no living quarters in nearby Manzanar at the time.

H: Were you then assigned to Manzanar?

C: I was assigned to Manzanar to help the project director, Roy Nash, who didn't have anybody assisting him. That's how I happened to be Manzanar's assistant director, because, as I say, I could easily have been the head of the motor pool, for instance. I was sent out to Manzanar to help get that operation going and try to get Nash organized--but not to correct any of his philosophies or any of his procedures.

H: They did have an assistant project director prior to you that worked with Nash by the name of Lewis Hicks, who apparently suffered a nervous breakdown.

C: I don't remember him. I went there to help set up the organization, or to fill a hole until that spot could be filled with a permanent person, and then I was to move on.

H: Had you been on the Manzanar site prior to getting this position?

C: No.

H: You didn't go there under the aegis of the WRA regional office to do anything?

C: No.

H: When you moved into Lone Pine, then, you started working as assistant project director, right?

C: Yes.

H: Had you known Roy Nash prior to coming to Manzanar?

C: Never.

H: How would you evaluate him both as a project director and as a man?

C: Nash was a short, fat man, and very verbose. Politically--and I'm
     not speaking of left or right, Democrat or Republican--he was inclined
     to benefit Nash. Hell of a nice little guy. I think he was rather
     shallow, not a heavyweight, and a good PR /public relations7 man. I
     remember how impressed he was when he was asked to speak at the Com-
     monwealth Club in San Francisco, and how hard he worked on his speech.

     When I first started to work there, I worked on a luncheon table--
     that was my office. I finally had to set up my own office and do my
     own organization out there. But I do not recall Nash being there a
     great deal of the time, or really running the camp in the true sense
     of the word. And by nature, if I see something that needs doing, I,
     like a damn fool, jump in and start doing it, trying to get things
     done.

H: From what I've heard, when Nash came to Manzanar he tried to liber-
     alize camp procedures. The previous project director, under the WCCA,
     was a man by the name of Clayton Triggs, and apparently during his
     tenure, the camp administration capitulated very much to the pressures
     of the local communities, and disallowed internees to go out of camp.
     Nash tried to liberalize that, and sought to allow them to fish and
     engage in other activities beyond the camp boundaries, and he even
     spoke at service clubs in the area revealing his plans for liberal-
     ization. But supposedly there was great reaction to his plans, and
     so he had to back down. The WRA office made him cancel these things,
     and it looked to the internees like he was breaking promises. The
     people in camp had liked him very much at first because he'd made these
     overtures toward liberalization, and then he was put in the embarras-
     sing position of having to say "No." But Nash increasingly became,
     so it seems, unpopular with both the internees and with his staff.
     How would you evaluate his popularity? Did you feel it was declining
     with time?

C: I couldn't make any comment on that. I have no remembrance of that
     at all--with the internees or with the staff.

H: But you do remember him as being absent a lot, and having a low pro-
     file in the camp, right?

C: Yes, very definitely.

H: Do you know why he ultimately left Manzanar?

C: I don't know. Nor do I know where he went, or the circumstances of
     his leaving. I do know that the camp was left in my hands off and on
     much of the time. New directors came in, and I found myself acting
     as the director while I was teaching them, and then they didn't stay
     long. For many reasons, I feel that if there is any blame or fame to
     have been gained during that interim in Manzanar, a great part of it

would have to be placed upon me. Nash was not a dynamic person, and certainly was not capable of grasping the scope of this organization to the point of really handling it. I would be curious to know whatever happened to him. He was a man in his late fifties or early sixties at this time. So he was not a youngster by any means.

H: Was he a civil servant?

C: I don't know.

H: I think, like you, he had a background in the Indian Bureau, didn't he?

C: I don't remember that, and I think I would remember that if it were true. Still, it may well have been the case.

H: I know when he came in, most of the people who were employed under the old governing agency, the WCCA, were let go. The only two people retained--at least that I can think of--were Joe Winchester and Bob Brown, while most of the rest were new people. So when you came in with WRA, you were essentially working with a new staff.

C: Don't forget for a moment what I've already expressed to you prior to taping this interview: my rather low opinion of the GIs that were in the perimeter guard detail. To a great extent this evaluation holds true for much of the personnel, but not exclusively. Most of the personnel we had were those who couldn't get a job elsewhere, or weren't needed by the Army, or some of the more vital wartime forces. So we were not getting the cream. We had some very outstanding people working with us, but they were in a minority. So, generally, we were not working with capable people. And that was why the director's or the assistant director's job was so vitally important there: you had to have somebody strong, someplace in the camp, who would make a decision, and carry forth.

Incidentally, one little thing that I do remember seems worthy of mention. There was a mayor or a chairman of the county board or something, up at nearby Independence, a German immigrant, who I understand--this is strictly gossip--was persecuted, in the same way the Japanese were being persecuted, during the First World War. He was one of the most vociferous, active, aggressive, and "down with the old slant-eyed Japs." He didn't even want them to cross the road to go down and work on the sewage disposal plant. He didn't want them anyplace. He was extremely difficult to deal with. He wouldn't listen to reason and you couldn't talk with him. I remember Bob had the job of trying to get along with him, and I think he did with only relative success.

H: Bob Brown?

C: Yes, because he was local and had known this man for some time. But I remember he caused us a great deal of trouble.

H: What kind of trouble?

C: Well, anything that we wanted to do, he was against it.

H: And then he influenced others in the Owens Valley?

C: Well, he was the county commissioner or mayor or something. He held some elected office, and was a hardheaded German. And as I say, he was just as adamant as could be. Anything we wanted to do that was the least bit outside the confines of the camp, he was very much against it.

H: I know Bob Brown, Ralph Merritt and Roy Nash spoke before service clubs in the neighboring communities of Independence and Lone Pine about what was going on at Manzanar. Did you ever do this?

C: No.

H: Had you met Ralph Merritt during the time you were at the camp and prior to his being hired as the director?

C: Bob Brown had told me of him, and his adulation of him, and had told me what a great person he was, and how much he'd done. But I had never met him, and in fact never heard of him, except from Bob.

H: Now, although you went to Manzanar without any other motive aside from simply getting involved in the war effort, and without any philosophy toward what was involved . . .

C: That's entirely true.

H: . . . you did say that you developed a philosophy, and certainly by the time you got enmeshed in the machinery of operating . . .

C: I had some very strong feelings.

H: What kind of philosophy--not simply a day-to-day pragmatism--did you develop toward camp management?

C: I think I strengthened my feelings of, "Christ Almighty, guys, we're in this, there's nothing you can do, or I can do, or possibly anybody could do, considering the political situation in the country"--and I'm thinking of the political situation from the terrible trauma of Pearl Harbor and how it had affected everyone; anybody who showed any friendship toward the Japanese Americans, or anybody that looked like a Japanese, was immediately castigated to the ultimate--"So listen, guys, we've got this place, it's a hellhole, I'll grant you, but let's do the very most we can to make it liveable."

I encouraged them to plant gardens in the firebreaks. They raised vegetables, far more than they could possibly use in the kitchens, and they would bring over great quantities of them to our family-- more than my wife, my infant son, and I could eat.

There was one man, a landscape gardener, who could take one of the

sewer manholes, sticking up three or four feet above the ground because
it had been constructed so hurriedly, and by taking some cement could
make it appear as a tree trunk. And we encouraged that. We allowed
them to turn some of their bath house toilets into sauna or hot baths.

We had a camouflage net factory there, and the internees were being
paid very poorly for their labor there. How poorly paid, I don't know.
It was something for them to do, a make-work project, and it was helping in the war effort. We had a little strike up there one time, and
I went up to speak to the strikers. One of the mistakes I made was
that I agreed with them entirely. Instead of backing up the Washington decision or acting as a shock-absorber to absorb some of the blame,
I just agreed with them and said, "Hell, we can't do anything about
this, so go on back to work." This was one of the things I was criticized for.

People were crawling onto a truck body there and talking to this
group, and I believe I have some native ability at public speaking,
as I've done a great deal of it, starting out with my Red Cross days,
and, as I recall, the strike ended up in a good laugh session.

H: I would like you to comment on this recounting of that situation, as
it was written by a former internee named Koji Ariyoshi. Maybe you
even recall him.

C: No, no. Names wouldn't mean anything to me.

H: I have his picture here. Do you recognize him?

C: No, I don't think . . . no.

H: Anyway, this recollection of Manzanar by Ariyoshi appeared in the
Honolulu Star Bulletin on April 8, 1971. He says that after returning
from Idaho, where he'd been topping beets during a furlough leave . . .

C: Yes.

H: "I worked full time at the camouflage net factory. We were told that
we outproduced defense workers outside doing the same work, and earn-
ing about $400 a month. We were paid $12 and later $16 a month. At
first, pay for laborers was $8; for semi-skilled, $12; and for professionals, like doctors, $16. The increase upped the pay to $12,
$16, and $19 a month. By working half a day, we outproduced net factory workers outside. We were on a quota basis; as we finished our
quota, we were free for the day.

"I went to Ned Campbell, assistant project director, and he told me
that camouflage net production was a defense project, and the factory
could not be idle half a day. He said it took considerable effort
and persuasion by people friendly to the Nisei to have the national
government introduce this war industry in camp. I reminded Campbell
that we were top producers. He said we must cooperate. The whole
country was watching us, and we must prove and show our loyalty.

Otherwise, we would remain in camp for a long time.

"He said a defense industry in camp doing well would help our position. He finally admitted that inspectors from the military headquarters at the presidio were coming to Manzanar for inspection, and he didn't know when. He didn't want the factory idle when they came. Our record spoke for us, I insisted, and he should back us up. We worked in an open, barn-like structure with enough heat and dust. We were doing our part. How could he tell us to prove our loyalty and say that our chances of relocation to inland communities depended on our cooperation, when he was primarily interested in protecting and enhancing his position? He declared that he would rig up a loudspeaker at the factory and make his announcement.

"The net factory workers were talking of walking off the job. On the day Campbell said he would announce the change in work hours, I went to him early in the morning. I was asked by others to do so. I pleaded, but he would not budge. He made the announcement from the platform of the truck. The faces of men and women turned up to him, turned away and the workers dispersed. The first defense industry and the first relocation center were shut down.

"That afternoon, a command car from the presidio parked outside the barbed wire fence. A few of us were taken out to be questioned. I explained to the officer why the factory was idle. No one had led the strike; workers just refused to work because they had been betrayed."

After listening to that account, how do you react to it?

C: I don't recall the details of the people from the presidio; in fact, I don't recall the details of my conversation, nor can I necessarily put any value on what argument I may have used. You can see my tendency toward a change in philosophy by that time. I wanted to get these people out as fast as I could, and I'm enough of a natural salesman that if I have to tell you that something's green when it's blue, I might have the tendency to say, "Well, that happens to be a bluish-green and not a greenish-green." It's entirely possible he's accurate in his account.

I do recall that from the bed of the truck we had a long discussion that day. It was open, and it was one where I met with quite a number of people. I agreed with them, but there was nothing we could do. As I have said, I feel this might have been my mistake—a basic mistake. When the boss tells you to do something, you either quit or do what you've been told to do. That's what I failed to do there, and was criticized heavily for my actions in Washington.

My sympathy was entirely with the Japanese at that time—maybe not entirely, I'll back up on that. There were mitigating circumstances; they were getting room and board—although they hadn't asked for it, they were getting it. If you get room and board, you don't get the same pay. However, I saw no justification for underpaying them to the extent that they were being underpaid, nor have I changed my mind about it today.

H: How much autonomy did you have at Manzanar; to what extent did you take your cues and commands from the Washington WRA office?

C: If they came out with a policy, I had no autonomy at all. But in the day-to-day operation, we were never interfered with, nor would they help or hinder us a great deal.

H: Did you feel hamstrung by policy directives that were constantly being altered in Washington?

C: Well, it certainly was frustrating. We had various experts, efficiency experts, that would come in with all the problems solved in their own mind, or with plans for preventing the problems from arising. It was frustrating to have these fellows come in who knew absolutely nothing about the day-to-day operation and the pressures that we were under. I'm sure I irritated them by saying that I didn't think they were omnipotent, and that they couldn't tell me a certain action was going to cause a certain reaction, that that was absolute absurdity. Even I couldn't foresee that because there were all these pressures within the camp.

H: Do you recall any of these?

C: No, but you felt them. There were people who felt strongly this way, and others who felt strongly another way. For instance, the little doctor that was there, Dr. James Goto, was a fantastic man. But there were people who said, "Don't ever go in there to get a splinter pulled from your finger, because you'll leave without an appendix; he'll operate on anybody for an appendix if he gets a chance." So, name a subject and there were very divergent points of view and very strong feelings on it.

I think one of the identifying features of the Japanese--maybe because under these circumstances of living in hovels and living as they were forced to live, or maybe it's part of their inherited nature--but they had very strong opinions that they wanted to act upon physically. I remember, with great pleasure, how I liked to sit down and talk with an intelligent man--and it's not hard for me to find one more intelligent than I--and I remember the "bull sessions" or "rap sessions" we would have with some of the young Japanese there. I remember this with great joy, although I can't recall anything in particular that we discussed.

H: Do you recall any of the people involved in these rap sessions?

C: Most of them were young people at the newspaper office. I was frequently in contact with them, and I think they became more friendly toward me. Therefore they came to me with--not tattletaling, but forewarning--as Tad Uyeno, a reporter on the Manzanar Free Press did.

H: Did you get any tattletaling?

C: No, not that I recall.

H: You don't recall somebody informing you about this or that person being pro-Japan in his sentiments and actions?

C: No more than what was said in these rap sessions. Well, they'd drop a name, like that SOB will do anything, or he's causing trouble, but never with a sense of disclosing information to me that I should take action upon. If it was done, I was too stupid to realize what they were telling me.

H: Did you have an informal espionage system or intelligence system?

C: Absolutely not.

H: What about the FBI? Did the FBI ever come into camp?

C: Oh, very frequently. They always checked in with me—as a courtesy thing—and I would get them an office and staff.

H: Why did the FBI come to you instead of the project director?

C: Well, as I say, I guess I was the de facto project director. It was through my own desire or aggressiveness or my stupidity, whatever you want to call it, or maybe it was just the flow of project directors. I've always felt that I was running the camp. That's been my feeling; anything that happened there during those days—in the latter days of Nash up to the day when Merritt came in and through the early days of Merritt—it was more . . .

H: Campbell's administration?

C: Yes, in my own mind. Now, I may be entirely erroneous in that, but I must accept the blame or the credit for anything particularly anything that happened there.

H: Former internees of Manzanar that I've interviewed have recollected you as the one among the staff with the highest profile in camp. They say that, if they were to identify a leader of the Manzanar administration, it would be you.

C: Whether it was pro or con, I think that's fair. I felt in my own mind, because of my own personality, and the situation there, that I should assume the authority to go ahead.

One disasterous incident I mentioned to you before we began to tape, I had an eighty-five dollar-plus phone conversation with Dillon Myer, attempting to get permission to take the known troublemakers out of camp. I was turned down even though I presented every possible argument as to why they should be removed. Dillon Myer said it would be undemocratic to remove them. I feel, had they been removed, the so-called Manzanar Riot might not have taken the shape it took.

H: How did these troublemakers operate?

C: I can't recall, except anything we wanted to do, any little decree or regulation we came out with, there was always somebody to oppose it, break it, or cause trouble with it.

Some of the Japanese wanted to start a soy sauce factory in there. They came to me, and I said, "Swell." We had bachelor quarters there, and I said, "Why don't we just use their bath house facilities to make soy sauce?" And I believe we also raised some bean sprouts, too. But if we were going to use it, the bachelors would have to go someplace else. This was acceptable with all the bachelors that I talked to. Then somebody started complaining about how I was doing the wrong thing to the bachelors--mistreating them because they were not aggressive, and they were older men and I was taking advantage of them. But the desire of the whole camp was to have their own soy sauce factory. Anything you attempted to do, these troublemakers were against it, and they were constantly stirring up more and more trouble.

H: Did they ever confront you openly?

C: No, only this man, this Japanese American that I told you of. They were just stirring up the embers as much as they could.

H: A man who figures very principally in the Manzanar Riot, the person whose arrest sparked it, was Harry Ueno. Apparently you had seen him a few times prior to his arrest. In fact, a lot of people recall times when you threatened to physically throw Ueno out of your office.

C: It's possible, but I don't recall it.

H: Ueno had floated an accusation within camp that you and Joe Winchester were two administrators involved in stealing rationed supplies and selling them on the black market. Some historians and former internees have claimed that because of this accusation you were so incensed at Ueno that you were ready to pick him up on the slightest pretext. So, when Fred Tayama was beaten on the night of December 5, 1942--the night before the Manzanar Riot--by masked men who he couldn't positively identify, you were so anxious to yank Ueno out of the camp, that you arrested him. At that point, you made an unprecendented move in the camp's history; you did not place Ueno in the camp jail, but removed him personally to a jail outside the camp in Independence.

C: I recall none of that, really. I can almost deny having taken him there, because I remember none of that. Now, I may have done it, but as I say, none of that sticks in my memory. A man accusing me of a thing like that would incense me.

H: Do you remember that?

C: No, but I can tell you this: if he did, I did. Those people had
     personalities, as I have a personality. He'd found my weak point.
     Don't accuse me of lying, or stealing, or you're liable to get a
     violent reaction. I'm sure if he did that, I was incensed. But
     to have used that as an excuse isn't a part of my nature, and I
     don't think it's ever been a part. I would tell you to your face
     what I don't like, and I will react to your face. But to do little,
     tricky things to trap you has never been my nature, and I hope it
     never becomes so.

H: But you don't recall these actions at all?

C: I'm absolutely blank on them, so I can neither deny nor affirm them.

H: You certainly can deny the fact that you took the sugar.

C: Of course! What would I have done with it? I was living in camp,
     I didn't know anybody in the Owens Valley; how could I have estab-
     lished--I'm just going about this logically--a contact with somebody
     to even do this, had I wanted to.

     When I was in Africa with UNRRA, I was approached by the Arabs.
     God, the opportunities were showered upon me there. Part of the
     time I was living in camps, but for a long time I was living in
     Casablanca. It seems to me that I was probably approached once a
     month, or once every two weeks, by some of the "merchants"--the
     Arabs are great merchants and anything is legitimate with them--
     during the war who were being starved and mistreated, but I had few
     contacts. As for the Manzanar situation, the few people I knew in
     Owens Valley were people Bob Brown introduced to me, friends of his.
     Most of them were very delightful people, but I could count those
     on three or four fingers.

H: After the accusation was reiterated and reiterated, the administra-
     tration finally agreed to set up an investigation to find where
     the sugar was going, and while they discovered shortages in the
     sugar supply, they were never able to pin down where they were
     going and who was taking them. But the rumor was given some credi-
     bility in the minds of the internees by the findings of the investi-
     gation.

C: They were looking for things, too. But one incident that I do
     recall was my first real contact with the Civil Service Commission.
     A man that I would call a low-grade employee was in charge of the
     motor pool there. He was a Caucasian, and I became aware of the
     fact that he had four U.S. government tires on his personal car,
     and so I summarily discharged him. First, I called him in and asked
     if it was true, and he said, "Yes," and explained himself, but I

fired him.

The next thing I knew, I was brought before the Civil Service Commission for I had not told him, prior to this time, that it was illegal to use government property and to remove the tires. Well, it seemed to me a grown man certainly should know that government property is government property. But I lost my case, for I had not given him prior warning after discovering this and allowed him time to adjust it. However, I refused to let him back in camp, and he was transferred. But that is the only incident that I know of. The sugar incident, now that you mention it, is a faint, faint cloud in my memory, but so faint that I couldn't even comment upon it.

H: Was it a cause célèbre at the time?

C: Well, it doesn't remain in my memory as such.

H: When you think back about that time and try to recapture the philosophy you were developing toward camp administration, you perhaps think, too, about your attitude toward the internees. Had you known Japanese Americans prior to taking this job?

C: If so, maybe one or two in my lifetime.

H: A lot of the criticism directed at you by former internees is to the effect that Ned Campbell did not understand the Japanese psychology. Would you care to comment on that estimate?

C: Well, that is 100 percent valid.

H: What do you think the Japanese psychology was?

C: I realize now that they are a far more sensitive people. As I say, I went out there a real babe. I went out there with the idea that here was a job to be done. I shall never forget how distressed I was when, as the assistant project director, I was assigned a big Chrysler, which I liked; everybody likes a big car to drive around. And I felt very happy about it. But then to have a boy, young man, come up one day and say, "You know, you're driving my car." He just wanted to look at it and touch it again. It was the first time I realized just how hard we were stepping on these people. Not only stepping on them but rubbing our actions in their faces. And I think probably that was my first realization that I was dealing with human beings, and this was just not a job to be done with so many bodies out there. Certainly I was very guilty of the fact of going out first with the notion that we have so many people--so many bodies, if you will, and we have a job to do: we've got to feed so many mouths, and we have so many people we have to get into the hospital, and we've got this, that and the other. But they were just numbers to me. And I think probably that instance was the beginning of my realization that I did have a human quotient to deal with. I don't know if I was mature enough--although I was old enough to be mature--to have developed a philosophy; but I will say, I left there with great admiration for the Japanese, and that has remained with me all my life.

H: Do you think most of the administrators shared the same sort of stereotypes and prejudices concerning the Japanese, or would you say they were different from the ordinary man on the street in their outlook? Were the people running the camp a particularly liberal, humane group or were they just ordinary people?

C: As I remember, I think they could all fall into about the same classification as I. I don't remember them making any verbal swings at the Japanese--like the "Japs," or the "slant eyes," or I guess the GIs call anybody that comes from the East the "slopes." I don't recall feelings of hatred, viciousness, or vindictiveness among any people I worked with, although it may have occurred.

H: Some people have divided the WRA administrators into two groups: those who were people-minded, who thought of the internees as people first and Japanese second; and those that were stereotype-minded, who thought of the internees as Japanese first and people second. Given those definitions, were most of the administrators stereotype-minded or people-minded?

C: I don't think it would be fair to even express an opinion--not that I'm refusing to answer your question, I just don't think my opinion would be valid.

H: Don't you recall bull sessions and the general sort of demeanor the administrators had toward the Japanese Americans?

C: Yes, I do recall a certain idealism. And since I am more or less pragmatic, I went in there and left there with the idea that this was a job to be done, and let's get it done, and make it as happy for all of us as we possibly can.

H: Do you think that was a generally shared attitude?

C: No, because as I told you earlier, I don't think the intellectual level of the majority of the employees there was such that you could categorize them. The camp was a two- or three-man operation, and by that I mean two or three peoples' personalities and philosophies. There was the police chief, Bob Brown, me, and to a lesser degree the people who specialized in various aspects of camp management, like the head of the motor pool and the head of the fire department-- and with those people with whom they came in contact.

H: Who was your closest friend on the staff?

C: I suppose Bob Brown.

H: How would you characterize him, how would you describe his role in the camp? Would you say that he played an important role?

C: Well, Bob played an important role as far as I was concerned. He was my information source on reactions to expect on the outside. He explained the Owens Valley to me, its people, and the personalities involved there. I don't think Bob had a strong conviction at that time vis-à-vis the Japanese. Again, remember this is over many years, and I could be very, very wrong. Bob was a hell of a nice guy, and I enjoyed being with him. He was certainly my intellectual equal, if not my superior, and I found him a stimulating person to be with. I think we had a difference of opinion on how to meet several particular situations that I can recall--but again, pulling rank on him, I usually went ahead and did it my way, erroneously or not.

H: Did you know, at the time, that he was angling to get Nash replaced as project director?

C: Nash replaced? No, I don't recall that--I can't even say whether or not it was true. I helped him bring Merritt in as director. I shoveled some coals on that fire, and that seemed so dastardly to me at the time, but now with greater age, well, I've seen it happen so many times in my life.

H: Could you explain how this happened?

C: No, only that I also recommended Merritt, on Bob's recommendation. My job was to get somebody strong in these jobs, so I could move on.

H: Why didn't they push you up into the position of project director?

C: I guess because I didn't have what it took. I don't think I did; I wasn't that mature at the time.

H: How old were you?

C: I think maturity is a relative term. I was born in 1905, so figure it out. I was thirty-five, because I didn't get married until I was thirty-four. My wife and I were old-fashioned; we were married before we had our child. Although I was thirty-five years old, I still feel I was very naive.

H: You have been described by some interviewees as "boyish" during your Manzanar days.

C: I think that would be a very accurate description. I feel I've matured rather late in life.

H: You have also been frequently described as "headstrong."

C: I think that would probably be true, and would still be true.

H: So you think the picture of a boyish and headstrong person who was willing to make a decision and who was quite open and frank in his dealings, would be a fair characterization?

C: I think the first part would have to be somebody else's evaluation of me. The latter part, I would be very proud to accept. Yes, I am willing to make a decision. The one decision I didn't make I've always regretted--when I called Dillon Myer.

H: Why don't you relate that incident again, for the record.

C: I became aware of ringleaders who were creating an increasing amount of trouble in camp. It was probably after the Fred Tayama beating-- although I can't correlate that in its proper sequence--when I called Dillon Myer, and first suggested that I be allowed to take four to eight people out of the camp and lock them up--just to get them out of the camp. He asked me what I would do with them. I said,"I'll figure that out, but with our association with the local authorities here, we can put them in something here, or take them someplace. Let's get them out of here, let's get the rotten apples out." His rejoinder asked me how we were going to try them, how were we going to weigh the evidence we had against them. I admitted we couldn't, that we would probably make some mistakes in this, and that we would probably take some innocent people out. In taking out the known rot- ten apples, however, we might get a few good ones in there.

H: How many are we talking about?

C: We're talking about taking out ten maximum, and I was thinking more about seven or eight.

H: Were they a special group in camp?

C: Not that I recall. I can't think of them as a group of well-organ- ized, well-knit, let's-get-together-boys-and-do-these-dastardly-acts types, like the IRA /Irish Republic Army/ today or anything like that.

H: Was it the reputed group alternately called the Blood Brothers of California or the Black Dragon Society?

C: I don't remember. Those groups may have existed, I don't recall, but I don't know of them. In my own mind I knew the several that I would have picked up and taken out. Anyway, Dillon Myer and I argued and argued, and he turned me down.

It's fixed in my mind: I shall never again in my life ask for permis- sion to do something that I feel should be done; I shall go ahead and do it and either lose my job or defend my actions for having done it. I think, had I gone ahead and done it, the riot would not have taken the form it did. It might have been far more severe, because I might have picked the wrong apples--ones who were not bad, and the bad ones would have used this as a tom-tom to beat upon. Maybe we would have nipped it in the bud. But the fact is, I didn't make the decision I should have made, and then defended it. I've always con- demned myself for it.

H: Before we started the taping, you made an interesting breakdown of the internee population in the camp. Could you relate this again?

C: These are just figures I'm grabbing out of the air. I've always said in discussing my Manzanar experience that probably something in excess of 90 percent of the people who were there just wanted to make the most of the situation. They didn't want to raise any smoke, they just wanted to live the best they possibly could. Of the remaining 8 percent or 10 percent, probably more than half of them were such loyal Americans that they would crucify their own grandmother to prove their Americanism--some of them were loyal almost to the point of nausea. The other 4 /percent/ or 5 percent were devoutly convinced that Japan was right and that Japan was going to win the war--they were the ones who were going to cause trouble.

H: How did you come in contact with these people who were so nauseous about their pro-Americanism?

C: Oh, they definitely made themselves known to me.

H: Were the people you ended up taking to Death Valley after the riot of this group?

C: Yes, there were a few in that group.

H: Are you talking about people like Tokie Slocum? Slocum was an outspoken patriot who got his citizenship as a result of fighting in World War I.

C: I'm confusing him with the Japanese American, Joe Kurihara. I'm making one person of them.

H: They were mortal enemies.

C: Their history is what I'm confusing into one person, in the name of Kurihara.

H: Well, the history of the two is quite similar. They were both decorated soldiers--in fact, Tokie Slocum had fought alongside Sergeant York. Kurihara and Slocum used to go at one another because Kurihara claimed all of his patriotism was for naught as soon as the war broke out. He had a fine paying job and he volunteered to be a navigator and work at defense factories, but none of these places would hire him. Then he ended up at Manzanar, and, of course, he was very embittered by it.

Tokie Slocum, on the other hand, became a sort of self-appointed vigilante committee, helping the FBI ferret out suspected pro-Japan sympathizers. He bragged around camp that he was working for the FBI, and so he was very unpopular with the people in camp, who used to call him an inu /dog/, and numerous attempts were made on his life. Joe Kurihara said he used to be an American, but Japanese blood flowed in his veins and now he would remember the spirit of Yamato Damashii and now he was a "Jap" 100 percent.

C: That I can remember.

H: Slocum claimed his commander-in-chief was the President of the United States, and that he was serving his commander-in-chief in Manzanar. Kurihara and Slocum had this common background, but there were dramatic contrasts in their actions.

C: Slocum would be one of the type of people I was talking about--one aggressive about proving his Americanism, and also creating frictions I'd rather not have had. To be patriotic is one thing, but to be vociferous about it is something else.

H: As an administrator, who caused more problems for you: the stridently pro-Japan internees, or the super-patriotic ones?

C: Certainly the pro-Japanese who were aggressively out to cause trouble.

H: But since almost all the reputed beatings and killings were directed at people who were outspokenly pro-American, didn't they by reiterations of their allegiance to the country and their attempts to circulate petitions cause the camp to be in a constant uproar?

C: No--but again, I keep hiding behind the cloud of years that have passed--I don't recall them as being real problems; they were just irritants. The things caused by the pro-Japanese created real and serious problems.

H: What kind of problems?

C: Any decision we made, as well-meaning or as good as it may have been, always found resistance.

H: Karl Yoneda was outspokenly pro-American. Actually, he was a Communist, and the first so affiliated to run for a state office in California.

C: Was he a longshoreman?

H: Yes, and he was a block leader.

C: I remember him. He was a great believer in Harry Bridges; he thought the sun rose and set on Harry Bridges' rear end.

H: You remember him, then.

C: I think I'd recognize the guy if he walked in today, as he was then; he's one of the few Japanese I think I would remember. I had some very interesting discussions with him.

H: He was married to a Caucasian who had been connected with left-wing organizations and politics for awhile before the war.

C: Yes, I remember, she was also rather vociferous.

H: Yoneda recalls times when a salvage crew used to take a truck around the camp, violating the speed limit, with a banner over it saying, "Black Dragon Society" or whatever. One day he was talking to Tokie Slocum on a stoop outside the barracks, when this truck came and tried to kill them. They jumped back into the building and the truck wiped out the steps. Yoneda claims that this was going on a lot, and that he complained to you, but you took a no-see attitude and pooh-poohed the whole thing. He said instead of trying to apprehend these pro-Japan elements, you and other administrators turned your head from it.

C: I recall nothing of that. But apply logic to it: if you are by yourself or in a very small group, in an isolated corner of an area containing more than ten thousand souls, you cannot occupy yourself with every little pinprick that occurs, although that pinprick may be very important to you. At the same time, if we ran after every pinprick, we could be trapped into doing very foolish things. We did have a police department that those things could be reported to. I make no defense for my lack of action; my answer to this is logic. It doesn't make sense that we would have done anything; we'd have been out of breath all the time, running here and there.

H: Yoneda wanted precisely what you wanted: to have those people involved in pro-Japan actions classified as troublemakers and taken out of the camp.

C: This conversation with Dillon Myer was one or two days prior to the riot, or maybe it was the same day. Things were getting pretty heated, and word was reaching me that there was going to be a problem. I don't recall the beating, but it might have been about that time. It may have been what triggered my call to Myer, I can't recall.

H: Let's talk about the Manzanar Riot: two people were killed and some ten people were injured on December 6, 1942. The press release Bob Brown wrote and distributed, under Merritt's approval, characterized it as a celebration on the eve of the anniversary of Pearl Harbor--a clash between pro-American and pro-Japan forces. This seems to me, from my research, to be a very poor rendering. What do you think?

C: I was going to use the very foul expression of "horse manure"-- it's a little more accurate. That's a bunch of horse manure! Bob ought to be ashamed of himself; he should have been ashamed at the time. It's absolutely untrue. The group causing trouble was beginning to get a bigger following, because they provided something to do, to listen to. The people followed them down the street one day and when I stepped out in front of them, I saw hatred as I've never seen before in my life in the eyes of four or five people crowded around me. They were followed by a bunch of teenagers along for a joy ride. "Let's see what happens when these four or five guys attack the big gringo." If you were sitting around the camp all day and had nothing to do, wouldn't you like to see a little action someplace? Sure you would. Bob was looking for words, looking for something to write, but he should be ashamed of himself. Merritt--now that I know the type he is--would never have been ashamed of himself; he justified anything he did.

H: Hadn't he just arrived?

C: That makes no difference; it's a part of his character. I knew very little of Merritt. I only knew him from the deification of him Bob Brown had given me.

H: Didn't you have a chance to meet him somewhat?

C: Yes, and he was a cold-blooded egoist who wanted to do things his way. He wanted things for Ralph Merritt; he was strictly an egoist.

H: When he first came to camp--he was there just a little over a week, six to nine days before the riot--he obviously had to depend upon you, since you were, in effect, running the camp. Nash left, then Harvey Coverley and Solon Kimball were there as acting directors, and then Merritt. Merritt was only there for a little while when the riot occurred. You were making most of the decisions, and providing a good portion of the information about what was going on and how to deal with it, so I imagine he was taking counsel with you quite frequently. Is it fair to say, then, that Merritt was pretty much relying upon you during this time?

C: In retrospect, I feel Merritt was, by nature, a conniving person. If only I knew how much he was relying on me and using my willingness-- which has always been a part of me, to believe a man when I talk with him--to get rid of me. I am now convinced in my own mind that he was indebted to Bob, and Bob was going to be his boy.

H: You mean he was going to hire Bob Brown as assistant project director?

C: Either that or some other very good thing. I'd have to be Jesus Christ in a chariot for him to want me, and I was far from that. I didn't have the depth of experience or many of the required characteristics. But I'm sure had I had them, he would not have wanted me, because I would have been a competitor of his at the time. He didn't want a competitor, he wanted a follower. He wanted somebody to idolize him, glorify him; Bob was his man, because Bob did idolize him. That's the type of people Merritt wanted surrounding him.

H: So when Merritt got there, for whatever reason--whether to give you enough rope to hang yourself, or legitimately as a successor coming in and finding out something from his top aide--you were in a position of acting director.

C: Undoubtedly.

H: Let's see if we can survey the situation: you don't recall picking up Ueno and taking him to the Independence jail, so at what point do you start having some memories connected with the riot? Let's reconstruct what you recall about that episode.

C: I really recall very little about it. There are little highlights
that stick out in my mind, but they're not necessarily in chronological order. News of the beating of Tayama reached me very quickly.
And then, I or Merritt said--I suppose it was Merritt--"Let's turn
this over to the Army, we've done all we can do." I was over at
the police station, which was right at the gate, when somebody said,
"Here they come down the street." The soldiers lined up across the
street with their guns and bayonets ready. Foolishly, I thought I
could talk anything down, and not wanting any confrontation with the
soldiers and the internees, I stepped out in front of them, and
stopped this group. It consisted of five or six people marching and
about fifteen hundred onlookers, or supporters, or just let's-see-
what's-gonna-happeners.

H: Would you see the fifteen hundred as part of a bound-together mob?

C: By no means; they were looking for something to do, some excitement.
There was a handful, and out of that handful were some of the people
I would have picked up. But I'm not sure my call to Dillon Myer
didn't happen after that. One of them said something to me, and I
remember my first reaction was to reach out and grab him by the
collar. I then saw this hatred as I've never seen before or since in
their eyes, in their faces, and in their expressions.

H: Was this the negotiating group that you were talking to?

C: This group wasn't negotiating. I can't recall why they came down or
what they were going to do or what they were demanding. My argument
was always falling back on, "Guys, I don't like this any better than
you do. Let's make the most of it, and why muddy waters we have to
drink?"

H: Did it work this time?

C: It didn't work this time and it never would have worked with that
group. I'm not sure I was even wise or logical in my thinking on the
thing. The logical thing to do would have been a thing I once suggested: to let these fellows demonstrate how great they are and put
them in a camp, then send their name through the Spanish legation and
let it be known that when the Japanese land on these shores and take
over the Western part of the United States, these are their boys.
Wave that big flag, and let them fly the Japanese flag if they want
to. I really think we would have eliminated a lot of our trouble
this way.

The 90 percent that just wanted to get along and didn't want to
make trouble--wanted to do things as near Japanese American as they
could and get this thing over as happily as they could--would have
become so predominant and said, "We don't want it. We're tired of
that. Why don't you go to camp X if you don't like it here?" I
think that would have been a constant threat with them. We would
have offered them an exit, and they could have made that decision for
themselves. But it was never acted upon until it was far too late.

Well, to start back, the whole thing was wrong; the people involved in it were not experienced in it. There was no firm or continuing philosophy handed down to us, because nobody had the basis for a philosophy. Everybody was interested in the war and they weren't interested in these Japanese Americans out there. They practically did the same thing during World War I with the Germans, and we learned lessons from it.

Hopefully, we've learned some lessons from this, because I think as a nation we have matured, and there are now more thinking people. By God, if we started a war against the Latin American people, and we started something like Manzanar for Latin Americans who were citizens or longtime residents of the United States, I'd become a vociferous leader against it. First, because of my great love for the Latin American people, with whom I have lived for twenty-five years and because I'm only using them as an illustration. I just don't believe in group classifications; in categorizing Japanese relocation camps we have made one of the greatest black marks in the history of democracy. If I were old enough to remember, I'm sure a similar thing happened to the Germans during World War I to a much lesser degree. We didn't go after the Germans in World War II. As I recall, the Office of Naval Intelligence and the FBI strongly opposed the Army proceeding with mass evacuation of those of Japanese ancestry. They said, "We know who they are, and how they're operating, and we can handle them, so just leave us alone, and leave them in a place where we can locate them." But General DeWitt, and, I think, President Roosevelt, made up their minds. I always blamed DeWitt for it, but I'm not sure he was really responsible.

H: Some say that in a democracy you ultimately must put the blame on the person who signs the executive order. In this case, Franklin Roosevelt.

C: He signed the executive order, but I could see how DeWitt would be frightened; I could see how all the Army and Navy people were frightened at the time. Behind their fear lay a reason. Some historians that I've read believe the Japanese could have moved right into the West Coast at that time, and probably could have made a very successful beachhead here, had they tried to then.

H: Were you ever frightened while you were in the camp that your life was in danger?

C: I don't frighten easily. I've been shot at close range; it hasn't frightened me--it's infuriated me.

H: So it wasn't something you thought about?

C: No, I don't think so. I think I became frightened that day after I went back to my room and began to think of how thin the walls were in the building I was living in, in which my wife and child--they were very dear to me--also lived, and I was frightened for them. One of those half-intelligent, 83 IQ soldiers out there could easily have pulled a trigger and one of those shots could have gone through the walls and through one of us en route. I was thinking more of my family, and certainly not of me.

H: Let's review the events during the afternoon and night of the riot. In the afternoon you met with some of the internees, and from what I understand, some of them were pushing and shoving you.

C: No, I don't think they ever laid their hands on me. One of them said something to me that infuriated me. I stepped toward him with the idea of laying hands on him, and I was prevented from doing so, not by their touching me, but merely by their surging toward me. We're talking about a surge of one step. They were either shaking their fists or making some gestures. At that time I realized I was looking at a hatred that was almost inhuman, and I would have been nothing short of a damned fool to have walked right into that--even with the soldiers standing two or three yards behind me. The only thing that did frighten me was--well, I've been disliked, but as far as I know I've never been hated, as I saw it that day.

H: So you think the soldiers were brought into camp on Merritt's recommendation and not yours? I had the feeling it was you who put out the order.

C: I don't recall. Knowing me, I doubt that it was me. I have a great belief that I can solve problems, and I doubt that I would be the one who yelled for help.

H: Were you in a position to see the riot itself on the night of December 6?

C: I don't even recall the riot. I was in my quarters when I heard the shots, and I remember I cried--my wife remembers that, too.

H: You weren't out there, so you didn't see the actual shooting?

C: No, I was in my quarters. I cry when I think about it today. It absolutely was not necessary. There were several steps I or others could have taken to prevent it.

H: What do you think you could have done?

C: The first thing would be offering to let those ringleaders be the Japanese they wanted to be. Let them wave the flag and march.

H: Do you recall, for instance, why you decided not to let Ueno out of the jail or why you kept Ueno in the jail?

C: I remember nothing of that incident.

H: Shortly thereafter, consequences followed from this--you were let go as assistant project director, forced to resign, so to speak.

C: I can't even remember the sequence or how I was informed. I don't think I was ever overtly informed of it. Somebody had to take these people over to Death Valley, and I was selected. Probably my first inclination was that they were looking for a way out. They gave me this "very, very important job." It was a miserable little job, living under miserable conditions.

H: Did they put you in charge of the Death Valley camp?

C: Yes, I set it up.

H: How long did you stay there?

C: A couple of weeks. Then it began to dawn on me that this great man that Bob Brown had told me about had feet of clay, regardless of how many halos he had around his head. He was looking after Merritt first, second, and third. After that, Bob would come in fourth, fifth, or sixth, someplace in there. I've met a number of men in my life like Merritt, but now I recognize them.

H: What did you do after you left Death Valley? Were you still with the WRA?

C: I went to San Francisco, to work in the WRA there. I found out they wouldn't let me work, so I resigned after a few months. They'd give me nothing to do. I was being castigated--they were trying to force me to resign.

H: As a result of the Manzanar incident?

C: Evidently. You see, Si Fryer had left, as had most of his close associates. After I resigned, I went back and talked to my old friends at the Red Cross because I wanted to go overseas. I was still determined to do something in the war. Meanwhile, Governor Lehman offered me this job with UNRRA. And since it was a far more attractive job-- providing a chance for a great deal more action than being a field director on some little atoll in the Pacific--I jumped at it. It proved to be a very, very interesting job--but also a very frustrating job, because again it didn't materialize. The cookie didn't crumble like everyone thought it would.

H: In the letter you recently wrote to me, you said you did not look back on this particular incident--your stay at Manzanar--as one of the prouder moments in your life. What were you referring to?

C: Being associated with the Japanese relocation, or internment, if you wish. I don't feel any pride in being associated with what I consider to be one of the great blemishes on American democracy. That's what I intended to convey to you.

H: Were you referring to specifics?

C: Oh, no, just the fact of the relocation--the way it was handled, the brutality of it, the inhumaness of it and everything else, that's what I was referring to.

H: Perhaps you've read somewhere in the newspapers that the Manzanar Committee and the Japanese American Citizens League /JACL7 had a plaque placed at Manzanar in spring, 1973. This state historical marker has raised some controversy because of the wording used on the plaque. For instance, they used the designation "concentration camp." Further controversy was sparked by saying, editorially, that the camps were caused by a combination of "hysteria," "racism," and "economic exploitation." What do you think about this controversial wording?

C: If you stop to think about it, "concentration camp" is a relative term. What do we use as a measuring stick--don't we think of German concentration camps?

H: Sometimes people like to call those "death camps."

C: Well, Manzanar was certainly a concentration of people in a camp, so it was a concentration camp in that sense. But, if we use the measuring stick of the German concentration camps, these WRA camps were not. I think the nature of the American people--as miserably as the Japanese were handled--is not to do the German camp type of thing. So I would differ on that, but the rest of the statement, as you reiterate it here, I think is damned accurate.

H: The part about racism and economic exploitation?

C: Yes, I think economic exploitation is what causes our little wars today.

H: Did you feel that sort of combination--of racism and economic exploitation--in operation among the local people surrounding Manzanar? Was there a lot of hostility from the locals?

C: Yes, there was.

H: Did you always live in the camp?

C: Before there were living quarters in the camp, I was living in a hotel in Lone Pine.

H: Did you know people in Lone Pine as a result?

C: I met the editor of the paper, whom I think Bob introduced to me, the person who ran the hotel, and a fellow at the bank; but they were very shallow relationships which only lasted a very short while.

H: Did they direct remarks to you concerning the camp?

C: Not that I recall.

H: So you weren't disliked because you were involved in the camp?

C: If I was, I was too blasé to see it.

H: Did you have friends among the locals?

C: No, because I made no attempt to create any.

H: So it was more or less a self-encapsulated subculture out there at the camp.

C: Yes, entirely. I remember occasionally going down the road to a restaurant because of their wonderful sweetbreads, but we left camp very infrequently. There was just too much work to do. I had a phone installed by my bed, and many nights I was called on because something was happening--mostly insignificant little things. But I wanted to be informed, and I was informed ad nauseam at times.

H: Well, I think we've pretty well covered everything. Is there anything you'd like to add?

C: The only thing I would like to add is that some of these people whose names you've recalled to me today, I felt very, very friendly toward, and I still carry a very soft spot in my heart for them. If you ever see any of them, thank them and tell them that, that's all.

I'm just sorry my memory isn't any more accurate than that, but as I told you in my letter, I am not a person with total recall. I remember the things I like to remember, and try to forget those things I don't like to remember. I had a difficult time remembering Merritt's name, either on the night you called or when I received your letter. I was trying to reconstruct this and Nash's name came back to me for some reason--I don't know why. And then during the night I remembered Merritt's name. I remember I played a great part in his being selected--at Bob Brown's insistence and because of my friendship with Bob--project director. At the time I was rather bitter about his treatment of me, but it's been a part of my philosophy not to retain memories of sad and embittered things. Why not carry the wonderful, beautiful things you've seen in others? I have very few enemies in my own heart, but I could have a hell of a lot of them in their hearts. See, I'm stupid and soft-hearted and illogical and all of the other things, but I don't have too many regrets. I do have some regrets at having gotten trapped into Manzanar through too energetic a desire to participate in the war effort.

By the way, whatever happened to Merritt?

H: He went to work for the War Assets Board after he left Manzanar, then he developed the rapid transit master plan in Los Angeles, and then he died in the 1950s. His son, Pete, who is the city manager of Redlands, California, is still a good friend of Bob Brown's. The Regional Oral History Office at UC Berkeley, began an oral history on Merritt

in the 1950s, and then a professor from UCLA, Doyce Nunis, finished
it up. When they were interviewing Merritt, he apparently couldn't
tolerate the interviewing, so he took the interview and converted
it into a narrative. It reads somewhat like an apotheosis of himself. And unfortunately, he never gets to Manzanar in his story.
The narrative stops with his prewar experiences. I understand from
Professor Nunis that he was very ill during this period and died
shortly thereafter.

C: Well, he was undoubtedly a very able man, but there are many of these
able men. If you look at the history of some of the big corporations
today, you'll find these are the people who are making successes.
Karl Bendetsen has certainly done very well for himself.

H: What happened to him after the war?

C: He became chairman of the board for Champion Paper, I think. Hell, six
months ago I read about him in Business Week. He's been a terrific
success in the financial and business world.

H: Do you know anybody else from the WRA?

C: I didn't follow any of them. But two or three of the people at UNRRA
joined me overseas, now that I recall. Bob Brown worked for UNRRA in
Washington, but he never went overseas.

H: So you really haven't crossed paths with too many of the people you
worked with at Manzanar. And I suppose the only person you still
see is Bob Brown.

C: We only exchange Christmas cards. He married Si Fryer's secretary, a
very, very charming lady. One of the good things that happened to
Bob. Have you met her?

H: Yes, I have, and I agree with you that she is indeed a charming person.

Mr. Campbell, on behalf of the California State University, Fullerton,
Japanese American Oral History Project, I would like to thank you for
your careful attention and considerate devotion to answering the questions to the best of your memory.

                        END OF INTERVIEW

Index

An Interview with
ED. H. RUNCORN
Conducted by Janis Grennaway
on July 17, 1973
for the
California State University, Fullerton
Oral History Program
Japanese American Project

(Cooperative Stores in Relocation Centers, O.H. 1332)

This is a slightly edited transcription of an interview conducted for the Oral History Program, sponsored by California State University, Fullerton. The reader should be aware that an oral history document portrays information as recalled by the interviewee. Because of the spontaneous nature of this kind of document, it may contain statements and impressions which are not factual.

Scholars are welcome to utilize short excerpts from any of the transcriptions without obtaining permission as long as proper credit is given to the interviewee, the interviewer, and the University. Scholars must, however, obtain permission from California State University, Fullerton before making more extensive use of the transcription and related materials. None of these materials may be duplicated or reproduced by any party without permission from the Oral History Program, California State University, Fullerton, California, 92634.

CALIFORNIA STATE UNIVERSITY, FULLERTON

ORAL HISTORY PROGRAM

Japanese American Project

INTERVIEWEE: Ed. H. RUNCORN

INTERVIEWER: Janis Gennawey

SUBJECT: Cooperative Stores in Relocation Centers

DATE: July 17, 1973

G: This is an interview with Mr. Ed. H. Runcorn, for the California
    State University, Fullerton, Japanese American Oral History
    Project, by Janis Gennawey at Mr. Runcorn's office at 7655
    Greenleaf Avenue, Whittier, California, 90602, on July 8, 1973,
    at 3:30 p.m.

    Mr. Runcorn, could you tell me how you got involved with the
    WRA /War Relocation Authority7 during World War II?

R: This takes me back over thirty years, to think about the War
    Relocation Authority. It really began on December 7, 1941,
    which is known as Pearl Harbor Day. I remember it so well. I
    was teaching world history in a high school in Albuquerque,
    New Mexico, and on that day my wife and I had dinner at the
    home of our dearest friend there, a principal in the school.
    It was a dark day, and the thing happened so fast that we
    were really shaken by what came. We knew that there had been
    bickering between the governments, our government and Japan,
    because of scrap iron and things like that, but this was a
    tremendous surprise. So the next morning, Monday, we had an
    assembly at the high school. President Roosevelt was speaking
    over the radio, and we all just sat there; we knew it was a terrific
    historical time, and there was going to be a change for millions
    of people. The first evidence that I had after that, that the
    Japanese American people were really involved, was one day in a
    hotel in downtown Albuquerque. Going up the elevator, I happened
    to notice standing beside me a very simple little Japanese farm
    woman with handcuffs on. And that experience was shaking to
    me. I told my wife about it that evening. Then we began to hear
    a lot of propaganda both ways, of course, that the Japanese people
    might be enemy aliens. Besides teaching, I had been trying to bring

my students along; the war had been going on quite a long time
in Europe. Some of the boys were getting restless to get into
the Army and so on.

Another interest I had was to teach in the Sunday school of the
Methodist Church there, for the young married couples. And the
other hobby I had was being the president of a local consumer
co-op store. I tell this because both of these things were quite
a factor in my life at that time. In the church group I was
on the peace committee, and I was opposed to war. I was a
conscientious objector, and the cooperative food idea was my way
of trying to correct some of the evils that lead to war and
tense competition between nations to the point of death. The
outcome was that, very shortly after war was declared, the superintendent of schools said that all the teachers would be expected
to pay into the government for war bonds. In my situation, I
said, "I will make contributions to the Red Cross and to the
American Friends Service Committee in Philadelphia." Well, even
though I'd been teaching there, that was the end of my teaching
career because I was told, very shortly, that my job would not
be carried on the following year.

So at the close of school in 1942, I went to work trying to help
the co-op store to survive. I wasn't a very good groceryman. I
worked very hard and did not do much reading that summer or anything. But in the meantime I had a co-op leader, a former minister from Kansas City, Dr. Merlin Miller, who had said he had an
offer to go to work for the WRA, which was establishing camps in
Colorado and a number of other places in the West. He said that
they needed men who had the co-op background. So, even though
I had lost my job in the school, the man who worked in the agricultural department called me. He knew that I was a conscientious
objector, but he said, "Are you blatant about it?" I said, "No."
And he said, "Well, come to the job in the next three weeks," or
something like that. This was after a good deal of interviewing
by the government. That was real enlightening and exciting to
me. In November I went to the relocation camp down on the Arkansas
River near Lamar, Colorado. There, during that summer, about
eight thousand Japanese American people had been gathered. They
had been brought mostly from California. There they were, in a . . .
we did not think of it at the time as a concentration camp, but
it had barbed wire around it, searchlights from the towers at
night, and was guarded by some military people. It was exciting
to us but tragic to those people from California. It took me a
little while to figure out what was up and what to do about it.
I was excited because I was getting about three times as much as I
had as a teacher in Albuquerque--$145 per month, for twelve months
a year. For awhile I wondered, "What am I doing here?" Then one
day a government man came out from Washington, D.C., and explained
how we were to develop some cooperative enterprises in that Amache
Relocation Center. I think how that developed was real interesting.

These camps were surrounded by barbed wire and, because of the
reaction of the people around in the community, the Japanese
people were not allowed to go out except in small groups. The
WRA was a little afraid, I suppose, that there would be some
incidents, or some cruel things would happen, so they would let
only a few out at a time. It wasn't until it became evident that
the people needed other things besides just a mess hall, and a
sixteen by sixteen foot barrack room to live in. The internees
needed some kind of enterprise for their barbershop, beauty shop,
general store and so on. It worked out that there were only three
ways the government could go: they could just treat them as though
they were all prisoners and just hand out goods paid for by the
American taxpayers; they could authorize somebody in camp or
somebody outside camp to come in and establish stores and, therefore,
make profit off these people; or they could let the people organize
their own cooperative businesses. It was decided--very logically,
I think--that the only fair thing to do was to let the people organize their own cooperative enterprises. I should say also that
these people were all paid a sum of sixteen dollars for whatever work
they did in the center. Of course, they were provided their meals,
and they had rather crude shelter in these barrack buildings. If they
were leaders or were on the police department helping the Caucasian
police, they might get nineteen dollars a month. If they were just
clerks, or barbers, or whatever, they got sixteen dollars a month.
Under this situation, it became advisable to form the enterprises.

Well, I was the associate superintendent of the Cooperative Enterprises. It was my duty to educate these people as to what a consumer cooperative is and how it would work in that center. That was
really a challenge because, as I said, I had been interested in the
co-op store back in Albuquerque. I was real enthusiastic about the
economic idealism of that, so it was a tremendous challenge, and I
enjoyed it immensely. I went up there in November 1942, and a little
before Christmas we began to have meetings with the older men, about
eleven of them, as I remember. One of them was a wealthy man from
Los Angeles, California; a produce man, Mr. Maruse. Others were
business people who had just had a few days to leave their business.
They were disillusioned, and they were afraid they were in a concentration camp. They didn't know whether they were going to ever
have freedom again. So it was a great pleasure to them to see that
there was going to be a possibility of some democratic control and
ownership in these enterprises. The management was to be handled
completely by them. When they learned all about it, I got along
with them beautifully. Also, I found that Japanese names are
pronounced exactly like Spanish names, and that helped. I had had
lots of Spanish American children in Albuquerque High School.

G: Did you have any Japanese American children in the high school, too?

R: We had a few there. However, my first experience with Japanese
    students was up near Greeley, Colorado. There were some Japanese
    families on very productive farms there. They were in a high school

where I taught prior to coming to Albuquerque. I remember very well what fine students they were, how they applied themselves and how they observed what their parents wanted them to observe. They were really fine people. So I had a fine attitude about the Japanese people. I think this is interesting: when I first went to Amache, it seemed so strange; here were these people—families, old people, young people—all huddled in this camp, but they took it. The young people particularly took it so well, I remember. It just seemed to be shocking. Here the young high school kids and the elementary kids going to the showers, singing, "Praise the Lord, and pass the ammunition," just like all other American kids were doing at that time. (laughter) As we discussed these matters about cooperatives and so on, the older men would be standing around. In the middle of the place, they had placed an institution-sized tomato can that they had used in the mess halls, and the brand was "Slap the Jap." (laughter) They put that out in the middle of the room and spit in it, put their cigarette butts in it, and so on. They just took it in stride very, very well. I was pleased just to see how they took the whole thing.

G: You had been teaching for some time prior to the war?

R: Yes. First I started in a Mexican school in New Mexico when I was eighteen years old, and I taught two or three years. Then I went to college at Colorado University. My second job after that was to be in charge of the English classes in a small high school near Greeley, Colorado, and there is where I first met Japanese American people.

G: When Pearl Harbor was bombed, what reaction did you get from the Japanese Americans in your class and from the community of Greeley at large?

R: I was in Albuquerque when Pearl Harbor occurred. I don't recall having any Japanese students in Albuquerque; I had them near Greeley. So it wasn't until I got into the camp that I saw a good many young people of Japanese ancestry again.

G: You've told how you got connected with the WRA. They approached you first; is that correct?

R: Yes. Well, I applied on the recommendation of this co-op leader from Kansas City. It took several months—while I was laboring away as a grocer there—for the letters and inquiries to come. Finally, it came in the form of a telephone call from the project director, Mr. James G. Lindley, right from the camp near Lamar, Colorado.

G: Was the WRA a civilian organization?

R: Yes, yes it was.

G: In your position, what training did you give the Japanese American people? Exactly what were they taught?

R: Well, this was a challenge to me because in the high school I had made it my custom toward the last week of school every year . . . I was interested in that consumer cooperative, and I had a conviction that our capitalist society needed the competition and the idealism of the cooperative movement to kind of balance things and to keep the monopolies from becoming utter dominating factors in our lives. So I rather insisted--though I know the principal was worried, but he let me do it--every year at the end of the year, I brought in a pamphlet which told about the Rochdale pioneers in Rochdale, England, where they began the cooperative movement in 1844. I had been using these couple of pamphlets to tell that story to my students in Albuquerque. So when I went to the camp, I used these same little pamphlets to help educate these men from California, the Japanese leaders. Some of them couldn't speak English very well, but they would talk back and forth and translate, and they got enthusiastic, more so than the students ever did. (laughter)

G: Did they? They were enthusiastic about setting up the enterprises?

R: Yes, they were enthusiastic about how it could be applied. They hadn't known anything about cooperatives, I don't suppose--maybe farmer cooperatives out in California, somewhat. But these were mostly businessmen from the Los Angeles area, so it was rather new to them. They were fairly well-to-do men and they said, "Well, this will really work in this camp because we can all buy shares in it, and we'll all have one vote. If we make any earnings out of it, they will be shared according to the way the barbershop is used, the grocery store, and so on." They were quite enthusiastic. I listened to many Japanese harangues back and forth. (laughter)

G: How were these men chosen to work in the co-ops? Did they volunteer their services or were they chosen?

R: Well, at the time I began there in December with these men, the project leader had told them that they were going to develop cooperative enterprises. "Well, what is that?" They didn't know, and it was my job to enlighten them as to what a consumer coopera- tive is. So they had been told, "Now you choose eleven men to be the group that will be a kind of committee to study this whole thing, and then present it to the people. Perhaps then we can form a cooperative."

At first the government had an idea, "Well, we've got a million dollars or so. If you want any help, we'll subsidize it for you." Ah, but I didn't proceed that way at all, and some of the govern- ment leaders, I think, were a little bit surprised that we didn't ask for a lot of money. We said, "Well, we'll put on a campaign, and we'll let all the people in the center buy five dollar shares." We had a great time putting up the canvas sign along one of those barrack buildings. Each block conducted a drive after this, after the education process had gone clear into the barrack blocks, so that people knew what was going on. And we had this contest; I think that was along in early spring of 1943.

G: And this was in Amache?

R: In Amache, right near Lamar, Colorado. Amache was the name of the center. So in a drive, for about three weeks, I think, they raised twenty-five thousand dollars, which was amazing at that time for these people who were limited in their incomes to sixteen and nineteen dollars a month--and then their own savings, in many cases. They were allowed to invest up to one hundred dollars in five dollar shares, and they would all be voters. Each one would be a voter in the enterprise. So it developed that it had a real advantage because many of the people had been very disillusioned. They were afraid: "My, we've lost our freedom; we've lost our property at home." They had been ordered out of their homes with just a few days' notice, and they had to turn their property over to white friends, if they had any, and most of them, I suppose, had some friends. But they were worried about their property at home. Many of the old folks didn't know when they would get home again. Some of them fell ill, went to the center hospital, and just sort of pined away. But the young people were having a great time. They had a lot more associations than they had ever had before. There were several hundred of them there, and they had a high school and other schools in the center. The young people were just having a great time; and the old people were suffering under it. Of course, the middle-aged people were wondering about their property at home, when they would get out, whether they would be treated fairly, and so on, because there was so much propaganda, of course, against Japan and "Japs" in general.

G: Yes. Did the Japanese Americans in the camps build the different stores, and where did they acquire their goods to sell?

R: Well, that was interesting. Through the fact that we had the government in back of us, they were able to have things shipped in. As soon as this twenty-five thousand dollars was raised, we began to use that to pay. So the people took right ahold of it, through their own money and their own businesses over the counters in those various buildings. Various barrack buildings were just remodeled a little to where they could put in counters, and a barbershop, beauty shop, print shop, and a general store. I can remember one of the most popular things was just crushed ice with various flavors: raspberry, strawberry, and so on. (laughter) That was a great delicacy, particularly for the young people.

G. And where did they acquire the goods?

R: We bought them from various wholesalers, and so on, around Colorado.

Finally, I put them in touch with the co-op wholesalers in Kansas
City. That was an exciting day, particularly for me, when they had
a truckload of canned goods, co-op labeled goods, brought from the
wholesaler in Kansas City. So they began to find out what co-op
food was like, what the brand meant, A-B-C grades, and things like
that, that they had at the time. It was bearing out the things that
I told them--how a consumer cooperative differed from just a usual
private enterprise.

In connection with that, there was a little story I thought was
real exciting. We told them, of course, that if they saved the
stubs from the little purchases they made in these various stores
and so on, that they would get a refund according to the earnings
of the cooperative. Well, naturally, if you're paying only sixteen
dollars a month wages . . . We were not allowed to pay any more than
the government was paying all other workers there, in the police
department, the fire department, in the schools and so on. So the
co-op paid wages of sixteen dollars for the clerks and nineteen
dollars for the managers. Naturally, there were earnings! We told
them, "Now to be fair on this, if you just keep your stubs, we'll
give you a refund. At the beginning, we don't know what it will be."
Of course, many of them never heard anything like this. They said,
"Aw, that's just a joke." So they threw their stubs on the floor of
the various places. The Japanese janitor, who was making sixteen
dollars a month, was one of those who said, "Well, I'll take them at
their word and save these." And he saved. He had three thousand
dollars' worth of these stubs. When it came time at the end of a
quarter or half of the year--I've forgotten which--he counted up his
stubs and presented them. They were able to pay a 10 percent refund.
Well, he had three thousand dollars worth of these stubs, so he got
three hundred dollars! (laughter)

G: Oh!

R: That was news in the Japanese newspaper there, that this man had
gotten a patronage refund of three hundred dollars from the co-op.
(laughter) So it wasn't very difficult to urge the people to save
their stubs from that time on.

G: No! (laughter) Who set the price structure on the goods sold at
the different stores and the different services, like the shop, the
beauty shop, and the grocery store?

R: Well, the board members. After this twenty-five thousand dollar
drive, of course, they had an election to elect a board of directors.
And the board was to set the policy and hire the managers, and the
managers would hire the clerks, barbers, and so on, to supply all
these services. The leaders were business people, and they, of
course, realized that there was no use putting prices too low or
too high. So they tried to find out what was fair under the circumstances. They considered that the people were living in the camp,

getting their food mostly in the mess hall, sleeping in these little barrack rooms, and didn't have a great deal of money, unless they happened to be well-to-do people, as certainly some of them were--at least, there were a few who were in this category. So they set prices fairly. Of course, they had to think about the white government people there, too, because they also patronized this co-op to some extent. They'd go and get their hair cut in this barbershop and things like that. I think we used to get haircuts for about a quarter in those days. My wife went to the beauty shop a time or two, I remember. It was a very modest price compared to today, of course. Still, the people--the board members that had been elected--set the policy of what was fair prices on these things. So far as goods that came from the co-op wholesaler or goods that they had to buy outside, like clothing, they had to pay the regular wholesale prices, of course. So they marked them accordingly. It worked out as a very fair, democratically controlled situation.

G: Were there ever any private enterprises set up anywhere in any of the camps?

R: No. I think not, excepting where some of the people . . . I don't know if it developed there, but in some of the centers, where they were able to get shells from the seaside or the streams, some of the people developed shell craft. And, of course, there were some that were developing art, and ceramics, and things like that, which they sold on their own. That was permitted. But it wasn't possible for a well-to-do man to set up a grocery store inside the camp and charge whatever he chose--that is, after the government had decided that the cooperative would be the best way to prevent a lot of bickering and exploitation. So the cooperatives were well accepted by the whole camp as the best way to supply those things.

G: I've read, too, that the internees used Sears Roebuck catalogs a lot.

R: Yes. That was interesting, too. I haven't thought of this for a long time. But for awhile we had a deal with Montgomery Ward, an ordering service for Montgomery Ward. So one of the co-op services was in a little office, where people could come and look at the Montgomery Ward catalog and order things. The co-op would order them, and then the people would pick up the order there after it was delivered. That got to be quite a difficult thing to do.

G: You had a lot of people going in and ordering that way?

R: That's right, for awhile. I remember one man particularly, a farm boy from California, who was in charge of that. He was having a time trying to satisfy people. Being wartime, of course they couldn't always get just what they wanted. He was trying his very best, in his courteous way, to please people. That man, E. J. Kashiwase, for the last twenty-five years, has been the chief accountant of the Associated

Cooperatives, a wholesale co-op in the Bay Area. So this farm boy got his first introduction to cooperatives there, and he has been in the business as an accountant ever since. (laughter) It's interesting.

G: How were these co-ops accepted by the people in the various camps?

R: Well, I suppose, there were some people that . . . I'm sure that in the beginning the business people said, "Oh, I never heard of this sort of thing." And I'm sure some of them were negative about it. Certainly the men that I had on the board, that were elected and the ones that had been nominated to set up the committee in the first place, were quite open to it. After they debated it and so on, they accepted it very well. Now, there were two groups of people in the center, which was another experience. The fellows from the city here in southern California . . . Some farmers from the valley in the north were not so well-educated, so far as English was concerned. So in the process of getting bylaws and getting established, there was considerable confusion. And the farmers said, "The city slickers are going to run this business, and we are going to get taken." (laughter) They put out the bylaws in English, and the farmers from the north couldn't read the English versions. There was quite a fuss about it. So one day, all of the men on the original organizing committee resigned to the city council. They just said, "Well, if that's the way they feel, here's our resignation." (laughter)

G: Oh, no! (laughter)

R: And the assembly leaders of the town council persuaded them, "No, we want you on there." So they came back on. They said, "Now we have got to have these bylaws all written up in Japanese. This was before we actually had the drive, you see, for the twenty-five thousand dollars. They put those bylaws out all in Japanese. That took another three weeks or a month or so for the print shop, and so on, to do this all in Japanese. After that, it was very smooth. Everybody said, "Well, this is something different."

G: Do you mean that they all accepted the cooperative?

R: They accepted it very well, yes.

G: That's great. In what camps did you set up the co-op?

R: My first job was at Amache, of course. I was there about two years. After the co-op was established and going well, the government authorities felt that they didn't need two government men. My immediate boss was the business head of the enterprises; I was the associate. My job was more educational. After the educational job was done and the co-ops were going successfully, the government asked me to go to Tule Lake Center, which is in northern California.

Of course, that was an entirely different situation. There were ten centers originally. By this time, from all of the ten, the majority of the young men were being drafted and volunteering to go into the Army. But there were a few that were so disillusioned that they said,"We will never again have a free life in America." They were disillusioned, and they began to be very critical. So it worked out that the government set aside Tule Lake as the camp in northern California to send those that were dissenters, that had become so disillusioned with this experience that they wanted to go back to Japan.

G: Could you give me the year that happened?

R: I'm sure it began at least by 1943. Some of the dissenters in the camps were feeling pretty bad about this. They said, "Well, our only chance of a good life is to go back to Japan." So under those circumstances Tule Lake, which had been just one of the ten centers, was changed into a real concentration camp [segregation center], you might say. I remember they had six hundred military men there all the time. They built the fences higher, more guard towers were built, and this sort of thing.

I was sent to help the cooperative that they had in Tule Lake, to replace the co-op enterprises superintendent who resigned. I arrived in June 1944. It was 1944 by this time, because I was at Amache for more than a year. When I got up to Tule Lake, of course, that was a different situation. There was tension, bitter anger, between the project director, Mr. Ray Best, and the people. The people inside the camp were rather furious about situations. They were locked into the camp. They were not allowed to go out into the communities. It was really a concentration camp. And the day I arrived there one man had been shot and killed at the gate. The guard said that the man reached for a gun when he asked him for his pass. Of course, that created tremendous fear and tension among the people and among the project director and the staff. They had cooperative enterprises there, so it was my job to go to the cooperative. It was a new experience for me to get acquainted with those leaders. The cooperative leaders, of course, were probably closer to the staff, the Caucasian staff, than most of the other Japanese people in the center. So we were sort of caught in between some of the angry people in the center and the white, controlling, government people.

G: Was it at Tule Lake that the cooperatives were accused of taking part in graft--both the internees and some of the WRA people?

R: It was a very serious thing, I remember. One thing that I was concerned about, I remember, was that the government people, who were getting good salaries, wanted the Japanese people to provide servants for them, private servants from the camp. And, of course, the co-op people said, "Well, now everybody is getting sixteen dollars in the camp, but why should we supply our young people as servants

for these government people at sixteen or nineteen dollars?" So
quite an argument developed while I was there in Tule Lake as to
what the co-op should do. They'd have it handled through the
co-op. The co-op would hire these people and send them out as
servant people for the staff. But the co-op leaders didn't feel
that they should get away with paying only nineteen dollars a
month. So there was quite an argument between the co-op and the
government leaders as to what they should pay for these people.
I remember, I was involved in that because I thought, "Well, now,
it's not fair for these government people, who are well paid, to
get these people at just slave wages." You see? So I had a little
difficulty with one of the assistant project directors there as
to what was fair on that.

In the meantime, serious things were happening at night. By this
time, some of the young people there were out of the control of
their parents. They were beating people up and trying to develop
fear in order that they all would stand together, have Japanese
schools, and not English taught in the camp; things like this.
It got very tense. Then one night, a sad thing happened. The
manager of the co-op, Mr. Y. Hitomi, an internee of course, was
caught somewhere outside the door, and somebody cut his throat.
He died that night. The tension was terrific. We didn't know whether
he was killed because he had been trying to work with the project
leaders or whether it was because of something else. We never
really learned why this man lost his life. He was a Buddhist. I went
to the funeral--the first time I had ever attended a Buddhist funeral service. It was a sad time and a disturbing time, because we
really had a concentration camp atmosphere there, and it was very unfortunate.

G: At that time did you have any contact with the Spanish Consulate? They
      were supposed to have helped the Japanese Americans in the camps.

R: The Spanish, from Spain, you mean?

G: Yes.

R: I don't know, as I recall there was some foreign group that tried
      to help. But I wasn't close to that at all.

G: I see. You weren't in any of the meetings or negotiations, trying to
      get the camp back to normal.

R: You mean in Tule Lake?

G: Yes.

R: No, I wasn't. It wasn't my job to be directly involved in that. Of
      course, we did have · · · When the death of the co-op manager there

occurred and uprisings like that in the camp, they . . . One assistant project director, Mr. Paul Robertson, was a personal friend of mine, a very religious man. He and I would go into the camp on Sundays and go to church together in the Japanese churches. There were Protestant churches, of course, among the Japanese people. So we were somewhat closer to the people in the center than some of the others. Some of the others were afraid to go, but we felt that the church leaders and the co-op leaders were on our side, so to speak; we understood them, they understood us. So when they had project staff conferences and so on about the conditions in the center, they called upon this assistant project director, and they called upon me, as the co-op supervisor, to give our views of it.

G: Oh, I see.

R: But I don't recall, I wasn't involved at all in any interference with any representative from another country. I do remember, for instance, what an exciting day it was in Amache when the Japanese Red Cross sent supplies in, foodstuffs like soy sauce. Then that was quite exciting to the people, to think that even Japan knew that they were in these camps and had sent some Red Cross goods through. The people were anxious to hear about outside things, because we didn't have television in those days, you see, so we didn't have much opportunity to know very much.

G: Could you tell me what the policy of the WRA was during the war?

R: Well, the main purpose, of course, of the War Relocation Authority was to relocate these people so that they wouldn't be so concentrated as they had been in California and on the West Coast. That was the prime purpose, at least that was the thing that was given to us as the reason why they were gathered into these camps; so that they could be redistributed in other American communities, spread out more. One of the prime purposes, then, was to help these people regain their confidence, to go out into other parts of America and find jobs. Most of them did. It was quite successful. They were well accepted wherever they went. Even though the war was still on, they weren't utterly mistreated or anything. They were fearful that they would be, but they were a very courteous kind of people, and they were well accepted.

G: Did you help in relocating some of your co-op workers?

R: Well, that wasn't my job. Of course, the WRA had a staff of people that were outside in various places--Chicago, New York, and so on--to find openings for the people. My job was to help them with their cooperatives as long as some people remained in the center. Of course, as time went on, the younger people were getting out. The older people were somewhat afraid to go and it was difficult to find jobs for them. So as it went, there were more and more older

people in the camps and fewer young people. My main job was just
to help and advise them, be a go-between in the cooperative enterprises, and to see that those businesses would be carried on successfully and ultimately wound up. I was up in Tule Lake for two
or three months, then I was sent to Washington, D.C.,to be a kind of
auditor supervisor. They called me to go to all of the centers,
nearly all of them. I went to all but the two in Arkansas. It was
my job, then, to be sort of a traveling man, to go to the various
co-ops, meet the leaders, get their financial statements, and report
to Washington as to how successful they were, what problems they
might have, and so on. In the latter part of my stay with the WRA,
my headquarters was supposed to be Washington, but actually I had
an office in Los Angeles, and I traveled from one center to another--
two or three weeks at each one--to work with the co-op people.

G: And this was what period?

R: Well, that lasted right up to the middle of 1945. The co-ops were
being wound up more and more as the people left the centers. They
had to be closed, so it was my job just to see how they were coming
along on their financial problems, so there wouldn't be losses and
unfortunate situations in that way.

G: So you saw the centers, then, just as they were being built and as
they ended.

R: As they were getting ready to close out completely. I didn't stay
on until the complete closeout of them. I was in one of the centers
in Arizona on the day that Japan surrendered. Stocks were being
reduced and the people relocated before V-J Day, August 14, 1945, the
day I left. I'm sure the co-op members got all investments with divi-
dends. I'll never forget V-J Day! (laughter)

G: What happened? Could you tell me about the day? How the people felt
that were still in the center?

R: These were not Japanese people in the sense that they had any relationship to Japan. They were really not any more related to Japan than
my grandfather was related to England, after he came from England and
had lived in this country for many years. They were American people,
and very few had sympathies for Japan. The ones that went to Tule
Lake, of course, were disillusioned, and they felt that they were
Japanese; they didn't want to be American anymore. But I think the
general result of that was that, after the war was over, only a few--
I don't know how many hundred--went back to Japan. But many of the
people that were in Tule Lake, I'm sure, got back into American life
after the thing was over; so it was just disillusionment for most of
them. There were a few hundred, I know, that went back to Japan. They
just gave up and said, "Well, we'd better go back to Japan. That's

our own country." But, for the most part, those were older
people and middle-aged people who had not integrated well into
American life. It was often said that, if the war had occurred
ten years later, this unfortunate camp experience probably never
would have happened, because the older people, the Issei, had been
. . . Well, they came here from Japan, and many of them had not
learned English very well. They lived pretty close to their own
groups, and they weren't very well known in many of the other communities. They lived in their own parts of town, and so on.
People were somewhat suspicious of them, especially if they were in
competition with them in their farm work. That was one reason why,
I think, all of this came about. But the Nisei, the younger
generation, the first generation born in America, were just coming
on. Many of them were just coming out of high school or college,
and they weren't old enough to have a wide influence in American
life. But had it been a few years later, I'm convinced they would
have sold themselves as American people and this thing wouldn't
have happened. The way it worked out, after they came back--they
had all accepted it so well--that they were accepted back. I think
even the Issei people gained property rights, and so on, after the
war was over.

G: So you feel mainly it was based on hysteria due to the war?

R: Yes, there was a lot of hysteria, that's true. And there was
      propaganda, ugly cartoons and so on, against the Japanese people
      because of the sudden attack on Pearl Harbor. It just overwhelmed
      the American people, and made some very terrified about what might
      happen. So it was a sad chapter in American history, but I think
      the Japanese Americans came through in a very heroic way. They
      accepted the situation and many things were bitter to them; but they
      took it. We often said, there in the Amache camp, that if we had
      gathered up a bunch of Kansas farmers, just east from there, and
      put them in a camp like that, we would have had some terrific brawls
      and murders and everything you can imagine. The Japanese keep very
      good control of their children, and they have good family lives.
      So we had very few incidents like that in my experience, except in
      Tule Lake, where things got out of hand, partly because of the close
      military surveillance there--they just were not allowed out of the
      camp. They were prisoners indefinitely, and they didn't know how
      long it was going to last. They didn't know how the war was going
      to go, and so everything was really a frightening situation.

G: Do you believe that the family structure of the Japanese Americans
      broke down somewhat with their internment?

R: I doubt it very much--not in the nine centers. In the Tule Lake
      camp, it was obvious that some of the young hoodlums there were
      out of control of their parents. And they were frightening their
      own people, and threatening and brawling. And, of course, this
      man was killed. We just figured that probably some bitter young man

had done that. But in the other centers, I wasn't too close
to the people, except in Amache, in that way. But I didn't see
much evidence that family life broke down at all.

G: How about the morale and the attitudes of the people during the
      course of the years? Did you find that that was breaking down?

R: You mean after they came back, in 1945, when they got out?

G: Yes.

R: Well, some of them suffered, of course. They would come home
      and find their goods had been stolen. They had stored them away,
      and there had been thefts; there'd been losses, and so on. They
      felt real sad about it, but so far as I know, the ones I've visited
      since then took it in very good stride. I've always found them to
      be a very courteous, a fine kind of people.

G: And throughout their internment in the nine camps, except for Tule
      Lake, their morale kept fairly high?

R: Yes, I think it did. Yes, and even many of them were quite patriotic,
      in sending their boys off to the Army, and so on. Of course, as
      everyone knows, the Japanese American boys--particularly from Hawaii--
      were in one special group that was over in Italy. They were a rather
      heroic type of people. The Japanese people followed that group, of
      course, with great interest.

G: Were you involved, during this time, as a Quaker?

R: Actually, I was a Methodist in Albuquerque and also a conscientious
      objector. I was unhappy when the Methodist Church voted, in Kansas
      City or somewhere, there in a big conference during the war. By
      just one vote, they decided that they would bless the war, so to
      speak. I was disillusioned with that, so I never remained in the
      Methodist Church. And as I traveled about for the various centers,
      I was able to visit the Quakers in Washington. The Florida Street
      Meeting in Washington was my first experience in a Quaker meeting.
      I remember particularly a fine old gentleman there was really giving
      us a terrific talk about the destruction of Dresden. Just a day or
      two before, the beautiful city of Dresden had been bombed, into the
      earth, practically, by American planes. He was, of course, very sad
      about that. So this experience in the relocation center caused me,
      of course, to think about these things more than I would have if I
      had stayed where I was before the war. It led me also to California.
      The young Japanese American people were always getting the football
      games on the radio in these centers, and I learned a lot more about
      California through that. (laughter) Then after coming to Tule Lake,
      of course, I decided that I'd like to come to Whittier, which is an
      old Quaker town. I've been here all these years since then.

G: So you were, of course, aware that the Quakers were helping at
     this time?

R: Yes. The Quakers sent people around from the American Friends
     Service Committee. Occasionally there would be somebody who came to
     the camps to try to understand the situation and meet with people
     there who were concerned along that line. And that brought me
     more in touch with that. So when I came to Whittier, one of the
     first things we did, of course, was to become members of the Friends
     Church. It was a fine experience for me to find that this was
     a church, even during the war, in which the minister was concerned
     about the conscientious objectors and the camps that they were in,
     as much as he was about the young men from the church who were in the
     Army. I didn't find that concern in most of the other churches at
     that time.

G: As a teacher, I wonder if you could comment on the schools in the
     camps?

R: Well, I wasn't too close to them. I got to know the superintendent
     of the school in Amache. They were trying to conduct a good American
     high school there, just as they would in any American community.
     The Japanese American children were greatly encouraged by their
     parents to do well in school, and they did. They were a fine bunch
     of students. As a whole, I would say, they were probably better
     than most students normally would be--that is, an average group
     of students--because they were encouraged by their parents to really
     succeed with their schooling.

G: In visiting the ten centers, did you observe the attitudes of the
     communities near each of these centers in the different states?

R: Well, the camp that I knew most, of course, was there in Colorado.
     There was a very small town right next to the camp--Granada, Colorado.
     It was just a small place, and some of those people were a little
     frightened by eight thousand people coming up on the hill above their
     town and taking over some of the bottom land. On the Arkansas River,
     there was the agricultural project for the Japanese. Some of the farmers
     had sold land to this government project, and they were worried about
     it and a little fearful, I think. But it wasn't long until the
     Japanese made friends with them, and pretty soon one man--his name was
     Tsuchia, I think--who had been a butcher, got a job in one of the stores
     in town. He also knew the fish business. They brought in fish, which
     I'm sure they never had had in that store before, and they brought
     in other meats. The town boomed, in a sense, because some of the Japa-
     nese people couldn't very well buy this in the co-op. We didn't
     push that sort of thing because the people were provided with their
     food in the mess hall. But if they wanted to buy a nice big fish,
     they had to go out of the camp and go down to the fish store, and
     things like that. So the Japanese, as they could find jobs out in

the local community, or nearby, or way off, were encouraged in every way to get out. So they were accepted quite well.

G: In Amache, then, the people could get out of the camp and go into the local town?

R: Oh, well, a few of them in the beginning. Then as time went on and the townspeople began to say, "Oh, well, these are just people the same as anybody else," and they weren't frightened, and then they were allowed to go out more; they were encouraged to go out more, especially if they could get jobs on the farms up and down the valley. So they were doing anything they could, of course, to encourage them to get out and find jobs on the outside. The people around the communities said, "Oh well, these are just Japanese American people. They're not Japs from Japan." (laughter) So as rapidly as they learned that . . . why, the resettlement process was going on all the time, you see.

I remember one experience down in Arizona: I went out one night to a restaurant with some Japanese people from the co-op group. Boy! The air was so intense there. You could just tell they thought, "Well, these are Japs. These are our enemies." We were afraid that they were going to hit us over the head before we could finish our meal! But nobody lifted a hand or did anything to offend anybody. We finally were allowed to eat and go. But I think I felt a little bit like a black man in the South must have felt eating in a white establishment, because you could tell there was fear, and there was hate in the eyes of some of the people around us. And they think, "Oh, there's one of these white men with them, too. What kind of a guy is he?" (laughter) You see.

G: How about in the community near Tule Lake camp?

R: Well, at Tule Lake they did not allow internees out of the camp because they took the attitude, "Well, these people are enemy people. They want to go back to Japan." So they did not allow them out. Of course, when Tule Lake first opened up, it was just one of the relocation camps. I'm sure the internees had some contact with people outside then. But I had to take the money from the co-op and drive into Klamath Falls every day because they didn't allow a Japanese man to do it. The administration was a little fearful that somebody would beat him up or something, so they were not allowed out. Of course, that made for intense feelings on the inside, because they felt that they were prisoners of war, you see. I don't know what the people around Tule Lake felt because I never saw them in contact with Japanese people there very much.

G: Can you cite any examples of Quaker involvement?

R: Yes. The American Friends Service Committee was very conscious of these centers. From time to time, they sent people to try to understand the situation. I remember Herbert Nicholson was one of the men who came occasionally. I saw him only recently, a very elderly man now, still rather excited about what he was able to do to comfort the people and to try and help them adjust. I remember some of the administrative leaders were a little worried when Herb Nicholson came, because he would sympathize with the people so much that the administration felt that they were being pitied a little too much, or something. They were afraid something would happen, but nothing ever did. The people needed friends, and they appreciated that. Many of the Japanese American people were church-minded people. I remember in Amache particularly that there were many different sects that wanted to have a church of their own. The assistant project director was a strong church man, but he had to sort of bear down, and he said, "Now, we've got only about thirty mess halls in this barrack city. And we can't spare too many of these mess halls for churches." So, he met again and again with them. They finally agreed that they would have one mess hall that was for all the Catholics, another for the Protestants. My wife and I often went to those meetings. One Sunday we might have a Japanese Methodist speaking, and the next time it might be an evangelist of some sort. They were very cooperative in just taking their turns in these various churches, you know. So it was an interesting experience from that angle.

G: Did the people feel abandoned by the general American public?

R: Well, I'm sure they felt isolated, and at first they surely felt mistreated. I heard stories of how they were mistreated here at Santa Anita, for instance. When they were first gathered up, they were gathered up in a very few days, very much like some of the Russian Jews were gathered up according to the show Fiddler on the Roof, which I just happened to see the other day. In that case, the people were given three days to leave. Now, I don't remember how many days the Japanese people had, but it was very short notice. Some from California were moved to the Santa Anita racetrack. They lived in the stalls where the horses had been. They had to clean those out and try to live there for several weeks, I think, while these centers were being built. One of my Japanese friends that was a leader in the co-op said, "Boy! It was pretty hard for me to see my old dad in one of those stalls. When they brought the food in, they just put it down on the floor and kicked it in under the door." So, some of the treatment at the beginning was very rugged and very alarming to the people. They didn't know whether they were going to be treated just like the Jews had been treated in Germany. But, of course, it never came to anything that extreme.

G: Was this initial movement into the camp at Santa Anita handled by the WRA?

R: No, that was done by the military. I think it was an order from the military that this be done, and they were brought into those places and kept there until such time as these barrack towns could be

built out in the deserts. That was another thing that was pretty
dreary for the Japanese people: they love flowers and plants, and
here they were put out into the driest parts of the country, you
know. Where the wind blew such dust storms, and cold winters, and
so on, that they were not used to. But, as I said earlier, they
came through with flying colors. They just did better than most
any group of American people, I think, would have done under such
stress. I'm very sorry that our country did this to them, but I
hope it will always be a lesson to us not to use such methods in
dealing with people. Because we're all people, and we all act
pretty much the same under various stresses of life. We need to
find a more humane way to treat each other.

G: I have a couple of final questions. Was Amache the first center
to have a cooperative or were there other camps that established
co-ops simultaneously? For instance, was there at Manzanar and
Poston, say, other men who had jobs comparable to yours? Do you know
any of their names? Was there any coordination of co-op policies
between the different camps? Was that your boss's job?

R: There was a superintendent and associate superintendent of the Cooperative Business Enterprises in each of the ten centers beginning
in 1942. Two or three times in the next two years both government
and co-op board members had co-op conferences. I remember one in
Salt Lake City and another in Arizona. Mr. Hugh H. Anderson, my
friend, still was the co-op enterprises superintendent at Poston,
Arizona. He manages a $2,000,000 San Gabriel Valley Postal Credit
Union in Alhambra, California, today. Mr. Lee C. Poole was another
co-op superintendent; he was at Manzanar for awhile.

G: Mr. Runcorn, do you think there is anything else we should discuss,
or do you think that we have coverered everything?

R: I think we've covered it enough from my point of view. (laughter)
I appreciate this opportunity to dig back and do this. It did a
lot in my life, I'm sure. It was exciting, as I say, for young
Americans to get government jobs like that, where we had a challenge.
It changed my life. As a result of that, I moved to California in
1944, and as soon as the government job ended I arranged a job as
field man for Associated Co-ops, which was the co-op wholesale here
in California. I did that for four years, as a field man, then I
moved into the credit union movement. So for the last twenty-three
years, I've been managing the Whittier Citizens Credit Union here
in the community. It is that office that we've been meeting in for
this interview today.

G: Well, thank you very much.

R: You're welcome.

END OF INTERVIEW

Aerial view of the Granada War Relocation Center, Amache, Colorado, in 1943, where Mr. Runcorn served as associate superintendent of the Cooperative Enterprises from 1942 to 1944.

The patronage refund booth offered rebates
to the internees from the profits of the
cooperative stores.

This photograph was taken at an inter-cooperative conference
in Salt Lake City, Utah, in 1945. Mr. Runcorn, who was then a
general auditor-supervisor, is seated in the front row center;
his wife, Mary Lee, is to his left. Seated directly behind the
Runcorns is Mr. Charles Belt, supervisor for the Poston Cooperative. Third from left in the top row is Mr. N. Kurita, Granada
Cooperative Board member; in front of Mr. Kurita, and to his
right, is Mr. K. Koda, president of the Granada Cooperative
Board.

A young Sansei--third generation
Japanese American--pictured in a
field at the Granada War Relocation
Center, Amache, Colorado.

Meals were served in mess halls such as
the one pictured here at the Granada War
Relocation Center.

Index

An Interview with
PAUL G. ROBERTSON
Conducted by Arthur A. Hansen and Reagan J. Bell
on August 12, 1987
for the
California State University, Fullerton
Oral History Program
Japanese American Project

(War Relocation Authority Administration, O.H. 1937)

This is a slightly edited transcription of an interview conducted for the Oral History Program, sponsored by the California State University, Fullerton. The reader should realize that an oral history document is spontaneous in nature, and portrays information and impressions as recalled by the interviewee.

Scholars are welcome to utilize short excerpts from any of the transcriptions without obtaining permission as long as proper credit is given to the interviewee, the interviewer, and the University. Scholars must, however, obtain permission from the Oral History Program at California State University, Fullerton before making more extensive use of the transcription and related materials. None of these materials may be duplicated or reproduced by any party without permission from the Oral History Program, California State University, Fullerton, California, 92634.

CALIFORNIA STATE UNIVERSITY, FULLERTON

ORAL HISTORY PROGRAM

Japanese American Project

INTERVIEWEE: PAUL G. ROBERTSON

INTERVIEWERS: Arthur A. Hansen and Reagan J. Bell

SUBJECT: War Relocation Authority Administration

DATE: 12 August 1987

H: This is an interview with Mr. Paul G. Robertson, who during World War II served the War Relocation Authority (WRA) both as the director of the Leupp Isolation Center in Arizona and as an assistant director of the Tule Lake Segregation Center in California.[1] The interview is being done for the Japanese American Project of the Oral History Program at California State University, Fullerton. The interviewers are Arthur A. Hansen and Reagan J. Bell. The interview is taking place on August 12, 1987, in the home of Mr. Robertson, at 4800 Oakfield Circle, in Carmichael, California. The time of the interview is approximately 10:30 a.m.

Mr. Robertson, you were kind enough, prior to this interview, to send us a thumbnail sketch in the form of a resolution presented to you by the senate of the state of California in 1969 on the completion of your service with the California Department of Agriculture. With it you sent me a letter which indicated something about your background prior to going to work for the state. But what we don't have is anything about your life up to the time that you were at Yale University and received a Bachelor of Fine Arts degree in 1929. So we would appreciate it if you could take a little time and talk about, not only your own early life, but your family background as well, both on your mother's side and on your father's side, and tell us a little bit about where you were brought up, when you were born, those types of considerations.

R: How far back do you want to go?

H: As far back as you possibly can go.

R: I was born in Arkansas City, Kansas, on November 18, 1903. My father, James Albert Robertson, was a railroad man, a train dispatcher. Both my grandfathers were ministers. On my father's side was a Christian minister, Richard Swanson Robertson; on my mother's side was a Methodist minister, Levi Gifford. So I was born in a Christian home and raised in a Christian home.

Being a railroad man, my father moved the family many times. In my real younger days, our home was in Marion, Illinois; Carbondale, Illinois;

and Chester, Illinois. This was in my elementary school days. Then I started in the first year of high school in Carbondale, Illinois, and my father was moved to Birmingham, Alabama. I moved to Birmingham for my sophomore year of high school. I don't know how long we were in Birmingham, but we moved from there to El Reno, Oklahoma, and this was where I graduated from high school. My brother and I, during school vacations, did house painting, contracted in house painting. I also worked for the Chicago Rock Island Pacific Railroad on a paint gang. Then we moved to Saint Louis, Missouri, and in Saint Louis I had a job as a street inspector, an inspector of new construction in streets. I did some graduate work, high school work there. I don't know what it was I took, but I went from there into Washington University in Saint Louis. My brother, Maurice Robertson, was in the architectural department there, so that's where I followed him. I was very active in the Union Methodist Church in Saint Louis, teaching Sunday school, singing in the choir. I spent two years in Washington University. My brother graduated from there in architecture. My father worked in the printing business and was in the printing business all the time we were in Saint Louis.

I got permission to go to Yale [University in New Haven, Connecticut]. You know, you have to send your resume and everything back to Yale before they'll accept you. And so I was accepted to enter my junior year at Yale School of Architecture. During my junior year, I met my wife, and we were married. She continued working, put me through my senior year. I graduated from Yale in 1929, with a Bachelor of Fine Arts degree.

I worked for the state of Connecticut in the highway department between school years. It's getting pretty hazy now. Then I worked for the New York, New Haven, and Hartford Railroad in survey work. I had to keep commuting back and forth to New York from New Haven. During my school years at Yale, I sang in the glee club, traveled with the glee club. I waited tables in the commissary for my tuition. And I was assistant to the pastor of Trinity Methodist Episcopal Church in New Haven [Connecticut], Reverend Roland Hill. Matter of fact, I lived in his home. When I first got to New Haven, I was trying to find a place to live, and I went first to him. He called around to various places and he said, "Well, why don't you come stay with us?" So I stayed right there till I was married. Of course, he married us.

After I graduated, I went to work with Sargent Hardware, a manufacturing company. That was the big manufacturing company in New Haven at the time. My wife [Harriette Anthony] had been a secretary for one of the vice-presidents at Sargent's, R. B. Gerard, and he got me a job. I established, through him, an annual meeting of the [Yale] graduates in architecture. Sargent Hardware gave them a big dinner, and gave them souvenirs and stuff, just to establish contact between architectural industry and the department of architecture at the university. I don't know whether they still do that or not. It's years ago, but at that time we got it established. Then the Depression hit. Well, I guess before the Depression hit, I was sent to California by Sargent Hardware Company. I got out here, and the Depression hit. And I was without work. We moved down on the ocean with my sister and parents, both. We occupied this tremendous house down there right on the beach.

H: Where on the ocean was this?

R: Playa del Rey [on the coast of southern California south of Los Angeles]. We had a house with four bathrooms and, I think, about six bedrooms. I went into the real estate business. This was during the Depression, you know, after I got laid off. I've got letters in there from R. Gerard, very complimentary letters, for my service at Sargent, saying how it was difficult to train men and then have to lose them because of the Depression.

"Fritz" Fitzgerald was the fellow I worked for in the real estate. During that time, one of the big producers at MGM [Metro-Goldwyn-Mayer] came by the real estate office. I was there alone. He wanted to look at some places for vacation. I took him around. He said, "Get in the car and drive with me." He took me back to MGM, and told the girl, "Make out a check from Buster Keaton's account." So I rented a place to Buster Keaton. During the same time, Charlie Chaplin and Paulette Goddard came by, and I took them through a house. So I had some good experiences there, and made some contacts at MGM. So my wife and I both did a little work at MGM, got acquainted with people there. And I very nearly got into the movies. Are you interested in this?

H: Yes, I certainly am. Please continue.

R: When this producer took me up to his office for the Buster Keaton account, I said, "Next time you need somebody--a singer, an actor--give me a chance." And he said, "Why, do you sing?" I said, "Yes." He said, "Walk over to the end of the room there and then walk back toward me. Next time you feel in the mood, come and see us." So it wasn't very long till I was back there, and they wouldn't let me in downstairs. They thought I was pulling a fast one. But he finally called upstairs. He said, "Sure, send him on up." I remember, when I was waiting to interview him, John Gilbert came in. Now that's an old-timer. He gave me a letter and told me to go over and see the casting director. I took the letter over. I didn't open it, but I handed it to the girl. She said, "Did you see this letter?" And I said, "No." She said, "Well, it was very complimentary." So the fellow who was the casting director took me in and said, "What would you like to do?" I said, "I'd like to do a scene from The Cuban Love Song. So he went out and got the scripts for The Cuban Love Song, and I took it home. He was going to call me for a screen test. He said, "When we get a prospect for a girl, we'll call you in." Time went on and on, and they didn't call, didn't call, didn't call. Oh, I did go over and have my voice tested, and I sang for them. I called him back, and he was just very discouraging. He said, "Robertson, you've got a good job. We haven't got any girls in here yet. I wouldn't get too excited about this. Just take it easy. You hang onto what you've got." Hinsdale, that was the guy's name. Oliver Hinsdale. I remember it. I just put that in the back of my mind, forgot it. But I learned later that this guy Hinsdale, that was his approach to young people coming in. He said in this article I read, that anybody who was born to be an actor, that wouldn't stop them. He says you couldn't discourage them. They'd just keep coming, coming, coming. So that's the way I was eliminated from that. I guess if I'd have pushed it, I could probably have gotten in. But I'm glad now that I didn't, because one of the fellows who was my pressman, Eddy Eckles, when I worked for WRA [War Relocation Authority]--he dealt with all of the newspaper reporters, and he had been with MGM--said I didn't know how lucky I was to get out of that. He said, "That's an awful life." So that part of my life I was glad I bypassed.

My sister, Alberta Robertson Gattone, was a deputy attorney general in the state of California. And she told me there was a job coming up in [the Department of] Agriculture. And she knew the chief of the division, who was C. J. Carey. He hired me as investigator in the Bureau of Market Enforcement [Market Enforcement Branch]. He was a bureau chief, that's what he was. Of course, eventually, I had to take the civil service examination. I worked in there from 1933 until 1942. In due course, I became district supervisor. I got real well acquainted with the state director of agriculture, William B. Parker. We went to a big Japanese blowout. We were the only two Caucasians there, the director of agriculture and myself.

H: By that you mean a big party that they had?

R: A big party that they had for the director and for me.

H: Where was that?

R: It was in Los Angeles. And that's where I got real well acquainted with the director. He later was the one that got me into WRA, because R. B. Cozzens, who was the regional director up here in San Francisco in WRA, had come to him and said that they were looking for someone to help out in the regional office. Mr. Parker called me and told me he'd already talked to Cozzens about me, so I flew up to San Francisco, and they hired me. I left the state service and went into WRA. That was when the ban was on. That must have been 1942.

H: Now, was Cozzens the regional director, or was he the assistant to [E. R. Si] Fryer at the time you joined up with the regional office?

R: I remember the name Si Fryer, but I didn't know him.

H: E. R. Fryer was the director of the San Francisco Regional Office, and previously he had been the superintendent of the Navajo reservation.

R: I guess Cozzens was his assistant.

H: But Fryer later left his position with WRA, so perhaps by the time that you got into it, Cozzens was the head of it. Okay. I know both of these men served stints as acting director over at the Gila [River Relocation Center] camp for a little while [in late 1942], when the WRA was looking for a replacement for Eastwood Smith who had resigned as director after only a couple of months of service in that capacity.

R: I don't know how long I was at San Francisco. It's difficult to remember the length of time. But I was called back to Washington to work in the Leave Clearance Program. I wish I could remember names, but it's difficult now.

H: Was it Rowalt?

R: Oh, yes. I remember Elmer Rowalt. He died, didn't he?

H: I'm not sure.

R: I think Elmer died. Of course, we worked on the release of people from the camps to go to work in industry around in the East. And I substituted on the Leave Clearance Board [Japanese American Joint Board] that was composed of G-2, the Army and the Navy Intelligence, and the WRA. I've forgotten who my immediate boss was, but he served on the board; and whenever he couldn't go, I went to the board. A guy that wore a coonskin cap, and I can't remember his name.

H: This was the fellow in charge of the Leave Clearance Board back at the Washington office of WRA?

R: He was my boss. I know he was not completely in charge. Thomas W. Holland was chief of the employment division.

H: The only person I've talked to about that is a woman by the name of Charlotte [Dixon] Brown, who married [Robert L.] Bob Brown, who was an assistant director at the Manzanar War Relocation Center in California [see O.H. 1375].

R: What was Charlotte's name before she got married to Brown?

H: I don't remember.

R: I've got a letter from her [in Robertson's WRA file], but it's just signed "Charlotte."

H: She lives now in Laguna Hills, down in Orange County [California].

R: Oh, she does. If you ever see her, tell her I said hello.

H: I will.

R: I knew her very well. I used to pick her up and take her to work once in awhile.

Now then, how in the world did I get into Leupp [Isolation Center in Arizona]? I guess that after a conference, Dillon [S.] Myer [WRA national president] sent me down there. Ray Best was the director at Leupp then, and the riot was just starting up at Tule Lake. And Myer was taking Ray Best out of Leupp to be the director at Tule. And I went down for, I guess, a week or two, to indoctrinate myself before he left, and get myself established, and get my family and my furniture moved from Washington, D.C. back to Leupp.

H: What was the size of your family at that time?

R: We had two children. Both of them were born in Los Angeles. One of them, Carol Louise, was born in 1933, and the other one, Judith Annette, was born four years later, in 1937. So they were both with us in Washington and at Leupp. They went to a little one-room school there in Leupp. They had several Indian fellows working around there. I used to take the fellows into Winslow [Arizona] for medical and, occasionally, dental work. But at the project itself, I'd go over when the fellows were sick or not feeling good. I'd go over into the compound and give them a rubdown, feed them aspirin, take their temperature. I was more of a father figure, I guess, than anything else.

H: Let me backtrack and fill in some details on your earlier life before proceeding too deeply into your experiences at Leupp, okay?

R: Surely.

H: You said that both of your grandfathers were ministers, but that your father went into railroad work. Was that because your father had reacted against the church?

R: No, I don't think so. You know, generally, preachers' kids don't follow in their father's footsteps. Usually they have to show themselves to be not as religious. They have to be sort of "macho" [i.e., stridently manly]. No. Dad was very close to his father, my grandfather. But he just wasn't interested, I guess, in preaching. He was always active in church. He sang in the choir.

H: So you didn't have a disjunction in the family in terms of a Christian background and a non-Christian one?

R: No. Matter of fact, I have a genealogy of my whole family that goes clear back to Cherokee Indian blood somewhere down the line.

H: You lived for awhile in the South, in Birmingham, and you also lived, actually in the Southwest, in El Reno, Oklahoma, where you graduated from high school. Later on you were going to work with an ethnic minority that's being discriminated against by public policy, and certainly you saw much of the same sort of discrimination, if not in El Reno, then certainly in Birmingham. I was just wondering what kind of impact this had on you, both as a young man who was brought up in Illinois and as a person who had a Christian background.

R: I can't say that it had any particular effect. I was in George R. Stewart's church in Birmingham--southern Methodist. And I played several instruments in the band there, both in high school and in college--saxophone and slide trombone. Played them all by ear. I can't see the ethnic influence at all.

H: I was just concerned if you were alerted to discrimination, manifestly so, in the South.

R: No, I don't think so. The reason I got into this work [WRA administration] was because I had dealt with the Japanese in my agricultural work. The produce market--dealers and farmers--was probably pretty close to half-Japanese, and I got real well acquainted with a lot of Japanese people in the produce business. And the reason that the director referred me to Cozzens is because I had a connection with the Japanese people in southern California.

H: I wasn't suggesting that because you lived in the South and been aware of racial prejudice that this predisposed the WRA to hire you. What I was suggesting was that you had become closely familiar with prejudice and the corrosive effects of prejudice, and that that might have predisposed you to these effects in your dealings with Japanese Americans, whether you're working for the state of California or whether you're working for the federal government through the WRA.

R: I don't think I was even aware of prejudice in Alabama, or in Oklahoma. It didn't enter my mind.

H: So the segregated system in Alabama wasn't something that hit you over the head?

R: No.

H: Okay. You were at Saint Louis, in Washington University, and you were in the architectural program there, and also active in the Methodist Church. You said you had a brother [Maurice] who graduated in architecture, and then later you mentioned a sister [Alberta] who must have had a law background or something.

R: Oh, yes.

H: Maybe you could tell us just a little about your brother and sister.

R: My brother's name was Maurice, but he called himself "Maureece" after he got into the architectural business. When we were kids, it was Morris. After, it was Maureece. He was twenty months older than I. He was much larger than I and, consequently, sort of my protector, you know, as we were growing up. He was a big guy. He was just really getting going--he had a rotogravure section of the Los Angeles Times with his architectural work spread out--when he had a heart attack and died. He had his headquarters in Palos Verdes [an affluent California community on the coast south of Los Angeles]. That's where he had his office.

My sister Alberta went to Southern Illinois Normal University first, then she went to Marquette University. And then she went to southern California. Her husband was a professor in southern California. His name was Belford. He went to a football game, got pneumonia, and died. Subsequently, she married a certified public accountant, Edmond Gattone, so that between them they had the law and the accounting business. Actually, he was a lawyer, too; he was a lawyer and a CPA. They're both retired and both living in Santa Barbara, [California] now.

H: Did you go to Yale for any particular family reason? Or was it just because of its school of architecture?

R: It was because of the school of architecture. My brother said, "Well, why don't we get you into one of the large schools on the East Coast? Yale has an excellent architectural school." He was in New York at the time. I'm trying to think of what that big church was that he helped work on back there. Oh yes, it was the Riverside Church. Anyway, he was there in New York when I got into Yale.

H: Your grandfathers, obviously, were college graduates if they were ministers. Was your father also a college graduate?

R: No, he wasn't. He attended Texas Christian University, but I don't think he graduated. My uncle, Walter Robertson, was an oil man, and he was a Thirty-third Degree Mason. My dad's family was pretty close. There were quite a group of them. I've got a picture of the whole family in there [the family photo album]. There must be four sisters and two or three brothers; it was a good-size family. And they were very close. Of course, they're all gone now.

H: Did your immediate family just consist of your brother, your sister, and yourself, the three of you?

R: No. I had a younger brother, Byron, and a sister, Mildred, who died very young, two or three years old; they died within a couple of months of each other.

H: So, effectively, you grew up in a family of three children.

R: Yes, that's right.

H: You met your wife in your junior year. Yale didn't have women students at that time, did it?

R: No.

H: So you met her in New Haven?

R: Yes. I met her in church.

H: I didn't get her name, either.

R: Harriette. H-A-R-R-I-E-T-T-E.

H: That's an unusual spelling of that name, isn't it?

R: Yes. Harriette Anthony was her maiden name.

H: And she was then working.

R: Yes. She was working for the New Haven Sandblast Company. Mr. Gerard was there at the time. She went to Larson's School for Girls [a private school] in New Haven. But I went to a church with this minister's son I was living with, and another fellow. The three of us went to this dance at the Congregational Church. And before I went into the church, I saw my wife and a couple of girls in the window, and I said, "Boy, there's a cute girl. I'm going to take her home." Sure enough, I did. She came with some other guy, but I took her home. I married her. One of the other fellows married another girl that was there at the dance. And the preacher's son proposed to another one, but she turned him down.

H: (Laughter) That was quite a night.

R: Yes, quite a night.

H: You graduated in 1929 with a B.A. in Fine Arts. A lot of schools of architecture programs are five years, and you got a B.A. in Fine Arts. Did you leave architecture before you graduated?

R: No. My fine arts degree was in architecture.

H: Okay. Then you went to work for the state of Connecticut Highway Department. Is this because we were already getting, really, the effects of the Depression and there were no jobs in architecture?

R: That was architecture.

H: It was.

R: Yes. It was drafting.

H: Okay. And then, also, when you were working for the New York New Haven Hartford Railroad, it was survey work, and that was drafting, too.

R: Yes. It was drafting, and it was actually fieldwork, too, surveying.

H: You were really into architectural work. I mean, you graduated and got a job, duly, in that field, and then when you got with Sargent Hardware

Company, that was also architectural work. You then came out to California.

R: I came out to California from Sargent's in sales work, really. I'd been through all the branches of manufacturing of Sargent Hardware. They sent me out here to work under a fellow by the name of E. F. Brittingham, who was [the Pacific Coast representative] in charge of California. Then the Depression hit, and I didn't have a job.

H: But you ended up living in a very palatial house in Playa del Rey. I'm wondering how, with the loss of a job, you all of a sudden found yourself living in a residence that I can't afford right now with a job. (laughter)

R: Well, my dad was in business and my sister had an income, and I went into real estate there. That home was owned by the . . . You know, the federal setup where they loaned money and then took homes back? I've forgotten what the . . . Like FHA [Federal Housing Administration] but it wasn't FHA. It was before. HOLC [Home Owners Loan Corporation], I think.

H: The precursor to FHA, okay.

R: And that home was owned by the government. So with our incomes, we were able to manage.

H: And then you almost got a chance at Hollywood, and then you said that through your sister, who was a deputy attorney general of California, you heard about this job that was coming up in Agriculture. Then you moved into something I doubt if you had any experience for, investigative work with the Bureau of Market Enforcement.

R: I went to Southwestern Law School for three years.

H: When did you do that, while you were working in real estate?

R: While I was working with the state. I got the job and knew that law would be a big help to me, so I went to night school.

H: When you said you went to law school for three years, does that mean that you did not pass the bar exam in California?

R: No. I never did even take the bar exam.

H: So you just took some legal coursework to help you in your job.

R: I took three years of law. I took constitutional law and torts. I took the things that I needed.

H: Why don't you tell us about your job as an investigator for the Bureau of Market Enforcement, precisely what it is that you did, and the degree to which this put you in contact with Japanese Americans.

R: We licensed the produce dealers. If a produce dealer made a contract with a farmer and there was an argument between the farmer and the produce dealer, the farmer would file a complaint with the Department of Agriculture. We would investigate it first. We'd get all the facts together. This is where the investigator came in. Then they would have a hearing and determine who was wrong. I think that a big part of my work was investigating fellows who were in the produce business without a license and taking them to court, prosecuting them for operating without license. So this was a big part of the work. That, in a gist, was what we did.

H: And to what extent did this get you involved with Japanese Americans?

R: Well, all those Japanese fellows were licensed, and I was in and out of there. I was down in the produce market all the time, in and out, and knew a lot of the fellows. Nearly every produce dealer down there, whether he's Mexican or Caucasian or what, I knew an awful lot of the fellows.

H: Did this put you in touch with, like, the Tenth Street Market and the City Market in Los Angeles?

R: Yes.

H: Was your area of coverage Los Angeles County exclusively, or did you go down to Orange County and San Diego?

R: Southern California.

H: Out into Imperial County as well?

R: Yes.

H: So wherever you were going, actually, you had contact with Japanese Americans.

R: That's right.

H: Okay. Did southern California take in Santa Barbara County, or was that regarded as being in central California?

R: No. We came up as far as the small town of Earlimart. You know where Earlimart is?

H: No. Is that Ventura County?

R: No, that's above Bakersfield [about thirty-eight miles]; that's Kern County. We had Kern County and we had Santa Barbara County. That's about where it was, though, right across there and south.

H: So you were traveling a lot, then, during that time in your work.

R: Yes. Now, when did I come to Sacramento? Oh, that was after the war. That's when I came up here and took on the whole state. That was after the ban on Japanese Americans living in California was lifted.

H: As a curiosity, did you, when you were at Leupp, meet any people that you had already met prior to the war in your capacity working for agriculture?

R: Not at Leupp, no. None of the fellows at Leupp were fellows that I'd had contact with before.

H: Or their families? Like the Oishi family, say, from Guadalupe [Santa Barbara County]?

R: No. I don't think I had anybody who was . . . Of course, I corresponded with the fellows that were in other camps, but none of them were sent to Leupp. Leupp was for incorrigibles, you know; they were supposed to be the bad boys.

H: So you worked, then, from 1933 to 1942, and finally you became district supervisor for the Bureau of Market Enforcement.

R: Sometime in that period, yes.

H: And this district that we're talking about is precisely southern California, then.

R: Yes.

H: You talked about attending this big Japanese blowout, or party, in Los Angeles, and how you got well acquainted with this fellow who was in a position to recommend you to Cozzens at the WRA's regional office in San Francisco. What did you do in San Francisco at the regional office? What was your capacity up there?

R: I'm trying to think. I wasn't there very long. It was in the agricultural field. As I recall, it was coordinating the agriculture operations in the various camps, finding outlets for produce, railroads and tariffs, this sort of thing.

H: You were in a rather unique position during the time interval spanning Pearl Harbor and the actual evacuation of the Japanese Americans to be able to understand what the Japanese people were going through, since such a preponderance of them were farmers.

R: You ought to read some of the letters I've got.[2]

H: Okay. Can you give us some insight into that particular time frame and what was going on in terms of your life and your work vis-a-vis the Japanese American farmers?

R: They were frightened. The younger people were astonished and rebellious. That's a bad word. They were shocked that, having been brought up in a democracy, all of a sudden everything they'd learned about freedom was yanked out from under them. On the other hand, there were some of them who felt more secure. With all this antagonism that was going around, they felt more protected. Here the government was pulling them out from all this turmoil, and some of the older people, I think, felt that way. I think I agreed with them. Personally, I felt it was a travesty of justice. That's about it, I think.

H: Did you have to serve as any kind of go-between with some of these people that you did know? They were dealing with the Farm Security Administration and trying to get their properties protected and leased, and in some cases get their harvests in and everything.

R: No. I had some letters from some of them, just telling me what they'd done, but not asking. Well, one lawyer there, Frank Kito, kept asking me to do things for him. He was an attorney. He was a good friend of mine, and he was trying to pull strings, but there was nothing I could do for him.

H: I just thought they might have turned to you in that instance on two grounds--one, your familiarity with their legal situation, and, two, your familiarity with their agricultural situation. Then, too, there was the matter of your own legal background.

R: I was pulled out of southern California and went to San Francisco. I had lost my contact with them. When I was hired by WRA, I left my state job and went immediately to San Francisco. I didn't have much time with any of them.

H: Okay, so you were up in the WRA regional office quickly, then.

R: Yes.

H: Okay. Then after several months you got yanked out of the regional office to work on the Leave Clearance Program in the national WRA office in Washington, D.C. When you were back in Washington, you had occasion to deal with many different people, but one person who might have talked a similar language as yourself was the then national director, Dillon Myer, who had previously been affiliated with the Department of Agriculture. You probably saw Myer quite a bit off and on. What was your impression of him?

R: I was very fond of him. I thought he was a very fine and very . . . Matter of fact, I think I've got a letter in here [Robertson's WRA file] to him, telling him what I thought of him. Yes, he was an excellent administrator. Well, we just hit it off, the two of us; I liked him very much.

H: Was he close to you during the time you were back there, or was he a distant figure to you?

R: No. I was in and out of his office. I called him Dillon.

H: So you had access to him?

R: Yes.

H: He has recently been characterized as a quintessential bureaucrat by Richard Drinnon,[3] who is high on Paul Robertson, but not so high on Dillon Myer. And yet the two of you were fast friends. Maybe you could give us a portrait of Dillon Myer?

R: When you say "fast friends" . . . We weren't, socially, on the outside; this is just in a business sense.

H: But you had a correspondence of sentiment--you could see eye to eye on things.

R: Yes.

H: But you had a chance to see him, and I think that Dillon Myer wasn't interviewed for this particular biographical study of him. I think what we need as part of the historical record are recollections of people who knew Dillon Myer.

R: My impression was that he was a fine administrator.

H: And what made him a fine administrator? What were the qualities that you saw at work that provided some kind of basis for this evaluation?

R: He would listen. When you made suggestions, he would follow through on them. I think that Dillon had a real understanding of the situation these people were in, and I think he was trying his best to help them.

H: He was the WRA national director when you went back there to Washington, right? The director was no longer Milton Eisenhower, is that correct?

R: Yes. Dillon Myer was the director.

H: Who else in the national office do you remember meeting, and what impressions did you have of them? The name of your immediate boss escapes you now, but . . .

R: There's half a dozen of them back there whose names escape me. I can't remember who they are.

H: But do some stand out in your mind, ones that you recall?

R: There was one fellow back there, but I don't know his name and I don't know what he did. He was a lawyer, but he was a pianist, and, of course, that attracted me to him. I've been out to his home for dinner. Boy, could he play piano, whew. And I had Christmas cards from him for awhile, but I don't remember what his name was. He was an attorney back there. I liked him much.

H: Philip Glick, was it?

R: Oh, no. I knew Phil after. I liked Phil, too.

H: He was the WRA's solicitor general there at the Washington office.

R: But I knew Phil after I was out here on the West Coast.

H: Did you know John Provinse [an anthropologist who headed the WRA's Community Management Division in the Washington office]?

R: Yes, I knew John Provinse. I knew him out at Tule Lake. See, these names I wouldn't remember, except when you tell me. Sure, I remember, I remember him. I couldn't tell you much about anybody in Washington. You know, when you mentioned Elmer Rowalt . . . I remember Elmer, and I respected Elmer Rowalt. In memory, I have a favorable opinion of Elmer.

H: Charlotte [Dixon] Brown told me that she had worked for the regional office. And then, when the regional office closed, she got sent back to the national office and worked on this same program that you were working on, the Leave Clearance Board programs, because it became one of Myer's highest priorities to relocate the people out of the camps and into the mainstream of American society, and Charlotte was heavily involved in this effort. You said that once in awhile you gave her a ride. Do you recall her very vividly back there and what her job was?

R: I don't remember her in Washington at all. I remember her in Los Angeles.

H: Oh, I see. So when you said earlier that you gave her a ride to work, you meant in Los Angeles?

R: Yes. Wait . . . you're right. I guess I did work with Charlotte in Washington, D.C., but I knew her much better in Los Angeles. It was in Los Angeles that on one or two occasions I drove her to work.

H: Mr. Robertson, before we start dealing with your two weeks of orientation from Ray Best, during the overlapping two weeks of your administrations at Leupp, I think my colleague Reagan Bell has some questions that he would like to ask you.

B: I want to ask you a couple of unfair questions. On that Leave Clearance Board you alluded to, there was a G-2, a Naval Intelligence representative. Do you have any recollection or impression of those people, or who they might have been? Were they difficult to get along with?

R: No. My impression there was that they were working in favorable cooperation with the WRA. No, I didn't have a bad impression of the fellows. I thought the board was doing a good job.

B: Was Dillon Myer getting any pressure to have a Leave Clearance Program, or was this a WRA idea?

R: I don't know what started that; I really don't know. I don't know whether anybody pressured him to do that or whether it was solely his idea. I just don't know.

B: Fair enough. You talked about your dealings with the Japanese merchants, farmers, before the war. Did you deal with any of the Japanese on a social basis?

R: Before the war?

B: Yes.

R: No.

B: But I get the impression you took a liking to them.

R: Oh, yes, I liked them.

B: They were honest, if I recall correctly.

R: Yes, sir.

B: They didn't go around without a license to do something.

R: No. I think that when we found them operating without a license, it was through ignorance rather than trying to do it maliciously.

B: Honesty is a virtue among them.

R: I think so. I found the Japanese people to be . . . They'd give you the shirt off their back when they know you and have confidence in you. I like the Japanese people; I think they're a fine race.

B: Seems you made an extra step that most people at that time didn't do in order to get to know and understand the Japanese people.

R: "Whatsoever ye would that men should do unto you, do ye even so unto them," and it always comes back to you.

B: Thank you. I figured I would get that type of response. I only have one other question right now up to this point. You're back there in the Disneyland [an amusement park in Anaheim, California] of the East, Washington, D. C. Do you recall just where in town the WRA headquarters was?

R: It was in the Blackstone Building.

B: What were your impressions of the Washington area at that time? It must have been rather frantic.

R: It was a hubbub. I wouldn't want to live there, although I did tell Dillon at one time that I thought that if you wanted to progress in government, that's the place to be. We enjoyed it. It was frantic, but we enjoyed the fact that we were in Washington for awhile.

B: Was your wife with you?

R: Oh, yes. The family was there. We moved back there.

B: Where did you live?

R: Anacostia.

B: There's the Naval Air Station there, right across the Potomac River, as I recall.

R: We were in an apartment building. You're going to get the real relationship I had with the military.

H: We'll get into that later in the interview, all right?

B: I spent some time in the Washington area myself. That's all the questions I have for you now, Mr. Robertson.

H: Thanks, Reagan. Mr. Robertson, when you were trying to recollect how it was actually that you ended up getting into Leupp, my mind was running in this direction: one of the things they [the WRA camp officials] had to do for the people that went to Leupp was, they had to deal with a clearance board in Washington, and I was wondering if the work that you were doing on the Leave Clearance Board got you entangled with some of the very people who were considering these different dockets on the people at Leupp, and that somehow or other that sort of got you involved in it.

R: It may have.

H: But who asked you specifically? Was it Dillon Myer who asked you to go to Leupp and tackle this job that Ray Best was abdicating to go to Tule Lake?

R: It must have been. I don't know who else back there would have had the authority.

H: Did it frighten you? After all, I know you had some investigative work, and you did have some work with the regional office, and you were back in the national office. But, boy, these men interned at Leupp were supposed to be the incorrigibles; these were supposed to be the baddest of the bad. Was this something that you thought you'd have the stomach for, or the experience for?

R: It didn't frighten me at all.

H: And why was that?

R: I think I knew the Japanese people. I knew I could get along with them. I had a Japanese secretary in Washington, Sally [Yamamoto] Tsujimoto. The last I heard from her she was a widow living in Sunland, California [a retirement community near Los Angeles]. She could give you a lot of information, too.

H: So the prospect of doing this was a challenge, but not one that frightened you. You got back to Leupp, Arizona, outside of Winslow on the Navajo reservation. And, in fact, where you went was a former Indian boarding school, which was quite a formidable structure in those days, even though it's no longer there now. And Ray Best had come there after heading up the camp at Moab, and so when you got there you were at least greeted, not only by Ray Best, but by the chief of internal security, Francis Frederick, and those two were in a position to be able to introduce you and to show you the ropes there at Leupp. Let's start with Ray Best. Had you known Best before this time?

R: Never met him till I got there.

H: When you met Best, what was your impression of him and how did the two of you get along during this orientation period? And did he give you a running start in the direction you wanted to go, or did you use him as something of a negative rather than a positive reference point, someone whose perspective and policies you didn't want to repeat?

R: No. I think we got along very well. I was using him more as an indoctrination: "Tell me what you've been doing and who these guys are and how you like them," this type of thing. It was a cooperative effort, and I enjoyed Ray at the time.

H: So he helped you, then, get oriented.

R: Yes.

H: Tell us about Best, give us a character portrait as you recall the way he was when you first encountered him there at Leupp.

R: Opinionated. I don't think that he understood the Japanese people. I don't want to use as strong a word as bullheaded.

H: Stubborn?

R: Even that's a kind of a strong word, but I think you know what I mean. He was . . .

H: Adamant or tenacious?

R: Yes. Socially, I was never very close to Ray Best. Even after we moved to Tule Lake, I never was really very close to him.

H: What was there as to differences in your temperaments and your life styles and your just general philosophical outlooks that made you not become close friends?

R: He was a Mormon and was close to the Mormon group up there [at Tule Lake]. There were quite a few Mormons on the Tule Lake staff. They sort of stayed aloof; they had their own little clique. This is as I recall. You know, there are certain people you're drawn to and certain people you're not drawn to, and he just wasn't one that I was particularly drawn to.

H: But neither of you drank. Probably neither of you smoked.

R: I didn't know that he didn't.

H: I'm saying, as a Mormon, ideologically, he wasn't supposed to. I don't know if he did.

R: I don't know whether he did, either.

H: So the chemistry wasn't there, for one or another reason. What about what he tried to impart to you during the two weeks that your situation overlapped at Leupp? What were some of the things that you can recall? Did he give you some guidelines: "Be tough"? What sort of advice did he offer, and what was the tenor of the advice?

R: I can't recall anything he told me, but if he did, I didn't pay any attention to it. I had my own method of dealing with . . . I didn't have any trouble with the fellows.

H: Let's move from Best to Francis [F.] Frederick.[4]

R: I can hardly recall Francis Frederick. I don't even remember what he looks like. You know, in what you wrote to me prior to this interview, you seemed so impressed with him, and I don't even remember him. I have a couple of letters in there [Robertson's WRA file] from him [actually, there is only one letter from Frederick to Robertson, dated 21 December 1943]. I think he asked me to try to find him a job after he got out of WRA, but I don't remember him. So I wasn't very close to Francis Frederick.

H: So you don't recall him? You can't draw a character portrait of him for us?

R: I don't see a picture of him, no.

H: It's odd, because I think in the documentation that exists on the Leupp period, it would seem that the two of you had worked very closely together, even though your temperaments seem so diametrically opposed. Why I say that is because he had written these dockets on almost all of the people interned at Leupp, and it was an armload of those that, allegedly, you took back to Washington and pretty much were able to use in order to convince people back there [in the WRA national office] that they had better close down Leupp, that there was no real reason for having that place, because most of the people who were there were there on flimsy pretexts that had very little to do with the reason that Leupp was originally established; and that the WRA ran afoul of being extremely unconstitutional in the sense that those interned in Leupp [American citizens of Japanese ancestry] didn't have formal charges leveled against them, they didn't have hearings, and they didn't have any kind of chance to answer their accusers or to be able to provide counterevidence.

R: Where did you get all this information?

H: Let me just read a little selection here from Richard Drinnon's Keeper of Concentration Camp: Dillon S. Myer and American Racism [Berkeley: University of California Press, 1987]: "Whirling up out of the desert air, Frederick's findings cut short this indefinite idyll. Matters no proper 'Caucasian' would put on paper had been highlighted in the files he presented to Paul G. Robertson upon his arrival. 'In reviewing the dockets of these evacuees,' the new Leupp director wrote Myer a few days later, 'I was very much amazed at the lack of evidence I had believed necessary to warrant a transfer to this center. . . . I expect to be in Washington around the latter part of August and would like to discuss these cases with you personally.' Robertson's letter arrived in the WRA headquarters just after Acting Solicitor Lewis A. Sigler had finished dictating an anxious memorandum for [WRA] Solicitor [Philip M.] Glick: 'We have had reports from several sources indicating that the Project Director at Leupp does not know why some of the men were sent there, and that requests for information go unanswered. . . . I should like to see a reexamination made of the advisability of continuing the Leupp Center. I think it is an un-American institution, corresponds to and is premised on Gestapo methods.' At the end of the month Frederick informed [Robert F.] Spencer [Japanese Evacuation and Resettlement Study research anthropologist] that 'Robertson is now in Washington and has taken an armful of my case histories which he says are so hot that there may be kickbacks but that he is going to show them to them anyway.' Ten days later he reported that the Leupp director had returned from seeing Myer and his aides: 'He went armed with my case histories which aroused them unfavorably toward me but still produced the desired results.'

"The brash young officer could lay claim to having changed history--a little bit. Frederick had put the 'WRA on the spot legally,' as he confided to Spencer, and thereby made a crucial contribution to the closing of Leupp. Without his case histories, the out-of-sight prisoners might have languished indefinitely in the old Indian school as jailer Myer patiently refrained from tempering justice with mercy" [pp. 107-108.]

This section of Drinnon's book is based, as is apparent, upon the following documentation: correspondence between you and the Washington WRA office and that between Frederick and Spencer. Along with the Frederick/Spencer correspondence in the JERS collection at UC Berkeley's Bancroft Library, there are copies of all of the personal dockets that were prepared by Frederick and sent surreptitiously to Spencer--that's how they ended up being housed there with the rest of the JERS materials.[5] Does any of this ring a bell for you, or not?

R: I'm sure that a lot of that is true, that I went back to Washington. And I'm sure that we sat down and went over the dockets written by Frederick. But I'm a little amused at Frederick's turning the history of the . . . I said I couldn't remember Francis Frederick. I have a faint recollection now of Francis promoting Francis. (laughter) I have a recollection of that characteristic of him. I wouldn't deny that maybe I did take some of his stuff back there [to Washington, D.C.]. But it struck me when you started asking me that that doesn't ring a bell with me, that I took his dockets with me and presented them to . . . But I can't recall. That's been a long time ago. I thought I had something in here [Robertson's WRA file] from Francis [indeed, a letter from Frederick to Robertson dated 21 December 1943 is included therein].

H: I asked you that because it figures as now a very crucial historical interpretation of why the Leupp camp was closed, and Richard Drinnon's reading of Francis Frederick[6] is similar to other people's reading of him, that he was mixed baggage to a very excessive degree, that he was capable of self-promotion, capable of deviousness, authoritarianism. But at the same time, for a number of different reasons, he was instrumental in being able to provide you with the sort of ammunition required to . . .

R: There's no question about that. He was a security officer, I guess, there at the camp. Coming in cold, I would have to sit down and go over documents with him.

H: Let me refresh you on a couple of things that Francis Frederick had to say about different items, because I think he writes very graphically. The letters from Frederick to Spencer start coming, really, even before you got to Leupp. He was writing to Spencer while Best was still director at Leupp, explaining something of his job and what was happening there.

R: You have his letters?

H: Yes, I have copies of the the letters that he was sending to Spencer. He and Spencer were, as I mentioned earlier, quite close at Gila. Spencer claims[7] that they weren't really close at all, even though their letters may seem like they were close. Spencer, like you, couldn't really form a very clear mental image of Francis Frederick. He just said that Frederick was a person who used to fix him with a steely sort of eye and made him feel very uneasy. He never quite trusted the person. But he was getting such wonderful information from him, as an anthropologist he wasn't going to turn from it. Frederick touts himself in his letters to Spencer. He says [in a letter dated 22 July 1943], "I . . . lived up to my reputation as the tough guy at Leupp. Et the ass of 'em." He's talking here about how he dealt with the internees at Leupp. He says, in this same letter, "There'll always be an England and there'll always be a Leupp, we are told." And further on: "Oh yes. Paul G. Robertson will be project director at Leupp and is here now—Best is leaving Saturday. Seems like a nice"—talking about you—"guy." This is when you had sixty-eight people at Leupp, and he had already begun to write up the dockets on the internees, which he's getting ready to give to you. And my impression is that the two of you sat down and went over some of these things. He says in an August 20 letter, at a point when you had been at Leupp for less than a month: "Paul G. Robertson is now director here and he's better than Best and is going to Washington next Tuesday and is going to try to get me deferred permanently. Seems that I am the only one who really knows these guys here, etc." Okay. And then, pertinent to his own case histories that he was writing up, he writes—excuse my language, I'm just quoting these things—"Every son of a bitch and his brother wants a copy. Naval Intelligence . . . Spencer, etc. I had to do many of them rather hurriedly but there is a lot of meat in them. Anyway, you [Spencer] could have them copied or get what you want out of them? Or if you'll guard them with your life, I will send them to you when I go into the armed forces and you can return them to my wife." And, as I mentioned earlier, his wife's name was Jane, and she was living there at Leupp, too.

He continues talking about these things in his correspondence with Spencer as time goes on. I'll just quote the most memorable sections. After getting confirmation from Spencer [letter to Frederick dated 27 August 1943]—"We're most interested in your case histories, and if you feel that you can spare a copy from prying FBI eyes, I wish you would shoot it out to us."—Frederick duly complied.

R: This is before I got to Leupp.

H: No, this was after you were at Leupp. He started to write some of those things, however, before you got there, and then he continued writing them while you were there, because there were seventy-some dockets that he was preparing.

R: He was writing to Spencer all this time?

H: Right. He says here [in a letter to Spencer dated 30 August 1943]: "There are only two persons who know why these guys from Gila were sent to Leupp. One is [W. E.] Williamson [the chief of internal security at the Gila center] and the other is me—and the latter takes the position that they were not legally sent. So how in the hell are they going to answer the questions? I don't mind admitting my perverted sense of humor makes me chuckle like hell over [Gila director Leroy] Bennett's predicament. Robertson went there [to Gila] with [George] Jyoji Yamashiro[8] and Bennett didn't even know who Yamashiro was—never had seen or talked to him." In other words, Bennett had remanded Yamashiro to Leupp and didn't even know the person.

R: George Yamashiro was a bigshot in Japan.

H: "So," continues Frederick, "if he [Bennett] didn't know the big shot, how in the hell is he going to write any kind of an intelligent report on a meek little shit like [Masua] Kanno?[9] Sweat, you bastards." That's what he says in here.

R: I didn't mean he [George Yamashiro] was a bigshot in Gila.

H: I know. You meant he was a bigshot in Japan, later on, after the war. But he was also a bigshot in Gila. "Robertson," continues Frederick in this same letter of 30 August, "is now in Washington and has taken an armful of my case histories which he says are so hot that there may be kick-backs but that he is going to show them to them [the WRA national leaders] anyway. He says that some of them would make his hair curl if he were in Bennett's shoes. He is also going to try to get me a permanent deferment but I doubt if he can. About the only satisfaction I can look forward to getting is that I have blasted that overstuffed bag of shit Bennett in such a manner that it is hurting him plenty. I usually lose out on these battles but not entirely. I know that I opened their eyes to [Lewis] Korn [assistant director of the Gila center] and [Morton] Gaba [assistant director of community services at Gila], and while they got rid of me (and I'm still with WRA) I also play a big part in the WRA getting rid of them. . . . Never a dull moment, and there is some fun attached to it." He goes on to conclude this letter by asking, "How in the hell can you Americanize the Jap when Gestapo methods are used in sending them to Leupp--no warrants, no trials, no sentence, separated from their families, etc.?"

R: I certainly agree with that.

H: This quotation comes from his September 9, 1943 letter to Spencer: "Robertson returned from Washington this week and was remarkably successful regarding the release of nearly all of our inmates. He went armed with my case histories"—you can see where I'm getting this phrase from—"which aroused them [the WRA national leadership] unfavorably toward me but still produced the desired results. He [Robertson] is trying hard to get me a permanent deferment and a raise. You see, I'm Acting Chief of Internal Security and receive the pay of Associate Chief. It is beyond question now that one of the reasons why I never was raised was so that they could get rid of me by having the army take me. The Chief job is on the key list for deferment and would automatically bring deferment. I honestly believe they are afraid of me—the sissies. The only slim hope I have is that Robertson is in my corner and says that he wants me to stay here."

Okay. The following derives from a Frederick to Spencer letter of November 29, 1943: "Robertson is a Jap lover by his own admission and I do not say this is any disparaging sense. He is highly thought of by the Japs here and they have entertained notions about circulating a petition when they arrived at Tule [Lake Segregation Center] to have Robertson replace

Best [as camp director]. Incidentally, they hate Best call him a bull-shiter [sic], meaning that he will promise you anything and never deliver the goods. . . . Robertson and Best are distinctly different types, and it will be very interesting to watch them when they are confronted with each other at Tule. I imagine, because of his recent bitter experiences at Tule, Best now dislikes strongly the Japs and the other guy is the other extreme"—meaning you, Robertson—"who feels that he can walk out among thousands of belligerent, angry Japs and alone and unarmed can placate them. Hmmm. Me, I am one of those guys that likes to be fully armed with overwhelming power that is very well known by the enemy and then be a nice guy." And, he continues in this same letter: "A teletype message from Myer arrived this A.M. telling Robertson what a fine job he had done at Leupp, that he will probably be sent on detail to Tule temporarily, and that they will place him somewhere later and where would he like to go, etc. Smells fishy to me but he is such a trusting soul that he will probably feel that a favor is being done him."

R: It was a favor.

H: Why don't we talk a little bit about some of the things that we've heard here. Anything that you wanted to comment on would be fine.

R: I can't say that, basically, there's any untruth there. There's no question that as security officer he made dockets on the various ones [detainees], and no question that I went over them with him. But in reading those, I recall an impression I had at the time that he was a builder of his own ego. And certainly I agree with him that the basis on which those fellows were sent down there [to Leupp] was very weak. I recall one fellow, Tom Tsuchita, I think was his name, that was sent down in a blacked out truck. I don't know whether you run across this anywhere in your . . . I think he had balls and chains on him. Tom took care of our kids. We'd go up to town shopping and leave Tom as a baby-sitter in our house. Worked around our yard. We saw a lot of him. And yet he was very dangerous, according to somebody else.

H: Was his situation representative or atypical? Were there people that should have been put in an isolation center that were under your charge?

R: You mean in a place like Leupp?

H: Right.

R: I suppose so. On the other hand, I had a fellow from—I can't remember what his name was—Sand Island in Hawaii.[9] He was very bitter; he used to snarl every time he'd pass me. But before we left Leupp, he told me, "I swore that if I ever got the chance, I'd slit the throat of any white man I could get my hands on. But I've changed my mind since I got to know you." So I think it's the attitude of the person who is dealing with them.

H: You have come across so uniformly in so many documents that I've seen as being a successful administrator—and I don't say this to embarrass you--that the Japanese Americans seem to have the highest of respect for you. And I wonder if you could just give us some sort of insight into what went on when you got to Leupp, what you found in the way of a camp disposition, and how you went about altering this and moving it to a position where, in fact, I think the authorities in Washington agreed that many of these people were not only safe to go to a camp [segregation center] like Tule Lake, but could be sent to one of the other camps [relocation centers], whether Topaz, or Granada, or whatever, or else even sent out into mainstream American society into work experiences. So what did you do there at Leupp? I don't want to call you a miracle worker, but it seems that the situation when Best was there, they had a lot of different kinds of things going on, and some of the internees were trying to burn down the barracks, and there were almost murders in there, and there were two very distinct groups at each other's throats. And something happened. It was either the heavy hand of Frederick or the velvet touch of Robertson, or the two of you working in tandem, to bring this about. This is what I want to fathom. I wonder if you could help me.

R: I don't know what caused the antagonism toward Best. I think generally people were afraid of him and hated him. I found that at Tule Lake, too. But my approach was one of friendliness, of empathy, of consultation, sitting down and finding out what their [the internees] thinking was and what the future held for them, and just discussing the whole situation with them. Caring for their physical needs. People think it's funny that I would go over there [to the internee barracks] in the middle of the night and give a fellow aspirin or really care about his pain. Actually, I rubbed some of those fellows down when they had a backache. And they still had this full company of soldiers with a man-proof fence, and guard towers, and everything in this compound. But with those fellows, I felt like they were friends, really. I mean, I didn't feel afraid of them. I think that's it. The more love you show for people, the more love comes back to you. I think that was the whole situation there. Just as I tried to understand the fellows and tried to treat them like equals and not have any harsh rules. We set up a little candy bar place where I could supply them with little things. What does the army call it when they have a . . .

B: Post exchange.

R: I set up a little post exchange there. The fellows had pretty much freedom. They're a clean bunch of people. You know, they take a shower two and three times a day.

I remember their catching rattlesnakes and taking the venom out of them, playing with them. We had one boy, his father was in one of the concentration camps up in . . . Missoula [Alien Enemy Internment Center in Montana],[10] was it? Somewhere. And his father died. He wanted his ashes. I wrote back and got hold of the funeral director back there that had performed the cremation and got his ashes, brought it [the urn] back to camp. Some fellow wanted me to get a steamer trunk for him, and I wrote around and finally got one for him. I'd just do little things like this for them, and I don't think Best had that personal relationship with them.

H: Did you, when you first got there, make a point of talking to them each individually?

R: Oh, yes.

H: I know you still have contact with some to this day.

R: George Yamashiro, we correspond all the time.

H: He was considered to be a very vociferous spokesperson.

R: Oh, George was a go-getter. Well, you know, about several years ago . . . Of course, it's been many years now, because I was still working. He'd call me on the phone, and he said, "Mr. Robertson?" I said, "Yes." "This is Yamashiro." I said, "Yamashiro? You mean George Yamashiro?" "Yes, sir." I said, "Where are you?" "I'm here in Sacramento. I want to see you." I said, "Well, I'd like to see you, too. Can you come out to the house?" So he came out to the house. I said, "What are you doing?" He said, "I'll show you when I get there." He handed me two business cards, and one of them [indicated that he] was on a board of directors of the Tokyo Railroad Company, and the other [that he] was on the board of directors at the Hilton Hotel chain back there. He was just that type; he was a go-getter. Nice guy. I liked George very much.

When we got to Tule Lake, the Japanese agricultural workers went on a strike. I went to George and said, "George, I want to talk to these guys, and I want to talk to them in Japanese. I need your help." So we sat down and I said what I wanted phonetically; he wrote it all out for me. And I went down to their mess hall at noon, when they're eating. I got up on the table and I talked to them in Japanese. Got a big hand, and they all went back to work. George was a big help to me.

Of course, George was the one who I took back to Gila. He was going to get married in Gila, to a girl he met down there named Sally, and on our way down to Gila I was going to rent a tuxedo for him for his wedding. We stopped in Phoenix, and I looked through the ads and I found a tuxedo for sale, just in the regular want ads, and I went over there and got it; it just fit him. We didn't pay much for it, I think $10. We went on down. Before we got there, however, we stopped in a restaurant. Some guy came up to wait on us, and he said, "You Japanese?" he said to George. George says, "No, me Hawaiian." (laughter) So the guy served us. He wasn't going to serve us. George got married, but I guess he hadn't been there but a month or five weeks and he was back at Leupp again; they sent him back. He was just the type of fellow . . .

You know, a lot of today's young people, if you did what they did to those Japanese boys, they'd have torn that camp apart. I thought the fellows were awfully good about it, accepting what had been handed to them. You know how boisterous some of our young people can be. Of course, old Harry [Yoshio] Ueno got himself in trouble by being a little too aggressive.

H: Why don't you talk a little bit about Harry Ueno, your recollections of him from the Leupp days.[11]

R: Of course, it's hard for me to pick out individuals at Leupp except in rereading some of the correspondence. Apparently, I held Harry Ueno in high regard at Leupp, because I know I wrote back to Dillon telling him that I thought Harry was one of the hardest workers we had in the camp. Of course, Harry and I have established quite a contact since. But as far as work at Leupp, I don't recall too much, just generally. That's forty years ago.

H: Sure. What about Joe Kurihara? Did you remember him at all?

R: Oh, yes. Joe was a philosophical fellow. He was a poet. As I recall him, he was an older fellow, and had more understanding than the younger fellows did. There were two personalities with Joe. I think he could be very firm in his assessment of something or he could be very sympathetic. I think I had something in here [Robertson's WRA file] from Joe. I can't remember all of it. I think what you'll have to do is look through this stuff I've got here and see if there's anything in it that you want.

H: Could I do that?

R: Yes. If there's anything in that you can use, you could duplicate it and then send the stuff back to me.[12]

H: Great.

R: Because there's a lot of letters in here from the Japanese boys themselves, explaining where they went and what they've done. I think you'll get a whole lot more out of the stuff that's in here than for me to remember stuff.

H: Okay. Let me ask you some more general questions rather than the specific ones. Could you tell us a little bit about Leupp? I mean, here it is, on a Navajo reservation. Tell us what physically you had in the way of buildings, and how the Navajos themselves reacted to this Japanese camp and the like, and who you had working with you there, and how your family got along there at Leupp.

R: In the compound was the school building. It was a large building. You have a picture of it?

H: I hope I do here. Let's see. This here (shows interviewee a photograph) is the living quarters, I think. And is this right here the mess hall?

R: That's it.

H: So they were the two buildings there.

R: Two buildings, the mess hall and the living quarters, and they were surrounded by a man-proof fence. And on the corners were the guard towers with machine guns. We had a full company of soldiers there, and they used to have drills on the outside to try to scare the Japanese boys, I think. But the Japanese boys sort of laughed at them, really, out there going through their maneuvers. We got along very well with the soldiers. The captain down there . . . I can't remember his name, but we ate quite often with the military, my family and I, and they ate at our house quite a lot, too, the captain and the other officers.

H: Where would they usually eat?

R: There was a mess hall on the outside.

H: The Japanese ate separately from the military?

R: Oh, yes. The military had their own quarters and a mess hall. Same type of food all the time: baked beans, peanut butter, and so forth.

H: But you would go eat with them [the MPs] at their mess hall sometimes?

R: Yes, we did. The officers came to eat with us every once in awhile. We'd invite them over to the house and my wife would fix up something for them to eat. We lived in the superintendent's home. There was a three-car garage and three bedrooms, a nice place. We lived in there. And we had a garden. As I said, Tom Tsuchita took care of our garden for us.

We had several of the Indians working for us in the heating plant. But the trouble with them was, when they got a little money ahead they'd go into town and get drunk and they'd be off of work for awhile. I think the Japanese were afraid of the Indians, too. I recall one time when some of the boys went in a truck with one of the camp staff over to get some soda pop at Flagstaff, [Arizona], and the car broke down. He went to get help, and some of the boys wandered off. They had waited so long that they didn't know what'd happened, and they were going to try to come back to camp. They were scared to death on their way back that the Indians would find them, but they got back okay. I took the fellows in one day to the dentist, I guess it was. And I went in to somewhere to get some soda pop, I think, and one of the fellows in there recognized me and said something about Japs out in the car. The fellows in the bar jumped up, and I had to run out of there and get going.

H: So the general attitude was . . .

R: . . . animosity.

H: Did you pick up any animosity from the surrounding Caucasian communities? They're not too close there like they are other places.

R: No. Winslow was the closest town, and we probably were eighteen, twenty miles out from Winslow. We were isolated; there wasn't anybody around there much but Indians.

H: You mentioned going into Flagstaff. Did you yourself have occasion to go into Winslow and Flagstaff and other places on a regular basis, or not?

R: Not too regular. But whenever the fellows had to have dental work, we went over. We shopped in Winslow, my wife and I. Yes, we went in there pretty regularly, into Winslow. We didn't go into Flagstaff so much; it was further away.

H: Did you ever have to go in to Winslow and give talks to Rotary clubs, Lions clubs, to explain what was going on out there at the camp at all?

R: No, I never did that. I got well acquainted with Mr. Magee, at the general store.

H: Where they had the post office and stuff?

R: Yes. And he didn't have any animosity toward the Japanese, although he dealt with the Indians all the time.

H: You mean he was a Navajo trader? So we're talking about a trading post.

R: Yes.

H: You mentioned earlier that your kids went to a little school out by Leupp. Was that an Indian school they went to, or what was it?

R: Yes, I guess it was mostly Indian kids. It was just a one-room school. That one building was still there the last time we went through Leupp. We got quite well acquainted with the Indians.

H: Tell us about that, okay?

R: There was a missionary there to the Indians, and there was a church there at that Indian school. She was serving the Indian population and, of course, we got quite close to her because we were interested in missionary work, too. My wife would go around with her to these Indian villages, and they got so they called her "the little nurse," because she brought aspirin and stuff with her. As a matter of fact, I've got several Indian rugs in here [in Robertson's home] that were given to us by the Indians down there. One night we went out to find a great big circle of wagons and trucks and just Indians, and they were having a ceremony. They were doing some sand painting inside of it, and they had medicine men there. We were the only Caucasians there. We had blankets wrapped all around us, and it was very interesting. Some of those Indians wrote to us after we left there for a little while, too. And the day we were to leave, our living room there in our home . . . was just full of Indian women. They came and just sat all around on the floor, just an expression of "goodbye, sorry to see you go."

H: In your house there at Leupp?

R: In the house at Leupp, yes.

H: You were mentioning some missionary work among the Indians. Aside from the social ethic and philosophical feelings and stuff that go along with being a Christian and dealing with the Japanese Americans, did you do any sort of Christianizing work with Japanese Americans?

R: I do this to everybody I meet. Are you a Christian?

H: Not an avowed Christian, but I was certainly brought up in a Christian church.

R: Don't put it off too long. I do that wherever I go. When you say "missionary work," I mean it just as a witness. Yes, I'm interested in the salvation of other people. I want people to know that Christ is there, and if they don't accept him, what they're facing. I do this even when I go to a restaurant to eat. I talk to the waitresses. In both Leupp and Tule Lake . . . I had a rather large group of Christian kids in Tule Lake. As a matter of fact, the Buddhist people invited me in to speak to a group of Buddhists. I said, "I'd come to talk, but I can't do it unless I can talk about Christ."

H: At Tule Lake, this was.

R: Yes.

H: At Leupp you had probably some Christians there already, didn't you? Some of the Japanese Americans were Christian, and brought up in Christian churches and things as well as Buddhist ones.

R: That was on an individual basis, though; that wasn't on a group basis.

H: So you didn't have any kind of services there at all.

R: Not for them, but for the Indians . . .

H: . . . you did.

R: Yes.

H: I'd hate not to ask a person who graduated from Yale as an architect what they thought about not only the architecture of the Indian school at Leupp that you were using, but even the architectonic forms of the area around where you were living. You were not too far from the Painted Desert and a lot of beautiful, scenic land formations. I'm wondering how a person in the fine arts, and particularly a person alive to not only spirit but to form, how you responded to that area.

R: It was different and beautiful. You mentioned the Painted Desert. We went there. Petrified Forest, we went to. Those were all lovely things. Of course, there's not much architecture to the buildings in the Indian school, just desert-type things. But we've done extensive traveling, my wife and I, and everywhere you go is different. People say, "What's the best place you've ever been?" Well, you know, you can't say. You think of Norway and Sweden, and that's so different than Italy and Africa. The last place we went was down in the jungles in South America visiting missionaries.

H: Is Robertson a Swedish name?

R: No, it's Scotch.

We had group spiritual meetings with the Tule Lake people; we had services there. The kids were allowed to come up on Christmas at our house. The Christian kids were allowed to come out of the compound; they'd come up into our house for a celebration. Of course, we got to the point where we didn't need any armed guards. Up there, if you went down into the compound, you had to take a soldier with you.

H: Just a small question. I always keep going back to look at the picture there of the main building at Leupp (displays photograph on dust jacket of Manzanar Martyr: An Interview with Harry Y. Ueno), and to me there's something so indestructible about its massive-stoned construction. And thus it was so sad when I got to Leupp [in 1985] to find that this seemingly permanent building had been razed. Did the form of that building or the form of the Navajo hogans or anything else in the area leave any kind of indelible mark on you?

R: We have some pictures around here somewhere of some of the hogans. When you say they had a lasting impression, of course, everywhere we've been has a lasting impression. We actually went out in places where there had been hogans. You know, you could see these mounds of earth, and we dug around for pottery. It was a different part of our lives that we enjoyed. I agree that that type of building, it would have been nice to have kept it historically. But that's the United States for you. Gee, we tear down beautiful things and erect stuff that certainly shouldn't replace them.

H: It's embarrassing.

R: Yes.

H: Reagan, I know you have some questions for Mr. Robertson about the military police, so why don't you now ask those?

B: You've already answered some of the questions I had, Mr. Robertson. But how large of a compound did the military police have that they lived in?

R: There was a building about like the compound that they occupied, and where we went to eat was over there in their mess hall. It's hard to judge. I don't know whether it was a two- or three-story building; it was a pretty big building, though.

B: You had about what, 130, 140 men?

R: One hundred fifty, I think.

B: So they had four or five buildings, then, they were living in and using for offices and the like.

R: Yes. It's very hard for me to remember. There were small quarters on the outside of the compound. I didn't pay too much attention to them.

B: This training you mentioned the Japanese would laugh at. That must have been riot training.

R: They'd go down with their guns and . . . Yes.

B: How did those MPs react to the laughter from the Japanese?

R: I don't think the Japanese said "ha ha ha" out loud. I think they thought it was kind of laughable.

B: Was there any provocation on the part of the MPs toward the men inside the compound?

R: No, I don't think so.

B: There doesn't seem to have been an incident at Leupp between the inmates and the guards.

R: No, there wasn't.

B: Did the soldiers have religious services on Sunday?

R: I don't think so. I don't recall that they did, and I probably would have known it if they had.

B: They must have had buses then to bring them into Winslow.

R: Yes, they had buses.

B: They had what, four towers around the camp, with machine guns?

R: Yes.

B: That must have been just very boring, standing up there day after day.

R: Oh, sure it was. I'm sure it was. There was nothing to do.

B: I realize you weren't on a day-to-day basis with them, but what was your impression of the MPs? Were they just plain old boys?

R: Good kids, yes. We didn't have incidents of drinking or the like.

B: When you had people to dinner to talk, did they exhibit any feeling at all about the type of job they were required to do? Did they ever question the necessity of being there, or did they just accept their lot in life?

R: I think they were just serving anywhere they were put. I don't recall their saying anything about having to be sent there against their better judgment. I think they just accepted their job. We liked that little captain; he was a real nice guy.

B: Was he an older person?

R: No. I'd say he was in his forties.

B: Then he was an older person for his grade.

R: That's young to me.

B: It is to me, too, now.

R: Probably I was pretty close to that then. That's forty years ago; yes, I was in my forties then, too.

B: I can remember being in my forties, also. (laughter) I guess that takes care of my questions for now, Art.

H: Okay. Thanks, Reagan. Mr. Robertson, was there any fraternization between the Japanese and the soldiers?

R: No.

H: So they were kept separate.

R: Yes. I think that was part of the military rule, that they weren't to fraternize with the Japanese.

H: Did you allow the Japanese to go out onto the reservation at all or not?

R: They stayed close. Just to my home and right around the vicinity.

H: What did they do during the day?

R: They played cards, just sat around and talked and played. I told you they caught rattlesnakes and . . .

B: . . . gambled.

H: You had a poet there, you mentioned, in part.

R: Oh, Kurihara, yes.

H: Did you have any painters or any musicians? Did you get a chance to ever have any evenings where some of them did some entertaining at all?

R: No. If they did, I wasn't there.

H: Did you ever invite any of the Japanese over to your house, a few at a time?

R: Not at Leupp, no. I did at Tule Lake.

H: But at Leupp you didn't feel it was appropriate?

R: I guess that was it, that these fellows were down there being watched by the [U.S.] Army. I guess it was just that maybe I was a little fearful that the Army would react if I took the fellows out of there. I guess that was just my reaction.

H: Tell me what you can remember about your trip back to Washington. Whether you had that armful of documents or not that Francis Frederick wrote to Robert Spencer about. You must recall going back there--maybe not specifically that one time, but the general tenor of discussions that you were having with the WRA Washington office about closing down Leupp.

R: I don't recall going back to Washington. I don't recall any specific discussion, except that the general tenor of the whole thing from the time I got there [at Leupp] until the time I left was that we were doing these fellows a terrible injustice by sending them to Leupp--many of them not knowing why they were sent there, and many of them not having any hearing of any kind at the center. It just appeared to me that they didn't like some kid, something he did, so they sent him to Leupp. Just the whole tenor seemed to be that there was no real justice, and that we ought to correct this thing. I know I talked to Dillon about this on more than one occasion, in correspondence, too. I wrote letters back there on an individual basis: "This fellow So-and-So, he hasn't done anything, and I think that he should be allowed to go back to wherever." I mean, this is just a common experience during the Leupp period. Now this stuff here that you've just read to me [during the interview] is stuff I didn't even know was going on, correspondence back to Spencer. That's why I said, "Where did you get all this stuff?"

H: Because he sent it to Spencer, it ended up in the Bancroft Library; therefore, it's been available to scholars who have been studying that stuff. Harry Ueno, when I showed him some of these letters, was amazed, because he had such a bad experience with Frederick. And even the report that Frederick did on Ueno. He had written a very damning report at Moab and even got Harry thrown into the clink there in Moab, the Grand County Jail, and then at Leupp he writes a letter for him, a case history in which he praises him in the same way you did earlier, as one of the most industrious people at Leupp. It was an amazing revelation to Harry, because he said they used to have this nickname for Frederick, "Seamy," because every time he spoke to one of the internees, he'd say, "You see me."

R: That's the only thing I remember about Frederick, that he was a pusher of Frederick. "I am it, I am it."

H: But you don't remember him having a wife there, and you and your wife don't remember having any dinners and things with them?

R: I don't remember he had a wife. Was he married?

H: Yes. Her name was Jane Frederick. He had not been married too long. He got married at Gila, just before he came to Moab, and then his wife stayed with him through Moab and Leupp.

R: Where did he live? I don't remember.

H: In one of his letters, he described who the personnel were at Leupp. I think he said there was a medical officer as well as somebody who was in charge of internal security. Now, he had a couple of guards, as well as the Army's 150 who were out there, so there were some WRA internal security people at Leupp, also.[13]

R: My recollection of that was that they were not professionals; they were just somebody that was hired to watch. But we didn't have any medical people on the staff there, because I had a doctor come in from Winslow. Once a week I think we had him there.

H: Caucasian?

R: Caucasian, yes. Anybody that had anything wrong, they'd come in at the time he came in. No, we didn't have any medical staff there.

H: In the last dated letter [in the JERS collection] that Frederick wrote to Spencer [9 December 1943], he deals with a couple of interesting things. He writes: "There was much consternation at Leupp when we learned that plans were made to place our guests into the stockade immediately upon arrival at Tule. Robertson opposed it strongly and intended to continue his fight after he arrived with them at Tule. Best was supposed to be in possession of written evidence that some of our boys were involved in the rebellion at Tule but would not discuss it over the phone. Robertson stated that he would let me know all about it. The Japs are very fond of Robertson and he is a very fine man. Leuup [sic] Japs plan to cause the circulation of a petition on his behalf at Tule requesting his appointment as Project Director."

R: I've never heard of that.

H: Frederick continues in this letter: "I am certain that this fact came to the attention of Best and I view recent developments re Robertson as being an effort to remove any possibility of his ascension to the position as head of Tule Lake. I know Best and his methods and am certain that he would cause Robertson to be placed in a position that would not jeopardize his (Best's) standing or position." And then he says later on in the same letter: "Indian Service plays a much more important role in this business than I ever imagined at first. What a bunch of racketeers! I believe their plans include the possibility of taking over the Japanese problem in the post war era—you know, reservations for the Japanese comparable to the Indians."

R: (laughter)

H: "There are many signs pointing this way—a possible solution of what to do with the Japs after the war keeping in mind the several factors including the antipathy of any state re taking them in and the attitude in California prohibiting their return, and making them government charges to checkmate any legal actions for damages, etc., against this government after the war for damages invoked because of the evacuation. Best has expressed the opinion that the Japs will be placed on reservations after the war and Robertson has expressed his desire to get into the Indian Service. The potent influence of the Indian Service within WRA and other factors give rise to my speculation that such a possibility of Jap reservations may become a reality.

"I know Best and Robertson very well and, especially in the case of the former, they did not gaze into any crystal ball and decide that Jap reservations were the answer to the post war Jap problem. Somebody told them and that somebody was undoubtedly Dillon Myer whom they both worship. Personally, I think he is one of the smoothest, suavest racketeers I have ever run across, and I know quite a few personally, and was probably selected because of his disarming speech and manners. He is fundamentally a politician which, in his case, makes him a racketeer for my money in his exploitation of this minority group for his own benefit and the benefit of others of his ilk such as Bennett, Cozzens, Best, etc." This is Frederick's final fillip in the correspondence, and there are several notable points made by him herein. Of course, one of them has to do with the contingency of putting Japanese on reservations; the second has to do with Best's, and possibly your, interest in being affiliated with the reservations for the Japanese after the war.

R: That certainly is news to me. I never heard of my getting into Indian Service. I never heard of that. That's all news to me.

H: The third is his accusation of Dillon Myer being a racketeer, and suave and smooth, and fundamentally a politician, and a person who got involved in the WRA so as to exploit a minority group, the Japanese Americans, for his own benefit.

R: That's false. That's not Dillon Myer at all.

H: So the characterization here is an assassination, really, of character.

R: Yes. This fellow was quite a writer, wasn't he? (laughter)

H: Yes, he was.

Mr. Robertson, when you closed up Leupp and headed over to Tule Lake to tackle a new job for the WRA, you accompanied some of the internees from Leupp who were going to be put in Tule Lake. You wrote at this time quite a long letter to Francis Frederick explaining your experience going over there.

R: I did, huh?

B: (laughter)

H: Would you like me to refresh your memory on the contents of this letter?

R: No. I have a faint recollection of my trip out to Tule Lake.

H: You write at one point in this letter about stopping at a particular place and buying some Chinese food for the internees. Maybe you could relate your recollections of that trip from Leupp to Tule Lake and what you were told by the WRA as to what your responsibilities were to be and what the disposition of your Leupp charges was to be once they got to Tule Lake.

R: It's awfully hard to remember. At the time, we put all of the evacuees on a regular passenger coach; we didn't have any sleepers on there at all. I think part of the time we were hooked onto a train, but part of the time we were just the luggage and the men. We stopped in Fresno [Stockton], I think it was. The fellows were very anxious for Chinese food, and so they took up a collection among themselves. I went into town and bought a <u>lot</u> of Chinese food. I guess Frederick helped me with that, bring the food in.

H: No, I don't think Frederick was with you, since apparently you wrote to him and told him about the experience.

R: Somebody went in and helped bring the food back. One of the other boys, I guess, one of the guards. We let the fellows out to walk around just for fresh air on the railroad platform. Then we got to Tule Lake. So I asked Best what we were going to do with these fellows. I guess most of them had relatives in the camp, but they were going to put them in a stockade until they could get straightened out as to who was going to be released and who wasn't. They put us up in a hotel--not a very nice hotel, either. There wasn't much in Tulelake anyhow. Then, when we started talking about distributing . . . Now, this is very hazy in my mind, but I remember that we had quite an argument about their not being allowed to go back out into the regular community, but they were going to keep them in the stockade. I lost out, of course; they kept them in the stockade. I don't know how long, but they started releasing some of them back into the camp. Some of them, it seems to me like they were transferred to some other camp. Some of them went back to Japan. But eventually that stockade was emptied, and I don't know how long that took, either.

H: One of the things you mentioned in the letter that you sent to Frederick after you had gone up to Tule Lake was that you felt very badly because you had an agreement that most of them would be released into the compound itself, and instead they were all put into the stockade. You said that a number of the Leupp inmates had felt that you had betrayed them, and that made you feel terrible.

R: Yes, simply because I had promised them that they'd go with their families out into the community. But I think I was able after awhile to convince them that they had agreed with me before they left that they would let them go out in the compound, and it wasn't my fault. There wasn't anything I could do about it. I just tried my best to change it.

H: What was your designation when you headed over there? Did you have a job at Tule Lake when you left Leupp, or was that something that was arranged later?

R: No. I think that I had been promised already, before I went up there, that I was to be in charge of operations, that I was to be designated an assistant director at Tule Lake. I think I had that understanding before I left Leupp.

H: Now, was that the assistant to Best?

R: Yes.

H: Was there only one assistant, or were there several assistants?

R: There were several. I was in charge of operations. Someone else was in charge of personnel.

H: You probably had still another person in charge of community management.

R: Yes, they had several. I think my responsibilities were as broad or broader than most of them. I had the motor pool; I had the construction unit; I had the furniture factory; and I had . . . I can't remember. It seems to me there were five or six sections of operation up there that I . . . I was in charge of agriculture, of all the growing of crops. So the responsibilities were pretty heavy at Tule. You see, I think there was . . . Did you have a figure of the number of residents?

H: I think there were about 18,000 at the time you were there.

R: I have [the figure of] 20,000 in my mind.

H: When you got to Tule Lake, it was late November, early December [of 1943]. Tule Lake had just been shaken by the first of a series of riots. Well, they had had some problems back when Tule Lake was a relocation center at the time of the registration in February 1943. But once it became a segregation center, the series of riots that actually dominate the public consciousness about Tule Lake began in November 1943, which, I think, was one of the reasons that Best reneged on his promise to release your Leupp people to the compound. Then all of a sudden there was this intervening factor, so there was a lot of anxiety about what was going to happen. But in any event, they all went into the stockade, and then, as you rightly pointed out, they started being released back into the community. Could you present for us an emotional portrait of what Tule Lake was like when you got up there? I mean, you came from Leupp out there on a Navajo reservation, and now . . . Granted, you were dealing with what was supposed to be the recalcitrants from all the different camps. But now you were up at a segregation center, and one that was rocked by this disturbance, and 18,000 people there. What was the configuration? What did it look like, and what did it feel like, et cetera, when you got there?

R: Now, again, you're asking me something that happened forty years ago. But from a faint recollection, it seemed to me like it was like an internment, that the military was in charge, that you couldn't do anything without permission, that there was antagonism between the staff and the Japanese. And the antagonism was, perhaps, fear on both parts. I think Best was fearful of his life. What started the military taking over, from what they told me, was that the Japanese people felt that they were taking stuff out of the warehouse. I think this proved to be true at one spot, of taking the meat and selling it in town. But a group of them started up to the warehouse to check, and they couldn't get into the warehouse, so they started over to Best's house. Someone was heard to say, "Let's go get Best." What they meant was, "Let's go talk to Best about it," but that wasn't the way it was interpreted. They interpreted it that they were going to get him. Then the military—as I understood, this was before I got there--they went all down through the colony and some of the stories you got was that the soldiers took stuff from the Japanese people, and just scared the life out of a lot of them. So things were pretty tense when I first got up there. I think it was some time before it settled down.

H: What about the appearance of the camp with the stockade and everything? You've described how Leupp looked. What about Tule Lake? So we can get a picture of what we're dealing with here.

R: The stockade was much smaller. Where's that stuff I gave you? I've got a map there of Tule Lake. It's on a blueprint. (Displays blueprint) Here's the colony, and here's the staff headquarters, and here was the stockade.

H: You mentioned off the tape that your housing was near the stockade?

R: Yes.

H: It was in the staff area.

R: Yes. I can't remember exactly where it was located.

H: Where's the entrance to the camp there, Mr. Robertson?

R: It's over in here. Here it is. That's where the military . . . I believe. It's all on here. If you can follow this with a magnifying glass, it'll tell you the whole layout. Our house is right in here somewhere.

H: But you were close to the stockade.

R: Yes, we were real close to the stockade.

H: Did you ever go into the stockade?

R: Oh, yes.

H: Could you describe the stockade, what that was like? Then there was supposed to be a bullpen within the stockade, an even smaller area within that area.

R: I don't remember that. As I recall, it was just a typical barracks-type building that they were in. I don't remember much about that. I remember the fellows getting out in the stockade yard, and they were within, oh, several hundred yards from the compound. And the Japanese people were talking sign language. The boys were motioning. I don't know how they were transferring information, but you could see them trying to communicate between them, the stockade and the compound.

H: You say when you went to Leupp, you didn't have any fear? What about when you walked into a tense environment that had lots of military presence and what sounds, from your description, like an angered, frustrated internee population? Was that a different situation or not, as far as your own reaction?

R: I don't recall that I had any fear. I think maybe I might have been a little apprehensive about the military being there and in charge. Perhaps how I was going to have a relationship [with the interned Japanese Americans] with the military between, I think that may have entered my mind. But I don't recall being afraid at all. I don't think I had the fear that Best had. But, of course, I think he may have had a reason for being afraid if all this business had gotten back to him about the hatred, and they're going to get him, this type of thing.

H: Frederick thought that Best looked at you as a possible sort of rival that had to be displaced or put in his place or whatever. Did you get a feeling that Best . . .

R: Resented my being there?

H: Yes, or just was apprehensive of your presence or whatever else.

R: I don't think I ever felt that. Of course, I'm not a very suspicious person anyhow. From way back when, from where I'm sitting now, I can't remember that I ever felt that he resented my presence. He was aloof. I never did feel very close to him.

H: He didn't take you into his confidence?

R: No. He ran a pretty tight ship.

B: Was this by nature his behavior?

R: I think so.

B: He was an ex-Marine officer or ex-Marine in World War I, wasn't he?

R: I don't know what his background was. More military than it was civilian. I think that his whole--"I'm in charge. This is the way it's going to be done."

H: Did he have a group of assistants there [at Tule Lake] that he tended to be closer to than you? I mean, people that were of a similar mind set.

R: I'm sure that he was closer to the Mormon group in his staff. We, at various times, have discussed this point. Because we have a Mormon neighbor, one of the best neighbors we've ever had. We're very fond of them. But we've talked to them ourselves about how when we were at Tule Lake we weren't very close to the Mormons up there; they sort of were aloof from the rest of the group.

H: Do you remember who some of the Mormon administrators were up there?

R: I don't remember anybody much by name anymore.

H: You mentioned earlier, off of the tape, Willard [E. "Huck"] Schmidt, who was in charge of internal security [at Tule Lake Segregation Center]. Was he somebody that Best was close to?

R: I think so. Yes, I think that they were pretty close.

B: When you got there, the military was in charge of the camp.

R: Yes.

B: Was Colonel Verne Austin someone you recall?

R: Yes, that name rings a bell.

B: He commanded the battalion there.

R: Yes. The name rings a bell.

B: Maybe you had the answer. All the other camps had one company and, yet, there was a battalion at Tule Lake. Is that because of the population?

R: The size of the camp, probably.

B: Or because it was a segregation center?

R: Was that battalion moved in after it became a segregation center?

B: Yes.

R: Oh, it was. Well, that's probably the reason.

B: Did you know Major John Hazlitt, who took the battalion over from Verne Austin? Great big bear of a man.

R: I don't think so. You know what year he left there?

B: In 1944.

H: Here's a picture of him. (Shows Robertson a photograph of Hazlitt)

R: Yes. Yes, I've seen him.

B: I understand when new military people reported to Tule Lake, he interviewed them to determine their feelings toward the Japanese.

R: I'll bet you he did.

B: And that if they had any bad feelings toward the Japanese, they were gone. Why did you just say what you said about him?

R: He just looks like a fellow who wouldn't let anybody get in there without an interview. I mean, he has that stern look about him: "Nobody's going to get in this camp unless they talk to me first."

B: Did the Japanese raise vegetables up there?

R: Oh, yes. Tule Lake? I was telling you about the farmers, the agricultural producers who went on a strike. I told you. When I got up and talked to them, they all went back out on the farm. Sure, we raised a lot of vegetables up there.

B: Was there a hog farm across the street from the main gate?

R: Yes, sir.

B: And occasionally the MP on the gate would have trouble just counting heads of people going across the gate.

R: I don't remember that.

B: Do you remember the border patrol? The border patrol was brought in [to the Tule Lake center] to calm the inmates down. They would come up and brag to the MPs how they'd taken care of those people inside.

R: Border patrol?

B: Yes.

R: You mean the federal border patrol?

B: Yes. Immigration and Naturalization Service.

R: I didn't even know they were there.

H: I think they came in when the people who renounced their citizenship [were removed from the Tule Lake center and taken] over to Santa Fe to the alien detention center toward the end of the war. Remember when they had a series of roundups, and they [some of the Tule Lake internees] had send-offs where they "banzaied" them [the renunciants], and everybody came out and marched, and treated them [the renunciants] as departing heroes?

R: I have a faint recollection of those fellows departing from the camp, those who had renounced their citizenship. But I don't remember the border patrol.

H: You mentioned earlier that when you were at Leupp you would occasionally have dinner with the officers from the military police there. Did this practice carry over to Tule Lake? Did you have that kind of relationship with the military there?

R: No.

H: Was this because there was this fear that you were talking about, that the military might take over and run the camp?

R: No. There was a much closer relationship in Leupp than there was in Tule Lake. We didn't have contact much with the military in Tule Lake.

H: When they had martial law, you didn't have much contact with them?

R: No. As a matter of fact, when they were in charge I had to have an officer go down in the camp with me. They wouldn't let me go in without someone with a gun to go down with me. But when we got inside the camp and I was visiting somebody, the guard would sit in there. He'd put his gun over in the corner and a woman would serve us all tea; then she'd go sit behind the screen. We all had tea together: the soldier, and the fellow I was visiting, and myself.

H: Tule Lake is portrayed in the historical literature as a place that was in constant turmoil almost during its entire history as a segregation center. Did you feel that, or is that an exaggeration?

R: There was an element, I think it was a small element, that kept things stirred up in there. When you say "in constant turmoil," it was woven throughout the whole time. There was this--not very many; I don't think there were too many. There was a murder or two up there, you know. These inu [informers], they kept calling fellows a dog, but this was a small element. As far as the whole camp was concerned, I think it was a very small element that tried to keep things in a turmoil, trying to get people to show loyalty to Japan.

H: Was there a paranoia on the part of the appointed personnel, a deep and abiding fear that they were going to be slaughtered in their beds or that there was going to be some kind of bloodbath?

R: I never sensed that.

H: You didn't.

R: No.

H: So the turmoil was never so great that . . . They moved tanks in up there and stuff.

R: Of course, that was before I got there. There were no tanks in the place after I got there. I don't think there was any paranoia. If there was, it was never expressed to me by the staff members that they were in danger of Japanese people coming into the staff area and doing them any harm. I always sensed that the director was fearful, but I can understand why.

H: You mean you felt that you could go about your job and that you could transact what it was that you had to do without looking over your shoulder and worrying about the slowdowns, and strikes, and dissident activity?

R: Well, I had my problems, of course. When one of the construction crew was murdered, there was a tense situation there. The Japanese people wanted to know why and what we were doing about it. When the strike came on, there was turmoil there, but it wasn't anything that I didn't think I could work out. I mean, I certainly wasn't fearful that the whole camp was going to blow up. I never felt that at anytime. On the whole, I thought the camp wasn't run too badly. Oh, if I were one of the inmates in there I probably would have felt like they do. They were short of coal in places; some complained about the food. The Japanese people, before this happened, were a pretty close family unit knit together; but when they moved into camp, the kids weren't dependent upon their parents. They were fed separately; everything was furnished to them. This had a tendency to separate the families. The old Issei people sort of lost control of their families. That didn't help for unity in the camps.

H: Did you get a chance to talk to some of those Issei people who perhaps you'd known from your work before the war with the Agriculture Department? Since Tule Lake was a segregation center, the people there were from all over the place--I mean, you had lot of people from southern California, northern California, Arizona, or wherever else who ended up being incarcerated there.

R: Yes. I talked to some of them in Manzanar; I talked to some of them in Tule; I talked to some of them in Gila. The older group, I felt, were pretty docile. They took it in stride. So it bothered me a little to hear the younger group clamoring for money recently. I don't think the old Issei would ever have done that.

H: You mean as part of the current movement for redress and reparations?

R: Yes. In my conversations with the Issei, they had accepted it. I mean, it was part of what the government had to do. They weren't really as resentful as I think I would have been. At least that was my feeling.

H: And then during the time that you were at Tule Lake, did you keep the same position as assistant project director in charge of operations?

R: I stayed right there until the ban was lifted and the Japanese were allowed to come back. And then Dillon asked me to go to Los Angeles to open up southern California for them to return.

H: Before you get into that, I'd like to ask you some more questions about your Tule Lake experience. What was your family situation while you were at Tule Lake. You lived near the stockade, but what type of housing did you have?

R: It was, I believe, a two-bedroom home, with a kitchen, and back porch, and a rather nice sized living room. Hallway. We had this sort of Japanese bath that the fellows had made out of cement for me. Nice quarters. I mean, they were clean and comfortable.

H: Your children, when they were at Leupp, had gone to a little one-room schoolhouse out there. Where did they go to school while you were at Tule Lake?

R: They went to public school in Newell, [California, next to the Tule Lake center].

H: Was that satisfactory for them?

R: Well, yes. They had to be bused over to the school from the project, but, yes, it was satisfactory. It was a good education for them.

H: You had to make a decision there, didn't you, because I know in a lot of the projects some of the appointed personnel's kids went to the schools in the project, and some of them were sent out of the project to go to school. Did you have that option in Tule Lake?

R: We had to send them. I don't think we had any option.

H: You might not [have had an option], since it was a segregation center and not a relocation center, but that's what I was wondering.

R: No. They were in elementary school, and so . . . I don't recall. I just know that we sent them to the public school. It didn't do them any harm, since they went on through and got their master's degrees. (laughter)

H: Did you talk to any of the people in the surrounding areas there, either the town of Tulelake, spelled as one word, or in Newell or anything? Did you have occasion to give talks to Rotary or Lions service clubs, or any similar organizations, in that area?

R: Never did. The people in Tulelake were worse than they were in Orange County, [California], I think. No, they had big signs. There was one guy said, "Jap lovers, we don't want your business."

H: In Tulelake?

R: In Tulelake, yes. No, they were pretty hostile in Tulelake.

H: What about in Klamath Falls, which is the larger community that's nearby in the next state, in Oregon?

R: I never got over to Klamath very much. We'd go in there for dinner once in awhile. But I don't know what the feeling was there.

H: That was a town where you would go for certain services, like restaurants and things?

R: Yes. And did some shopping there once in awhile. But it was further away, and Tulelake was just a wide place in the road.

H: Did you ever fan out as far as Portland, [Oregon]?

R: No.

H: You didn't. So you stayed closer to the camp area?

R: Right.

H: How would you describe your duty there at Tule Lake relative to what you had been doing during the months you were at Leupp? Would you draw an invidious comparison between the two, that whereas one was an enjoyable experience the other one was not enjoyable?

R: No, no. I enjoyed both of them.

H: You enjoyed both of them?

R: Yes.

H: Like you were saying earlier, when you go on trips you see different things in different places, so you derived different kinds of pleasures out of Tule Lake.

R: But at no time did I feel that I made a wrong move to go into Tule Lake. I enjoyed my stay there. It was cold in the wintertime. They did have a garage, but it wasn't much of a garage. Car got frozen once in awhile. Little things. But that was a physical thing; it had nothing to do with my mental attitude up there. No, I enjoyed Tule Lake. Matter of fact, I wouldn't trade my four years with War Relocation for anything I've done. That was a real experience for me. Looking back on it, I loved every minute of it.

H: So you enjoyed working for the WRA during the war.

R: Yes, I did.

H: Was it largely because of the people in WRA? You've shown me a nice little brochure that they put together for you when you retired, which seems to be full of good cheer and fellowship. Was it that, or was it the Japanese, or a combination?

R: I think it was a combination of all of it. I enjoyed it because I accomplished something. When I looked back on it, I felt that something had been accomplished by my having been there. I don't want to sound like Francis [Frederick]. (laughter) But you asked me what my feeling was, and I guess because I knew the Japanese people and I liked them. And I got along well with the staff members. I can only remember one fellow at Tule Lake that every time I came in where there was a group of them, he'd grab a book and put it under his arm and say, "Here comes the preacher."

H: Who was that, a Japanese?

R: No.

H: A staff member?

R: It was this kid. "Here comes the preacher." (general laughter)

H: Did you do quite a bit of testifying in a ministerial sort of way?

R: Not so much among the staff, but, yes, we had regular services with the Japanese people. They had a Japanese minister there, but we worked with them.

H: My understanding was that in the last couple of years, especially at a segregation center because this was supposed to provide a Japanized environment and a lot of people were preparing to go back to Japan, whereas in the earlier years of the evacuation there were more people that affiliated themselves with Christian churches, in the course of time, and especially at Tule Lake, there was a movement toward Buddhism and toward Japanese forms of worship. Did you find that to be the case, that there was maybe some greater resistance to Christianity because it was affiliated with Westernism and Americanism, or not?

R: No. There had always been a strong Buddhist element there. I attended several Japanese Buddhist funerals there. There was a young fellow by the name of Tom Grubbs, who was a missionary assigned to Tule Lake by his church. He was a single young man in his twenties. He had a burden on his heart for the Japanese people, and after the Tule Lake center was closed, he went to Japan as a missionary. He there met and married a young girl who was also a missionary to the Japanese. But we had a very strong Christian—young people, mostly--group at Tule Lake. There must have been, I'd say, thirty-five or forty who were regularly active in the Christian Church there, meeting in a barracks, of course. And they had a Japanese fellow--I don't know whether he was a minister or not--[who] sort of coordinated all the activities there.

H: Were you dealing with a particular sector of that population, because, as I understand it, a lot of the reason there was tension in Tule Lake had to do with the fact that those people who were there that had said no, no, on question 27 and 28 [during the February 1943 "loyalty" registration] had felt that there were a lot of people in the camp who for one or another reason did not share their outlook. Some of them were what they called "old Tuleans" who had been there when Tule Lake was a relocation center and simply never bothered to even register, because they didn't want to move. This was one of the things that fueled this movement for resegregation, that element in the camp wanted it to be pure Japanese. Did you then end up dealing with those people who were characterized as inu or were seen as kind of carriers of American traditions and were deemed by some as un-Japanese?

R: I don't think that I made any distinction as far as my relationship with them was concerned, because I dealt with some of the fellows who were considered troublemakers. I think you'll find a letter in here from a girl whose husband had been in trouble. It was a letter to the Spanish Consul [Francisco de Amat]. She wouldn't work through the staff or WRA at all; she didn't have any use for them. But in that letter she said that "the only one in WRA we can trust and depend on is Paul Robertson, but he doesn't have too much authority." (laughter)

H: Was that a result of your work over at Leupp?

R: It may have been a result of the fellows after they got back out into the compound, although I can't recall at any time before they were released into the compound that I had any difficulty with any of the fellows there. It seemed to me that my relationship through the whole of WRA, as far as the Japanese people were concerned, was cordial, was friendly. I don't know of anybody that I had real difficulty with.

H: It seems to be borne out by the documentation, because I haven't seen any reference to people having difficulty with you, either. What about these former Leupp inmates? Once they got released from the stockade, did you reconnect yourself with them?

R: Yes. I talked to them. And George Yamashiro was one of them. He was back out in the colony when I went down to ask him to help me out. I couldn't name them, but I recall that I did talk to them after they were back in the compound.

H: Did you have contact, say, with Joe Kurihara and Harry Ueno at Tule Lake?

R: I'm sure I did. I don't recall specifics, but there's a letter or a card in there [Robertson's WRA file] from Joe Kurihara to me after we got out, so I'm sure I kept contact with him.

H: Of course, there were 18,000 people now instead of less than 100 at Leupp, right?

R: Yes. But, after all, we had established a pretty fair relationship at Leupp, so that wouldn't be dropped just because they were stuck out in the compound. They'd still send a note in that they wanted to see me. We kept contact.

H: Francis Frederick had used that term "Jap lover" in relationship to you, which was a common kind of expression at that time. I'm wondering if at Tule Lake other appointed personnel felt that way about Paul Robertson.

R: Did you ever have any indication in your research of having had anyone indicate that?

H: No, I haven't. I'm just wondering.

R: I never felt it on the part of anyone there.

H: The reason I even asked that question is because there seemed to be a lot of concern about fraternization during that period of tension, and it could have seemed to some of those people who were becoming paranoid that anybody who would be friendly with the Japanese, perhaps, needed to be watched a little bit; and I just wondered if you'd felt that or not.

R: No, I didn't. Of course, in the staff meetings I think that would have been very evident to me if there had been any indication that people felt that I was fraternizing too much with the Japanese. And I never had that feeling from any of the staff. What was that fellow's name that was in charge of community services, sort of public relations type thing?

H: I'm not sure.

R: Oh, yes, his name was Martin P. Gunderson; he would probably have been in a better position to have relayed this type of feeling to me than anybody else there. I never had that at all. I thought I got along very well with all the staff.

H: As you look back through the forty years, who on appointed personnel did you and your wife socialize with, have fellowship with, or feel close to? It wasn't Ray Best.

R: No, it wasn't Ray.

H: And it wasn't Schmidt.

R: Not Schmidt, no. We got along very well with this young doctor and his wife at Tule Lake.

H: [Dr. Reese M.] Pedicord [Chief Medical Officer of the Tule Lake Segregation Center]?

R: No, not Pedicord. He was younger than Pedicord. His name is almost on the tip of my tongue, but I can't quite remember it. Okay, now I've got it, it was Dr. Jack Sleath.

H: But Pedicord wasn't somebody you had a close relationship with, either.

R: No.

H: You mentioned off tape that you knew Marvin Opler, the War Relocation Authority's Community Analyst at Tule Lake.

R: Yes. We weren't real, real close, but we socialized with the Oplers. Gee, that's a long time ago.

H: Were you lonely, then, for four years without any social companionship? You talk about your years of experience with WRA with warm recollections, and when we try to ferret out who the warm connections were with, we're having some difficulty. So I'm wondering, was it then more the Japanese than the appointed personnel?

R: My warmth toward the WRA personnel was more a business type thing than it was a social fellowship. I think you'll see in some of the correspondence here in this [WRA file] that people I worked with . . . We had a very warm relationship. Earl Barton was my assistant in Los Angeles, and we got along very well together. Eddy Echles, the newsman in contact with all the news people down there, was a very good friend of mine. As a matter of fact, we carried on correspondence. He's dead now, but for several years we corresponded with each other. I didn't know his family, but I had a very high respect for him.

H: What about the image of WRA personnel? You mentioned the Mormon group, which would suggest, actually, a kind of moral purity to their behavior and things. But I've heard interviewees tell me who were associated with different camps--not Tule Lake so much, speaking of that specific situation--that there was a kind of thing you might have found among the British in India, people who socialized a lot, drank a lot, played cards a lot, caroused a lot . . . even bedhopping back and forth between different families. Was that a part of that life, too, or not?

R: If that existed, I wasn't aware of it. They wouldn't have included me anyhow. (general laughter)

H: But I was just wondering if you were put off by that thing, if you knew about it, and that's why you had respect for them on a business level but [did] not socially interact too much with them.

R: I think that may be true because, as I recall, we weren't particularly interested in going to their blowouts in the "rec" hall up there at Tule Lake, their dances, and their liquor, and so forth. This type of thing didn't appeal to us, and it wasn't because we disliked the people; it's just that we didn't care about that type of thing. No, as far as fellowship outside . . . I'm trying to think. What was it that we were so active in . . . this little Community Presbyterian Church in Tulelake. We had fellowship with people outside. I think that was Tule Lake, too. I know we were invited out to dinner several times by different people outside the camp that were members of the church. Can't remember their names, either, but I remember they'd go out in the backyard and shoot a pheasant and have it for dinner, right in the backyard.

H: Reagan, you probably have a few questions you'd like to ask about the military, don't you?

B: I only have a couple questions. Once you got to Tule Lake, you didn't have many relations with the military police.

R: No.

B: And after the tensions were relaxed, you had no reason to meet with them.

R: No.

B: I understand they escorted you in and out of the camp.

R: When we first got there.

B: One question. I saw it happen in other camps. When the WRA staff would have their staff meetings, they would include the CO [Commanding Officer] of the MPs.

R: Would or would not?

B: Would include him. And he wasn't there as a member of the staff, but he could answer questions; he could also give out information.

R: He could audit the conference, in other words. That's about all he was there for.

B: Yes. You know, if they're having a problem with the MP's, you know, he could . . . Was there such a thing as that at Tule Lake?

R: I kind of think so. I kind of think we had an Army man at our staff meetings. I don't recall specifically, but I think we did. And our relationship with the Army at Leupp was very good.

B: I understand that the military police at Tule Lake, their biggest thing in their life was getting off and going to Klamath Falls at night.

R: (laughter)

B: That they really didn't have any particular feeling either one way or the other toward the Japanese, that they were behind two rows of barbed wire . . .

R: As far as I was concerned, I really don't know how they felt. But I never saw anything that would indicate that there was strong animosity between the soldiers and the camp.

B: That's about all of my questions.

R: The Army post had a theater, and we used to go to their theater all the time, attend the shows.

H: Did you ever go over there to purchase things at their PX [post exchange]?

R: No. We had our own PX at Tule Lake. We had a co-op.

H: The evacuee head [Yaozo Hitomi] of it [Tule Lake's cooperative store] got shot.

B: I understand some of the MP's went out for awhile and picked potatoes to help the farmers out and to make a little extra money.

R: Gee, I don't recall that; they may have. First you tell me that they didn't grow any crops, and now you tell me the military . . .

B: No. This is the local civilian farmers.

R: Oh, I see. Not in the camp. They're helping the local farmers. I wouldn't question that. Probably did.

B: My question was, did the Japanese raise vegetables in the camp?

R: Oh, yes. You betcha.

B: But not out of the camp.

R: No. No, we raised a lot of vegetables there.

B: What was this hog farm that was across the road?

R: I don't know. I just remember that there was a hog farm there.

B: I get the feeling, from reading and from talking to people, that the WRA—and this is not intended as criticism; it's just seeking an answer—lived in one world, the Japanese lived in another world, and the military police lived in a third world, and that their meetings were few and far between.

R: I can understand how an outsider might feel that way. One who wasn't on the inside would think that. As a matter of fact, I don't think it's too farfetched, really. I don't think that the Japanese people had much to do with the Army, and I certainly don't think the Army had much to do with the Japanese people. They were separated. There could have been a relationship between the staff and the Army. And there certainly was a relationship between the staff and the compound. I don't think you could separate the three of them completely and say none of them had any relationship with each other. Sure, there were elements both in the compound and in the staff which were not completely cooperative. With 18,000 people out there, there's bound to be some of them that resent everything that's going on there. And I'm sure that on the staff there were people who, like Best, were a little fearful and apprehensive about what the future holds. I'm sure that there must have been feeling, but as far as being completely separated—that the three separate units didn't have anything to do with each other—I don't think that's true.

B: Was there any hostility between the WRA and the Army? Jealousy, maybe, would be a better word. Sometimes you get the feeling that some of the WRA staff really didn't want anything to do with the Army; they'd stay away from it. And in other camps, you see where there was a close interface. There were a couple of camps where the MPs played softball against the Japanese. The CO was invited to speak to a group of Japanese women.

R: Yes, but you must remember that Tule Lake was different than any of the other camps. It was a segregation center, and the Army moved in there and took over. Of course, they came in at the request of the administration, but if what these people said happened was true, I can understand how they would have no use for the Army. If they went and robbed them and took their watches, jewelry, and stuff . . . Those are just stories; I don't know whether any of that happened or not. But if it did, you can understand how there'd be a strong feeling against the Army [personnel]. But we had so little to do with the Army; they ran their show and we ran ours.

B: Was that fairly common? I realize you weren't at all the camps all the time. Was that fairly common among the ten camps, that there was very little to do between the Army and the WRA?

R: I couldn't speak for the other camps, because when I went to the other camps it was merely to check the agriculture operation and report back to Washington to the Leave Clearance [Board] Program. And I was there, what? Two or three days, maybe, and I was gone. I couldn't evaluate as far as the other camps, because I spent most of my time at Tule Lake or Leupp. And again, our relationship with the military at Leupp was excellent.

H: You were close to a number of Japanese at Tule Lake, and there was, during the time that you were there--during a part of the time, anyway--what has been characterized as a reign of terror, that there were different types of groups that intimidated and coerced people into making decisions which oftentimes were against their will, and there was just a pervasive kind of fear that people would be branded as inu and beaten. Did anybody come to you and ask for protection, or alert you to this kind of thing, or in any way did this reign of terror make itself manifest to you?

R: I was aware of it, but I think that the people who were intimidated were that much intimidated that they were afraid to come to the staff. We were all aware that there was an element that was stirring up trouble in the camp. I think this woman, the one I referred to earlier who wrote to the Spanish Consul, was indicating there that they had come to me for help and there was nothing I could do; I had no power to control it. So I'm sure that at the time I was there that the word got back to me from the camp as to what was going on.

H: But you weren't taking any people in on a protective custody basis or something?

R: No. I would have been afraid to do that.

H: In the best of situations, the Caucasian would be referred to as the hakujin, and in a less happy situation referred to as a keto. Did you ever hear the term keto either applied to you or to others while you were at Tule Lake?

R: As a matter of fact, I don't know that word keto.

H: It just means "hairy beast." Just a kind of a word of ill-repute. But you didn't hear that at all?

R: Inu, I knew. They used that a lot.

H: Did you see much symbolism dealing with the inu? Because I have done some research on that, and in some camps they would symbolically do things like put bags of bones on people's doorstep.

R: I heard of this. I didn't see it done.

H: You didn't see any of that done.

R: No. But I heard of it being done.

H: I guess we're ready to explore your WRA work in Los Angeles. Could you tell about how your experience at Tule Lake wound down and how you got involved in the final stages of the Evacuation, and what that involvement consisted of?

R: When the ban was lifted, we were faced with trying to smooth the area down before the people moved in. I suppose it was Dillon [Myer] again who asked me if I would go to Los Angeles. Now I'm just surmising. He was in charge, and I don't think there's anybody who would have the authority to move me from up there to down there except him. We moved down.

H: This was before Tule Lake closed down, too, right?

R: Yes. We established offices on Broadway and about Eighteenth Street, I think. We took a big part of that building, a couple or three floors. So we had a pretty big staff. When I first arrived, I was a little apprehensive, because the newspapers were hostile about the Japanese coming back in.

H: And did this hostility carry over to the WRA for helping to bring them back in?

R: Sure. We would hold press conferences, and I'd have maybe ten or twelve newspaper reporters there. We'd have our conference, and the next day, when the news releases came out, you wouldn't recognize what we had said the day before. That's the reason I've had difficulty in accepting what I read in the press, because they print what they think the public wants to hear. They thought the public wanted to hear, "We don't want these people back here." You'll see in the stuff I gave you a report on meetings I had with the Produce Dealers Association down there, and I sensed that they were very reluctant to have the Japanese people come back into the produce market at all. We had incidents of shots being fired and going through a window or something--scare tactics.

Oh, you asked me if I had anybody that had ever said anything against my operation. There was a Buddhist priest in Los Angeles . . . I think he sort of felt like, because I was a Christian, that I was doing something to harm the Buddhist Association. And it seems to me like this . . . Yes. (Reads a newspaper clipping from the Los Angeles [Herald] Examiner dated 31 December 1944) "Pictures show exterior of former Japanese Buddhist temple, now housing colored workers at First and Central, which may figure in court as Japanese Americans return to the Coast from relocation centers. The first attempt of returning Japanese Americans to oust the Negroes and regain possession of Little Tokyo and move to evict the Providence Baptist Church from the Hongwanji Buddhist Temple was made yesterday and immediately gave indication of the coming court battle. Following disclosure that the church and seventy-five Negro war workers now housed in the temple located at First Street and Central Avenue have been given until January 5 to vacate the structure, Dr. L. B. Brown, pastor of the First Street Baptist Church and president of the Providence Baptist Institute, announced that the church group has retained an attorney. 'We have made a $7,200 down payment, thinking that we were purchasing the temple building and that we have $25,000 to put down,' Dr. Brown said. 'We are not opposed to the Japanese returning, but we believe, since many of our people are war workers engaged in work vitally essential to the war effort, that we are entitled to certain considerations. We are not opposing the government in its plans of relocation of Japanese Americans here, but we do want our rights as American citizens.' The Reverend Julius A. Goldwater"--that's the one I was talking about--"a Buddhist priest who was given power of attorney by the Japanese owners to act as temple custodian, said that he had given the Negro groups occupying the building until January 5 to vacate, and he said the lease expires on that date. Twenty, possibly twenty-six, branch offices are to be established in California by the War Relocation Authority to assist evacuated Japanese Americans who wish to return to the state, Paul Robertson, WRA supervisor for southern California, disclosed yesterday. Robertson, who is in charge of the Japanese relocation in the area extending from San Luis Obispo to San Diego and including Arizona, also admitted that indigent as well as self-supporting Japanese Americans will be permitted to return. 'If indigent evacuees wish to return, we cannot bar them,' Robertson explained. 'They'd have the same civil rights as any other American citizens.' He said that he does not expect the county and state relief load to be greatly increased by the return of Japanese indigents, however, as most of the evacuees have means of support. 'In fact, we do not expect any mass return of Japanese Americans,' he added. 'But because we are unable to determine the number, we do not know just how many centers will be required to handle them. The number of such centers,' he said, 'has been set tentatively by the WRA at twenty-six. The purpose of the proposed centers,' he said, 'is to assist the returning evacuees in whatever way possible. We would like to limit the returnees to those who have a planned program and means of support, but we cannot bar indigents from returning, if they wish to come in on their own. They have the same civil rights as any other American. However, I don't think you'll find any coming here unless they do have support.'"

H: Now, this sounds like it might be accurate reporting. Is it?

R: Yes.

H: Is this the Los Angeles Times that you're quoting?

R: No, the Los Angeles [Herald] Examiner.

H: That's very interesting, because I tried to get a handle on this, because during World War II, Little Tokyo became a residential area for blacks, and they renamed it Bronzeville. I was wondering how, after the war was over, the Japanese were able to reclaim what was really their commercial and cultural center. Some of this that you were reading here from this article gets into some of the tensions that were incumbent upon this.

R: (Reads) "Robertson declared that many of the evacuees released recently from the WRA centers have gone to the East and Middle West, and that the shipments of goods which they left stored in the government warehouses here bear out that trend. Charging that the WRA planned for setting up the twenty-six relocation centers in California as a part of a deliberate plan to force California communities to accept the Japanese, Dr. John Lechber"—have you run across him yet?

H: No, I haven't.

R: ". . . executive director of the Americanism Education League and other groups opposing the return of the Japanese Americans for security reasons, yesterday forwarded new protest to Congress. 'The WRA,' Lechber charged, 'has a secret order to unload internees, many of them indigents, on California from various relocation centers. They will be given six months to come back to this state, where the taxpayers of California will have to support them,' Lechber asserts. Arrangements also were completed yesterday for a meeting of the executive committees of three farm groups to formulate plans to discourage those of Japanese ancestry from re-entering agricultural occupations on any extensive scale in southern California."

H: So this is what you were dealing with, at least on a couple of grounds. One, you had a lot of resistance to the return of Japanese Americans to California. Secondly, when they did come back, a lot of them didn't have money and didn't have jobs, and what you had to do was to develop public relations to accept them back and then also to help them get established in housing or whatever else.

R: And it was a heart-rending thing to see those old people come back to the . . . really, as bad or worse than the accommodations at the center. I know one particular old fellow, his wife was an invalid, and he had to carry her to the bathroom, and he had to carry her down to give her a bath, to a central location. It just hurt you to see those old people have to go through that.

H: Would it be fair almost to characterize this last job that you had with the WRA as the toughest of three different assignments that you had? Even more so than the Leupp and Tule Lake, which I would have perceived before we started this interview as the hardest? But I'm starting to sense from what you've related here . . .

R: I think probably I felt more resistance, more difficulty, in doing my job there than elsewhere. Because here I was dealing with people that I knew pretty well, in both places. Here I was dealing with antagonists, people who don't want these people here.

H: Like Lechber.

R: Yes. Here. (Reads) "Almost at the same moment when the first citizen action was taken against Japanese Americans returning to Orange County, the local post of the American Legion today adopted a resolution which, although deploring the return of the former residents, urged complete cooperation with local authorities and offered services of its 600 members for law enforcement purposes in case of outbreaks. The first trouble in the county was reported in Talbert District, west of Santa Ana, when a sign stating 'This ranch operated by a pro-Jap' was placed on property owned by George Iwakoshi, an American-born Jap who returned to the county this week from an Arizona relocation center. Hiyo Moneki, who has been operating the Iwakoshi ranch under lease since the owner was taken to Arizona, today said he has completed with the owner for purchase of the property and that Iwakoshi is returning to Arizona immediately."

H: Mr. Robertson, I'm working on something dealing with the Japanese Americans in Orange County [14] for their centennial history right now, and I'd certainly appreciate getting copies of the things that you've just been reading. Is there any way that you might Xerox some of those things for me and send them to me? Because I don't want to break up your scrapbook there, but just these relevant pages at the beginning. Because they include some very interesting information, and I think this would be helpful. Our Japanese American Project [of the Oral History Program at California State University, Fullerton] is also doing something dealing with Bronzeville, and I think this one would be helpful. Then this other thing on Orange County was extremely helpful. Could you do that?

R: Yes. I can Xerox those for you.

H: Thank you very much. I appreciate that.

So how long did you work in the capacity of the head of the southern California effort to resettle the Japanese back to the West Coast?

R: What was the date of that thing I just read? It doesn't say. Yes. December 31, 1944. So it was at the end of December I went in there. The thing I gave you,[15] that "Farewell Party," would give you the date on which I left there.

H: Sure. It says "March 18, 1946," which is just about the time [two days before] Tule Lake closed down.

R: Yes. Very shortly thereafter. And it was in 1946 that I returned to state service.

H: And then you came back to state of California?

R: Yes.

H: And did a series of things, some of which involved you . . . It looked to me as though you were dealing with cattle thieves or something like that.

R: That's right. I got a letter from the chief of the Bureau of Markets [William Kuhrt] while I was still in WRA, asking if I would be interested in setting up a new enforcement unit within the Bureau of Markets. The Bureau of Markets was a cooperative growers' means of curtailing production or limiting distribution of their product by law. For instance, a peach association would get together and say, "For the coming year, we'll establish a certain number of acres of peaches that can be produced." And we had all kinds of them. We had turkey associations, orange associations--we had them all over the state, all different kinds of crops. I came up to Sacramento and talked to Bill Kuhrt, and I said, "Yes, I think I'd be interested." I had known Bill Kuhrt before, so he set up this unit within his bureau, and I came up as supervising enforcement officer for the Bureau of Markets. I was in that thing for quite some time before I got into cattle.

I became a hearing officer. We'd hold a hearing on determining whether or not they were going to form an association and whether or not anybody had violated the terms of the agreement. And so the director gave me authority to hold the hearings, and I held hearings all over the state. Sometimes there were as many as four and five attorneys on both sides, so I was really just like a judge. I was a supervising enforcement officer.

Let's see, I moved from there to being the assistant chief of the Bureau of Livestock Identification, which had to do with the sale and branding of all cattle sold in California, and the control of cattle rustling and this type of thing. I had fallen out of a tree when I was pruning and broke my neck and wasn't expected to live. But I was in a cast from here [half way between the hips and knees] clear up to cover my head--I just had a little face-hole--at the time the Personnel Board Examinations were being held. So I called in and asked them if there was any way for me to take the examination, and they said, "Yes." So they sent an examiner out to the house. I lay there in bed, and he asked me the questions, and I answered them through this little hole. (laughter) And I came out on top of the list, so they gave me the job of assistant director.

H: Was there a lot of rustling going on in California, then? Was it a major problem?

R: Oh, yes. There was never a week during the year that we didn't have somebody up for stealing or shooting. Yes, they would go out and shoot a cow, and just take the hindquarter and leave the rest of it. You see, they're in a hurry; they just take the whole hindquarter and leave the rest. They steal calves, you know; they were easy to steal. They get in and take young calves, two or three of them, put them in a truck and away they go.

H: Was this a dangerous job for you? We talked about the dangers at Tule Lake. Was this more dangerous?

R: No, it wasn't, because I was assistant chief of the bureau, and the brand inspectors were all out in the field.

H: The field people had the more dangerous job on that, then.

R: Yes. I'll never forget. This is kind of hazy, but I remember one of the brand inspectors saw his own calf going through the chute, being sold, so he went back to see who had consigned that calf in to be sold. And it was a couple of high school girls. They had stolen his calf, and they were trying to sell it where he was a brand inspector.

H: You developed some kind of manual dealing with this subject.

R: Yes, California Brand Book. Do you want to see a copy of it?

H: Yes. Was that adopted in schools or something? Did they use it for the field agents?

R: They used it for identifying cattle.

H: I know you retired in 1968 from the state.

R: But before I retired, the chief of the Bureau of Livestock Identification got into trouble and resigned under pressure, and I was made chief of the bureau. Then we had a reorganization.

H: Were you working out of Sacramento during this time?

R: Yes. I was in Sacramento all of this time. The fellow I worked with when I was supervising enforcement officer, Dr. James Ralph, was a marketing specialist in the Bureau of Markets. We both had the same bureau chief. We became rather good friends, and he became director of agriculture. So he reorganized the department and set up the Division of Compliance, and I was made chief out of that division. I had three: I had the bureau I used to work for a long time ago as a supervisor, the Bureau of Market Enforcement; and I had the Bureau of Livestock Identification; and I had the Bureau of Weights and Measures [Division of Measurement Standards].

H: That's not a bureau you ever worked for before.

R: No. The weights and measures was probably the largest bureau I had, because that had to do with the sale of anything by weight, measure, or count.

H: In the entire state?

R: In the entire state. We had all of the filling stations in the state, all petroleum outlets. We had a division of electrical equipment. And we even went so far as counting the number of tissues in a toilet paper roll, or the number of pins in a package of pins. I mean, this is the type. I recall that one time we stopped 42,000 turkeys for the holiday season which were underweight because, when they wrapped the cellophane around the packages, they vacuumed them. And in vacuuming them, they pulled some of the liquid out and it reduced the weight, so that the weight that was shown on the outside was incorrect.

H: So you had to stop that, right?

R: Oh, yes. Then I recall one group of cosmetics. I don't remember what they were, but I remember that they had a false bottom; the bottom went up like that rather than straight across, so when you picked up the bottle it looked like there was a whole lot more stuff than there was in there. So we wrote back to the manufacturer and said that he was going to have to redo this stuff. He said, "Destroy it. It wasn't worth it."

H: How do you get involved with that through agriculture?

R: No, through weights and measures.

H: But isn't weights and measures part of the agricultural . . .

R: Yes.

H: Well, how does weights and measures of perfume or products like that . . . Is it because there's an agricultural base?

R: I don't know why it's in agriculture, but it was part of the . . .

H: But weights and measures covers things outside of agriculture anyway, then.

R: You betcha.

B: There isn't anyplace else to put it.

R: How about petroleum? What does that have to do with it?

H: Yes.

R: But all of the sealers of weights and measures were under our supervision. Each county sealer of weights and measures was under the division.

H: But the other two bureaus in there were strictly agricultural things, right?

R: Yes. They were.

H: This one had somehow just got into the Division of Compliance.

R: Of course, that would have to do with the sale of produce, too, if it was underweight or if there was cheating on size or whatever. But that covered a broader area, a larger area than anything else that we had.

H: Now, was there a persisting involvement on your part with Japanese Americans in your postwar work? Did you still have contact? I mean, after you'd left WRA and the resettlement thing?

R: No.

H: You didn't.

R: No. Only those fellows like Harry Ueno and George Yamashiro, and the little girl that was our housekeeper up at Tule Lake, Dorothy Ito, she lives here in Sacramento.

H: But nothing through the agriculture thing, farmers and things like that?

R: No. See, that's forty years ago, and I got completely away from any of that when I got into the law enforcement programs with agriculture. And I didn't have anything to do with that because, after all, I was a division chief. I was removed from the actual contact in the field. I had a bureau chief, and assistant chief, and several supervisors, and then all the field men under them, so they were the ones that had the contact that I used to have a long time ago.

H: Now, you retired in 1968 and got a resolution from the [California] Senate in 1969. Then, in a letter that you wrote to me recently, you noted that in 1975 you took on some responsibility with the First Baptist Church here in Sacramento. Maybe you can talk a little bit about that. I know you had been doing missionary work of one sort or another from your early years back at Yale, and this seemed to be a culmination of that.

R: Well, I taught young adult married people for eighteen and a half years at the First Baptist Church of Sacramento, I got my license as a Baptist minister and preached around at the various outlying churches, when the local minister was on vacation or something. I married my daughter, married my granddaughter, and buried my son-in-law's mother. These little things I did on the side. I never took a pastorate of my own; there were too many things to do. Oh, I guess it's been about ten years ago, after we retired, we found that going back and forth into town--which is about ten miles--two and three times a week was quite a chore, to church activities, so we moved out to Arcade Baptist Church on 3927 Marconi Avenue in Sacramento, which is a conservative Baptist Church. I've been on the board of elders, and a deacon, and sang in the choir, and done some church calling, and handling Bible study groups and stuff. That's my activities here now. But that, I think, brings us up to about now.

Of course, after we retired we started traveling because we hadn't done much before that. Well, you name it. I guess we've been nearly everywhere. We haven't been to Russia, and we haven't been to Red China, although we've looked over from Hong Kong into Red China. It wasn't open at the time we were there.

H: Is that a trip that you intend to make in the future?

R: Friends of ours said it wasn't worth it. They said that it's pretty rugged in China. The accommodations, they said, are pretty bad. We're going on a Caribbean trip this October, which we haven't been on before. One of the most interesting trips we had was down to South America to visit . . . You remember when these five missionaries were killed by Auca Indians?

H: Sure do.

R: Well, that's where we went. These young missionaries--they're not young, but they're young to us--Marion and Ralph Stuck were first-name friends of all those five fellows. They worked with them down there. And they met us at Quito, Ecuador, and drove us, oh, for several hours, down to the end of the paved road. Then we went on a dirt road for several more hours, and got down to Shellmera, Equador, which was a Shell Oil Company place that they had tried to develop [as a] source of oil. Little town. There we took a private plane--that's Missionary Aviation Fellowship plane--and flew for a couple of hours down in the jungles to Chupientsa, Ecuador. That was, I guess, one of the most interesting trips we had, just to go down in and see what the missionaries were doing in this country. I got some beautiful pictures of the vines all hanging down, Tarzan type of stuff.

H: You went to Japan once, too. I know that you mentioned off tape that you saw George Yamashiro's wife, Sally. But I'm curious if when you went there you saw any of the people who had renounced their citizenship at Tule Lake and who never did come back to the United States? Most of these renunciants, of course, did return [to the United States], and were able to get their citizenship back.

R: No. They had a court case in Los Angeles—I think you'll find some of that in the material I've loaned you—where a couple of people were trying to get their citizenship back. And a firm of attorneys had subpoenaed Dillon Myer and they subpoenaed me, too.

H: Was this A. L. Wirin? Or was it Wayne Collins?

R: No, it was Fred Okrand [of the legal firm of Wirin, Rissman, and Okrand, 257 South Spring Street, Los Angeles, California]. But it never did materialize. We had some correspondence, but he never did call me down there. Now there were several of the fellows that renounced their citizenship and then got their citizenship back, but I never had contact with them. They never contacted me. And the only contact I had in Japan was a missionary and the Yamashiros. It was a very interesting trip, though. Africa was a very interesting trip, too. Of course we were on a tour. I prefer to go on tours, really, because you go on your own, you spend half your time trying to find places to stay and trying to find food to eat. You go on tours, they know where the places are you should go.

H: Then you can focus your attention on what you want to see.

R: You go to your hotel and your luggage is there, and they hand you the key to your room. Next morning you put your luggage out in the hall and away you go. You don't have to worry about passports. They take care of all that for you.

H: Changing currency, doing all the other things that are so troublesome.

R: Yes. I like a tour type thing best.

H: Reagan?

R: Reagan? That's your first name?

B: That's my first name.

H: It's spelled just like President Reagan.

R: Just like Ron does, huh?

H: Reagan, do you have any closing questions?

R: What's your interest in the military, Reagan? You keep talking about the military. Are you connected to the military some way?

B: I was. I spent twenty-nine years in the Army.

R: Are you writing something on the military?

B: I'm working on my master's thesis, and it's the Army's role in the evacuation and relocation of the Japanese that I'm exploring.[16]

R: My nephew is a general in the Air Force. He was; he's retired now. He was a chief of chaplains, General Richard Carr.

H: In which branch of the service?

R: Air Force.

B: That's almost like a friendly foreign power when you're in the service.

R: Yes, I realize that. We went back for his retirement.

B: The chief of chaplains in the Army is Catholic, then a Protestant, Catholic, then a Protestant.

R: Same in the Air Force.

B: They change it off. And the deputy, then, is the opposite.

R: That's right. We were there at his pinning and then again at his retirement. That's when I got that thing hanging on the wall there, that United States Seal or something.

H: Mr. Robertson, it's been eleven years since I first read Michi Weglyn's book [Years of Infamy: The Untold Story of America's Concentration Camps].

R: Has it been that long ago?

H: Yes, that book was published in 1976. And she alluded to you in a way there that was so favorable and so warming that it, at that time, excited me about the possibility of someday making your acquaintance. And then I had the good fortune to work closely with Harry Ueno, who you knew from several contacts, both from Leupp and Tule Lake and afterward, up to the present, and he spoke so warmly of you. Since that, other books have come out, and nice things have been said. And I'm especially pleased to talk to you, because I think that usually we carry around stereotypes that sometimes lead to public policy mistakes, like stereotypes toward the Japanese Americans, which led to the disaster we had there. But stereotypes can lead to historiographical mistakes, intellectual mistakes--for instance, to perceive people in the Army who were connected with the Evacuation through tightly managed images, and this is one of the things that Reagan is trying to correct. And then I think the other is to see people that were working for the WRA in terms of tightly managed stereotypes. Personally, I think that organizations don't act in a completely determinating way to produce a particular social type, whether it's an ethnic group, a governing body, or whatever. It's been a pleasure to see that someone like yourself who has moral values and has an integrity of purpose, and a concern and a love for people, can persist through great temptations to reduce oneself to being power hungry or to being opportunistic, arrogant, or whatever, and actually see a thing [like the Evacuation] through with an incredible amount of decency. It's been a wonderful experience talking to you, and just making your acquaintance.

R: Well, I thank you, but I just hope that you haven't felt that your taking the time and trip up here has been disappointing. I didn't see how I could give you much.

B: This trip has not been disappointing in the least. It eliminated a stereotype I was developing about WRA people. It renewed my faith in man. You've been an inspiration to listen to. I don't say this to embarrass you; I say this because you had your fellow man uppermost in your mind, and you kept it that way. You don't hear much of that about World War II or the Evacuation. Everything's been negative, but you've had a positive approach to everything throughout your life, and I think it's remarkable and wonderful.

R: I think it [the Evacuation] was a travesty, an injustice, this whole business. There was no danger. There never was danger from these people. I know on the joint board in Washington, the Naval Intelligence knew who these people were; they had them all behind wire the day after Pearl Harbor. They had the potential enemies all coraled the day after Pearl Harbor. We didn't have to have all this internment stuff. [Lieutenant General John L.] DeWitt [Commanding General of the Western Defense Command] had a bad name.

B: He saw his friend, [Major General] Walter [Campbell] Short, Commander of the Hawaiian Department at the time of the Japanese attack on Pearl Harbor on December 7, 1941] , crucified. I can imagine him saying to himself, "It's not going to happen to me." And he had a lot of instigators, I think, that swayed his thinking.

R: I never met the man; I didn't know him. But I know that generally they felt DeWitt pushed this thing.

H: I certainly don't feel like my time was wasted. In fact, I feel doubly blessed, not only to have received information, but also as Reagan pointed out, to receive inspiration. I thank you for your hospitality, for sharing your life, for sharing not only your testimony but your testament. We appreciate it very much.

R: I haven't shared my testimony. If either one of you died tonight, you know where you'd be tomorrow?

B: I have a good idea.

H: And I don't.

B: I know where I'm hoping I'll be.

R: You ought to know where you're going to be tomorrow. You never accepted Christ as your personal savior?

H: I haven't.

R: The only way to eternal life is through Christ, and you shouldn't put it off, because that's the only way you're going to know where you're going to be tomorrow if you die tonight.

B: (laughter)

H: That's why he said he had a pretty good idea.

R: Yes.

B: I know what I'm hoping for.

R: I don't hope; I know where I'm going to be tomorrow.

H: Well, you two have me outnumbered. Thanks again.

END OF INTERVIEW

Photo by Harry Y. Ueno

Mr. and Mrs. Paul G. Robertson

Staff Housing, Leupp Isolation Center, Leupp, Arizona, 1943

Mess hall, Leupp Isolation Center, Leupp, Arizona, 1943

School children in front of Navajo Indian School building near
Leupp Isolation Center, Leupp, Arizona, 1943

Navajo Indians and their sheep, with hogan on right, near
Leupp Isolation Center, Leupp, Arizona, 1943

Navajo woman weaving rug near Leupp Isolation Center, Leupp,
Arizona, 1943. This rug was on the floor of the family room
in the Robertsons' Carmichael, California, home at the time of the
interview with Mr. Robertson in the summer of 1987.

Harriette A. Robertson
Tule Lake Segregation Center
Newell, California, 1944

Carol Robertson, daughter of
Paul G. and Harriette A.
Robertson, Leupp Isolation Center,
Leupp, Arizona, 1943

Paul G. Robertson, Tule Lake Segregation Center, Newell,
California, 1944, at the time of his service as one of
that center's assistant directors. Note man-proof fence
and internee barracks in background.

Courtesy of the War Relocation Authority

Paul G. Robertson, pictured at far left, receives the first prize award presented in 1946 to the War Relocation Authority's Southern California Area Office for "outstanding accomplishment" in the 7th War Loan Drive. The presenter of the award, shown on the far right, is Wright L. Felt, regional coordinator of the U.S. Treasury's Bond Committee. At the time, Robertson served as the WRA's area supervisor for southern California. WRA topped all federal agencies by oversubscribing its quota by 621 percent. Because everyone of Japanese ancestry working with the WRA area and district offices in southern California--a few of whom are seen here with Robertson and Felt--purchased bonds, the WRA easily came out on top in the contest.

Photo by Harry Y. Ueno

(l-r) Yaso Ueno, Harriette Robertson, Paul Robertson, Harry Ueno, at a reunion at the Robertson home in Carmichael, California, 1986. Mr. Ueno was interned at both the Leupp Isolation Center in Leupp, Arizona, and the Tule Lake Segregation Center in Newell, California, during the time that Mr. Robertson served, respectively, as the director and assistant director of these centers. Mrs. Ueno was interned, also, at the Tule Lake facility. Mrs. Robertson shared staff housing with her husband and children at both centers.

ENDNOTES

1. As the interview clarifies, Paul G. Robertson also worked for the War Relocation Authority during World War II in several other capacities. During 1942-1943, he was employed first within the WRA's regional office in San Francisco and later assisted its Leave Clearance Board Program at the national office in Washington, D.C. Following his stints as director of the Leupp Isolation Center in Arizona and as an assistant director of the Tule Lake Segregation Center in California in 1943-1944, he concluded his WRA employment in 1944-1946 at Los Angeles, California, by serving as supervisor there for the agency's southern California office charged with assisting evacuated Japanese Americans returning to settle in that area.

2. The letters referred to here are contained within Paul Robertson's personal WRA file. Copies of these letters are archived with this interview in the Japanese American Oral History Project (JAOHP) of the Oral History Program (OHP) at California State University, Fullerton (CSUF).

3. See Richard Drinnon, Keeper of Concentration Camps: Dillon S. Myer and American Racism (Berkeley: University of California Press, 1987).

4. Following service as Assistant Chief of Internal Security at the Gila War Relocation Center in Arizona, Francis Frederick was transferred in early 1943 to the WRA's newly created temporary isolation center outside of Moab, Utah, where he was Chief of Internal Security. When a permanent isolation center was opened at Leupp, Arizona, a few months later, he continued in the same capacity there until the camp's closure in December 1943. Thereafter, Frederick was inducted into the Army. Shortly before the liquidation of the WRA in 1946, Frederick was again an agency employee, this time in the position of Senior Internal Security Officer. For further information on him, see Francis S. Frederick, "Personal Narrative Report" (March 13, 1946), folder S.100, Leupp Isolation Center (LIC), Japanese Evacuation and Resettlement Study (JERS), Bancroft Library (BL), University of California, Berkeley (UCB). In the same collection of documents are four reports written by JERS field anthropologist Robert Spencer that shed light on Frederick: "Political Pressure Groups" and "Administrative Organization," folder K8.62; "Pressure Groups and After," folder K8.54; and "Tada Case," folder K.8.65.

5. See folder S1.10, LIC, JERS, BL-UCB.

6. See Keeper of Concentration Camps, p. 100, where Drinnon notes that Frederick was "no stranger himself to the arrogance of power."

7. See interview 1958 conducted with Robert Spencer by Arthur A. Hansen for this project on 15-17 July 1987.

8. George Jyoji Yamashiro was a twenty-nine year old internee from the Gila center where he had been the head of the Gila Young People's Association and considered by the Gila administration to be an active leader of the alleged pro-Axis faction in that camp; for further information, see the docket on Yamashiro prepared by Francis Frederick in folder S.100, LIC, JERS, BL-UCB.

9. Masua Kanno was mistakenly confused by the Gila administration with his cousin, Minoru Kanno, a member of the board of governors of the Gila Young People's Assocation, and incarcerated in the Leupp center; see Francis Frederick's docket on him in folder S1.00, LIC, JERS, BL-UCB.

10. In the summer of 1941, the United States Department of Justice (DOJ), under the aegis of its Alien Enemy Control Unit, designated special camps for the internment of "potentially dangerous enemy aliens." One such camp, which included citizens of all Axis countries but was preponderantly comprised of Japanese nationals, was located in Missoula, Montana (which until 1941 was an Army camp, Fort Missoula). By an agreement struck on 18 July 1941 between the DOJ and the Army, the DOJ was assigned responsibility for the arrests and loyalty hearings of aliens listed as potentially dangerous, while the Immigration and Naturalization Service was charged with their custody in Missoula and the other internment centers. For a detailed overview of these camps and a series of in-depth oral history interviews with former internees and administrators, see Paul Frederick Clark, "Those Other Camps: An Oral History Analysis of Japanese Alien Enemy Internment during World War II," M.A. thesis, California State University, Fullerton, 1980.

11. For more about Harry Ueno at the Leupp Isolation Center and in other WRA facilities during World War II, see Sue Kunitomi Embrey, Arthur A. Hansen, and Betty Kulberg Mitson, eds., Manzanar Martyr: An Interview with Harry Y. Ueno (Fullerton, Calif.: Japanese American Project, Oral History Program, California State University, Fullerton, 1986).

12. In addition to the correspondence noted above (see fn. 2), copies of newspaper clippings, government reports, and miscellaneous items in the interviewee's WRA file have been archived along with his interview in the JAOHP, OHP, CSUF.

13. In a letter to Robert Spencer dated 20 April 1943, several days prior to leaving the temporary isolation center at Moab, Utah, to take up his duties at Leupp, Francis Frederick wrote: "I have seven broken down Caucasian guards under me and no one I can depend on to leave in charge for any length of time. I've been Mess Operations, fiscal maintenance, housing, and other departments as well as Internal Security to say nothing of being Acting Project Director. Talk about a one-man band. One thing is that I've had my way on everything so far." See folder S.1.10, LIC, JERS, BL-UCB. In his subsequent correspondence with Spencer, Frederick makes no mention of the personnel at Leupp.

14. Honorable Stephen K. Tamura Orange County Japanese American Oral History Project, jointly sponsored by the Japanese American Council of the Historical and Cultural Foundation of Orange County and the Japanese American Project of the Oral History Program at California State University, Fullerton.

15. The interviewee is here referring to a booklet entitled Here's How We Feel About Paul G. Robertson, dated 18 March 1946, that was compiled by the "War Relocationeers." For a copy of this booklet, see Robertson interview file in JAOHP, OHP, CSUF.

16. See Reagan J. Bell, "Interned Without: The Military Police at the Tule Lake Relocation/Segregation Center, 1942-46," M.A. thesis, California State University, Fullerton, 1989.

Index